MOVING ON MOVING FORWARD

MOVING ON
MOVING
FORWARD

A GUIDE FOR PASTORS IN TRANSITION

MICHAEL J. ANTHONY and MICK BOERSMA

ZONDERVAN®

ZONDERVAN.com/
AUTHORTRACKER
follow your favorite authors

Moving On — Moving Forward
Copyright © 2007 by Michael J. Anthony and Mick Boersma

Requests for information should be addressed to:

Zondervan, *Grand Rapids, Michigan* 49530

Library of Congress Cataloging-in-Publication Data

Anthony, Michael J.
    Moving on, moving forward : a guide for pastors in transition / Michael J. Anthony and Mick Boersma.
    p. cm.
    Includes bibliographical references.
       ISBN-13: 978-0-310-26776-8
       ISBN-10: 0-310-26776-5
    1. Clergy — Relocation. I. Title.
    BV664.A58 2007
    253'.2 — dc22
                                             2006100429

Interior design by Mark Sheeres

Printed in the United States of America

07 08 09 10 11 12 13 • 10 9 8 7 6 5 4 3 2 1

*We dedicate this book to the individuals who have made
it possible for us to fulfill our dreams and pursue life's greatest joy—
serving the body of Christ as a pastor.*

*To Michelle Anthony
and our two children, Chantel and Brendon.
Together, you compose the center of my universe,
and I appreciate your support and encouragement—
especially during those long hours
when I'm called out to minister to hurting people.
I couldn't do it without you!*

*To Rolane Boersma,
my lifelong ministry partner,
for your incredible support and gifted counsel
while writing this book.
And to our two wonderful daughters, Cara and Riva,
whose lives consistently reflect the love of Jesus.
You are my richest treasure and dearest friends.*

CONTENTS

Part 4: Getting There from Here

INTRODUCTION

A few years ago, I (Michael) packed up my family and headed for a small Bible college in East Africa for a three-month sabbatical. The time away from the seminary gave me occasion to reflect, train national pastors, and get caught up on some much needed writing.

Toward the end of our stay, I took my wife and young daughter to the Masai Mara Game Reserve to experience a genuine African safari. It was springtime on the savannah, and the great wildebeest migration was in full swing. Each year, wildebeest and zebra travel by the tens of thousands for hundreds of miles across treacherous territory in search of fresh grass and cool waters. Along the way they encounter lions, leopards, alligators, and an array of other natural predators. Not every animal that begins the trek completes it. Many succumb to the perilous journey and die along the way.

Each year across North America a migration of a different kind takes place. Men and women who have committed their lives in service to building the kingdom of God find themselves on their own perilous journey. Some have been preparing for it during years of Bible college or seminary training. And although many have entered this populace with forethought and planning, some, through circumstances beyond their control, find themselves thrust out into a landscape with far too few resources given the miles that lay ahead. These travelers have heard that 10 percent of their fellow pastors who are forced out of office leave the ministry altogether and become casualties of a harsh and unforgiving world. Consequently, they face the future with fear, anxiety, and uncertainty. What kind of journey is this, anyway?

The landscape of the twenty-first-century church has changed dramatically. Our grandfathers, and even fathers, had the privilege of graduating from seminary to find themselves fulfilling thirty to forty years of faithful service to the same congregation. During the past few decades, this possibility has rapidly declined. Shockingly, the average tenure of some senior pastors is measured in months rather than years. For other pastoral positions (e.g., children's, youth, singles, associate, etc.), the length of service is far less than for our forebears. For many churches, the picture of a revolving door on the pastor's office is an accurate portrayal of life in the ministry.

What are the causes of this shifting landscape, and what are the effects on those who are on this journey? How will you know when this shift will affect you and your ministry position? How will you know when it's time to leave and when it's time to navigate the treacherous territory? Numerous surveys, interviews, and denominational studies have given us the answers to these questions over the past several decades. Several factors can be unearthed, but two key factors are *conflict* and *unrealistic expectations*.

Conflict between the pastor and members of his congregation or church board is one of the most common reasons for leaving a ministry position. For the associate pastor, the elements only increase for potential conflict between this position and the senior pastor or other associate members of the pastoral staff. Unrealistic expectations on the part of both the pastor and the church also play a role. Churchgoers in today's society get a weekly dose of enthusiastic television preachers, experienced radio Bible teachers, and enlightening, authoritative authors who present God's Word with the skill and precision generally associated with neurosurgeons.

When laypeople walk into their churches on any given Sunday morning, they expect to hear a message with the same degree of depth and clarity as these ministry moguls. It doesn't matter that these TV and radio personalities aren't available to come and hold their hand or pray for them when they face a personal or family crisis. The fact remains that the bar has been set. They have a clear standard of performance in mind. Anything less is a disappointment. So when the pastor's contract comes up for renewal, it is little wonder that many churches cast their pastor aside in search of a "new and improved" model.

A recent *Christianity Today* article[1] reported that one-third of all pastors currently serve congregations who either fired or forced out their predecessor. Surely we should realize that if it happened once before, it can happen again. Take, for example, the Southern Baptist denomination, which reports that 225 of their senior pastors get fired every month while another 250 offer their resignations.[2] That's 475 pastors each month starting the journey of career transition in just one denomination! Multiply that by the number of other pastoral positions (e.g., children's, youth, singles, worship, associate, missions, etc.) and by the number of denominations, and the final total becomes almost overwhelming. What a profound impact this has on the church and its professional leaders! Is it any wonder that some denominations are facing a shortage of trained clergy? It leaves one asking the obvious questions, "How are these people (and their families) able to survive?" and "Why would anyone become a pastor in the first place?"

Again, being in ministry isn't for the faint of heart, and neither are the inevitable career transitions that accompany it. Pastoral ministry is a journey fraught with risk and danger. But it doesn't have to end that way. With the right kind of preparation and resources, this journey can also be an enriching time of renewal, professional development, and personal healing. Many have come through this season of their lives with better focus, a deeper conviction about their calling, and a renewed vision for the contribution they want to make in the kingdom for Christ.

Looking for a new position in ministry is similar to dating after a divorce or the death of a spouse. One experiences the pain of looking back mixed with the apprehension of what the future holds. Getting back into the "pastoral job market" is not what it used to be. There was a time when a simple phone call to a well-placed colleague was all it took to find a new place of service. Today's fast-paced global culture has changed all that.

Contemporary Pastoral Perspective

Survey Composition. To get a better glimpse into the life of today's pastors, we distributed a survey to pastors whom we knew personally. We received responses from nearly two hundred of them scattered across many miles. Some even came in from four foreign countries, but the vast majority were from the United States. Pastors responded from seventeen states and twenty-four different Protestant denominations. No particular denomination dominated the group, and many surveys came from pastors serving in nondenominational churches. We wanted as wide a theological swath as we could reasonably pull together. The end of the survey allowed participants to make personal comments about their experience as a fellow traveler, and they were generous with their responses. They wanted to help their fellow travelers learn from their experiences. Some were straightforward in their observations, saying clearly, "Don't do what I did!" We weave their responses and observations throughout the book as supporting thoughts and reflections.

Full-time vs. Part-time. To help provide some perspective, the pastors included in this survey were mostly serving full-time. The number of years they had served in ministry ranged from "just began" to thirty-four, with the average being thirteen years. When asked how many full-time positions they had served in during those years, the range was between one and sixteen, with the average being a little over two. For those serving part-time, the numbers changed to six positions as the maximum number, and one was the minimum; the average was a little less than two.

Job Title. Regarding job title, the distribution was senior pastor, 29 percent; associate pastor, 18 percent; youth pastor, 7 percent; and executive pastor, 4 percent; with worship pastor and children's pastor coming in at 1 percent each.[3] The greatest surprise was that the category "Other" was represented by 40 percent of our respondents. Upon closer examination, it was revealed that their titles included terms such as senior associate pastor, co-pastor, English ministry pastor, missions pastor, pastor of small group ministries, Christian education pastor, or chaplain. Clearly there is far more variety in titles than there ever has been before. The trend seems to be in specifying a selected area of ministry rather than using the more inclusive "associate pastor" designation.

Tenure. It has been widely reported that the average tenure for a senior pastor is twenty-four months, while other pastors (e.g., youth, children's, singles, etc.) serve an average of eighteen months before moving to another ministry. In our sample, the average length of time senior pastors had served in their preceding ministry was fifty-four months. The average length of time they had been serving in their current ministry improved a bit to an average of fifty-eight months. For nonsenior pastors, the average length of stay at their preceding ministry was forty-six months. The average length of time they had been serving at their current ministry was forty months. Although those serving as nonsenior pastors had much longer stays than the traditional eighteen months, they still remained in their ministries for a shorter period of time than their senior pastor colleagues.

Denominations. We tried to gather a broad spectrum of denominational representation for our survey. Altogether twenty-four denominations were represented. The largest percentage were the nondenominational pastors (34 percent) followed by various kinds of Baptists (30 percent). There were also those in the Free Church tradition (11 percent), Presbyterian (5 percent), as well as a few from the Lutheran (1 percent) and Methodist (1 percent) denominations. The category "Other" had a total of 16 percent altogether. A closer look at these revealed denominations such as Calvary Chapel, Grace Brethren, Friends, Reformed, Foursquare, Christian Missionary Alliance, and Covenant churches.

City Size. Our survey participants provided a balanced perspective in terms of city size. These ranged as follows: metropolis (1 million+), 25 percent; large cities (500,000–1 million), 12 percent; medium cities (100,000–500,000), 28 percent; small cities (25,000–100,000), 20 percent; small towns (10,000–25,000), 8 percent; and rural (less than 10,000), 5 percent. Overall, we were pleased with the balanced location demographic.

Discovered Ministry. When we asked pastors how they discovered their current ministry positions, 35 percent said they found their ministries through the resources of a friend, 33 percent cited "Other" (e.g., ministry job fair, ministry conference, a visit to a church, previous service on the church board as an elder), 10 percent said they responded to an Internet posting, and the rest said they were connected to their position through a denominational leader, seminary placement office, or family member.

Unemployed. One of the major fears of pastors is being unemployed for a prolonged period of time. This fear causes many pastors to stay in what might otherwise be an intolerable ministry setting. When asked how long they had been unemployed before finding their current ministry position, the range was from one month (19 percent) to over one year (8 percent). For the vast majority, it was between one and six months (62 percent). The overall average length of time a pastor was unemployed was a little less than three months. This confirms the advice of financial planners who recommend that everyone should have at least ninety days of income set aside in a contingency fund.

I Quit! "Never resign on a Monday" is a famous admonition quoted among pastors. In other words, give it some thought; don't leave without giving your decision the reflection that's warranted. Among our survey participants, 17 percent took less than a month to decide, 19 percent took from one to three months, 17 percent took from four to six months, 8 percent took seven to nine months, and 10 percent took about a year. Overall, the average amount of time it takes a pastor to decide to leave his or her ministry is about four months.

Reasons for Quitting. Although the reasons why pastors quit vary, the major reason can be summed up as a sense that they were no longer useful at a particular church. Beyond that, the second largest reason was disagreement over the direction the ministry should take (23 percent). The third reason boiled down to conflict — either between themselves and a staff member (75 percent), a church board member (15 percent), a denominational leader (5 percent), or a congregation member (5 percent).

These are among the discoveries we made as we examined the surveys. More insights are woven throughout particular chapters. Our hope is that pastors on this career transition journey will find comfort by reading the reflections of others who have also made the trip.

Overview of the Book

The first part of this book deals with preparation for transition. We begin with a look at one's ministry from God's perspective instead of from the world's viewpoint. From there we address the important issues of one's personal mission and vision for ministry involvement. The remaining chapters in this unit address laying out a goal for where you want to go in life and then developing a plan to help you get there.

When you feel as if you can't go any further, part 2 is where you need to invest some reading time. Chapter themes help you take an objective look at your life and ministry to determine if you're simply having a bad day (or month) or if it really might be time for you to pack up your office after all. In the case that you decide it is time to move on, we'll help you lay out a God-honoring and well-planned exit strategy. We'll help you write that all-important letter of resignation, including what to say and what is best left unsaid. Finally, we'll look at the real-life nuts and bolts of negotiating your severance package, securing ongoing medical coverage, and exploring options after you resign.

The third part of the book handles the topics that most pastors never hear about in seminary. They will make you sit up and pay attention. It's not uncommon for the pastor who is departing to get so wrapped up in transition issues that the emotional, physical, spiritual, and relational needs of the family go unmet. Spouses and children feel the pain of departure every bit as much as the departing pastor. Family members may verbalize it differently (or not verbalize it at all), but the pastor must never underestimate the importance of monitoring their well-being along the way. We'll also take a little time to share some principles of resume writing that will make your material stand out in the crowd. Additional chapters deal with networking with friends and colleagues, networking on the Internet, and looking seriously at midlife career transitions.

Part 4 is the stuff of ministry that most pastors dread—the business end of the career search. These are the issues of concern once you send your application materials to the search committee and begin the arduous task of meeting, interviewing, and negotiating with them. In today's competitive climate, a representative from a professional search firm may be the first individual the candidate hears back from. If you have never entered into this unique relationship, sit down, pour yourself a cup of coffee, and get prepared for some surprises.

We have found over the years of helping pastors get appointed that many prefer to leave the financial compensation details in the hands of God and the search committee. They prefer to sit back and accept whatever is offered to them by the committee without giving serious thought to the part they ought to play in the process. To them, refusing to negotiate is proof of their living by faith. Perhaps. But it may be proof of ignorance too. For once they accept the job and receive their first paycheck, they live with the constant reminder (and regret) that too many things were left unsaid and unwritten during the final stages of accepting the church's call.

For those who find themselves on a journey of pastoral transition, the material in this book may prove life saving to both them and their families. In addition to the materials we've brought to the discussion, we also surveyed and interviewed hundreds of pastors who have taken the journey and lived to talk about it. They reveal their own personal feelings and emotions about the trek. They provide those still in process with perspective and hope.

It's our desire to remind each pastor making a career transition that God is still on the throne. His sovereign power and wisdom are available to guide you and sustain you through the fiercest of storms. Remember, at the end of the day, you are his beloved child, and he has promised to care for you and see you safely to the end of the journey.

We encourage you to view this as a resource handbook. You need not read through the whole book in one sitting but pick it up during different seasons of your career transition and select the chapters that apply to your current need the most. Different chapters will be relevant to your needs at different phases of your ministry.

Let's get started! It's time to begin. Take this book, clear the list of "things to do today," and let's go for a ride on this grand adventure, stopping at times to sit under a tree to enjoy the process of discovery. This journey, like the one that began years ago in the life of Abraham, will reveal your own character and God's omniscient power to preserve and protect you as his child. Let the journey begin.

Michael J. Anthony, Ph.D., Ph.D.
Mick Boersma, Ph.D.

ACKNOWLEDGMENTS

Many people have contributed to the development of this book. We especially want to acknowledge the input we received from the two hundred pastors who responded to our survey request for information. We spoke with many of them personally, and they were helpful in providing us with significant insights and meaningful perspective. Thank you for being so vulnerable and open with us while sharing your stories and professional expertise. You invested in this project because you care about what other pastors are going through on their career transition journey. We hope that we represented you well and that your involvement will help others along the way.

We would also like to thank the dean of Talbot School of Theology, Dr. Dennis Dirks, who provided us with significant resources to aid us in purchasing books, printing and mailing surveys, and funding sabbatical leaves. Thanks, Dennis, for all you do to make our lives as professors so meaningful and fruitful.

This book would not have been possible without the wise counsel of our editor, Paul Engle. Paul has been a senior pastor himself, so he understands full well the challenges that leadership in ministry can bring. Thanks, Paul, for partnering with us in our goal of making a contribution to pastors all across North America.

Several student assistants helped us as well. Ryan Keen spent countless hours doing the data input from our survey. He managed to keep all the important numbers organized and made the data useful for us. Thanks for all you did to help make this book possible, Ryan. Katherine Schuster was also helpful in typing out the open-ended responses. This provided us with comments and anecdotal materials that found their way into the text. Thanks so much for your help, Katherine.

Finally, we would like to acknowledge the assistance of many of our current students and alumni pastors. Their journey helped us envision and complete this book. It's our desire to provide all pastors serving Christ's church with a resource that will ultimately make a contribution to the kingdom of Christ. Being a pastor in the twenty-first century is not for the faint of heart, and we want to partner with those who serve the church during long, lonely hours of dedicated ministry leadership. May the material in this book bless your lives and lead you to a successful arrival along your career journey.

PART 1

PREPARING FOR THE JOURNEY

CHAPTER 1

TRAVELING BY THE BOOK
A Christian View of Vocation

MICK BOERSMA

I was made a minister, according to the gift of God's grace which was given to me according to the working of His power.
Ephesians 3:7

It was a clear and sunny midsummer's afternoon. Six weeks had passed since graduation from seminary without so much as a call, let alone a rejection letter. I had heard nothing from any of the numerous churches that had received my resume. I was working a part-time job making furniture, just trying to make ends meet, while waiting for the phone to ring with an offer that would confirm God's will for my life. But the phone wasn't ringing. I slumped down in our only living room chair and began wondering out loud if I'd made a terrible mistake. "Why did I spend the last four years earning my seminary degree? Did I just waste all that time and money? Am I really called to pastoral work? Why isn't God doing something?" The questions rocked my world as the weeks passed. This constant soul searching and second guessing of God's will was taking its toll on my peace of mind.

So began my first pastoral transition during which circumstances would cause me to question a most fundamental assumption — one faced by all pastors at some point during their journey: *Has God really called me to vocational ministry?* Indeed, pastors around the world often question their calling. It's nice to know that nearly every minister questions his or her call at some point in life. A recent study conducted by Duke Divinity School reveals several factors related to why pastors sometimes doubt their call to pastoral ministry (see sidebar).[1]

Surveys consistently show that ministers consider their call to ministry to be a key factor keeping them in their job when the going gets tough. It allows them to focus their efforts and even helps them to thrive.[2] Over the last twenty years, I have counseled a great many pastors transitioning in ministry who lacked a clear sense of God's call on their lives. Perhaps part of the reason is a misunderstanding of what constitutes a call in the first place.

Biblical Evidence of a Divine Call in the Old Testament

A number of high-profile personalities in both the Old and New Testaments heard God's voice call to them. God gave Noah a specific call to build an ark and make preparations for the end of sinful humankind (Gen. 6:13–14). Noah's response was an obedient acceptance of that call: "Noah did according to all that the LORD had commanded him" (Gen. 7:5).

Later God called Abraham out of his ancestral land of Ur to a new frontier known as Canaan. He had plans for him that were wildly beyond anything he could have dreamed possible (Gen. 12:1–3). We read Abram's response to God's call in Genesis 12:4: "So Abram went forth as the LORD had spoken to him."

Years later Moses, who had presumptuously misunderstood his call, received God's call on his life as he walked in the lonely desert. God got his attention through a burning bush. We read, "When the LORD saw that he turned aside to look, God called to him from the midst of the bush and said, 'Moses, Moses!' And he said, 'Here I am'" (Ex. 3:4).

After Moses brought God's people into the appointed land, God spoke to an unassuming wheat farmer named Gideon. God used an angelic messenger to inform Gideon of God's plan for his life. Gideon was less than enthusiastic and needed some convincing (Judg. 6:11–40). God was patient, and Gideon

Ten Factors Related to Why Pastors Doubt Their Call

- People treat me differently because I'm a pastor.
- The congregation makes too many demands on my life because I'm a pastor.
- My spouse resents the amount of time the ministry takes.
- Church members disagree about the role of a pastor.
- I have difficulty finding time for recreation and personal renewal.
- Congregational criticism is causing me lots of stress.
- My spouse resents the lack of family finances.
- I feel so lonely and isolated.
- The ministry is having a negative effect on my family.
- I find difficulty having a private life apart from the clergy role.

reluctantly accepted his invitation. Gideon fulfilled his assignment and resisted the nation's desire to make him their ruler. He replied to their insistence, "I will not rule over you, nor shall my son rule over you; the LORD shall rule over you" (Judg. 8:23).

A number of years later, God sent the prophet Samuel to Jesse's household to anoint the man who would become king of Israel. David was a most unlikely candidate. In fact, he wasn't even invited to the feast by his own father, who instead left David in the fields to watch the sheep. God, however, had other plans. God's words to Samuel give us a glimpse into the reasoning behind God's call: "For God sees not as man sees, for man looks at the outward appearance, but the LORD looks at the heart" (1 Sam. 16:7).

Once we move beyond the period of the kings, we meet another unlikely candidate for God's call into service. The prophet Jeremiah rose in prominence as a spokesman for God, but his beginnings were less than impressive. Jeremiah could have been the poster child for reluctant servants. He tried to beg out of his calling by telling God, "Alas, Lord GOD! Behold, I do not know how to speak, because I am a youth" (Jer. 1:6). God's response was simple, "Do not say 'I am a youth,' because everywhere I send you, you shall go, and all that I command you, you shall speak.... Behold, I have put My words in your mouth" (Jer. 1:7, 9).

One of the more humorous glimpses into an Old Testament ministry leader is seen in Amos's response to a prophet by the name of Amaziah. In a self-effacing revelation of his own reluctance to enter into the ministry Amos responded, "I am not a prophet, nor am I the son of a prophet; for I am a herdsman and a grower of sycamore figs" (Amos 7:14). In essence, Amos responded in the face of opposition, "Hey man, don't blame me, I'm just the messenger here. I didn't apply for this job. I was busy minding my own business with a stable career when God interrupted my life and called me into his service."

Biblical Evidence of a Divine Call in the New Testament

The New Testament also provides us with biblical insights into the ways and means of God's calling people. Jesus selected his twelve disciples from a vast array of backgrounds. Some were minding their own business and leading productive lives when they had an encounter with Jesus. Their lives were never the same. Jesus' call to Levi, a corrupt tax collector, was direct and unequivocal: "Follow Me" (Luke 5:27). Each of the disciples received a personal invitation to follow him along the journey set before him.

Perhaps the call of no other New Testament figure illustrates the mysterious workings of God more than that of Saul. While on a journey to fulfill what he wrongly thought was God's will (i.e., extermination of the sect known as Christians), Saul was knocked nearly senseless on the road to Damascus when he heard the voice of Jesus saying to him, "Saul, Saul, why do you persecute me?" After a brief verbal exchange, during which Jesus told Saul to wait for further instructions, God provided a somewhat reluctant servant by the name of Ananias to come and bring healing to Saul's eyes. After Saul was healed and baptized, he embarked on a lifelong quest to spread the good news that Jesus is the Messiah (see Rom. 1:1; 1 Cor. 1:1).

A little while later, Barnabas and Saul, now named Paul, began doing ministry together in Antioch. While in this ministry partnership, the Holy Spirit set them apart with a specific call to become the church's first missionaries (Acts 13:2). A few chapters later, God called Paul and his companions again, only this time it was to take the gospel to Macedonia (Acts 16:9–10).

Forming a Theology of God's Call

Time and space don't allow for more detailed descriptions of each individual who received a call from God. I could give many more, but for the most part, they simply would reinforce what we have already uncovered. In forming a theology of a call to ministry based on these passages, a few guiding principles would include the following:

1. *God does the calling.* We have no biblical examples of someone rushing into God's throne room, asking for a ministry assignment, and receiving such a position. In fact, those who try to push their way into divine appointment suffer severe consequences (see Miriam and Aaron in Num. 12:6–10 and Korah, Dathan, and Abiram in Num. 16:1–35). As Gordon MacDonald puts it, "Calls were not classified ads so that anyone could volunteer. Persons, sometimes strange persons, were selected while others, seemingly more worthy and capable, were not."[3]

2. *God's method of calling is unpredictable.* We would love to reveal some prescriptive formula for how God calls men and women into service. Then we could hold our ministry call up to this litmus test and compare. If only it were that easy. God, however, doesn't fit his ways into some preconceived system. Elisha was called while plowing a field, Levi while sitting in a toll booth, and Peter while fishing. If there is anything we can say with confidence about the manner in which God issues a call, it is that God is unpredictable.

3. *God's call is compelling.* Recipients of God's call were compelled to serve even if they knew it would lead to pain and suffering. They had become so convinced of God's call on their lives that they no longer cared about their earthly existence. They lost sight of earthly treasures and lived focused on their eternal destination. This world was not their own, and they knew it wasn't their final destination. They were men and women of whom the world was not worthy (Heb. 11:38). Their response to God's calling was unwavering dedication.

4. *Recipients of God's call serve out of a heart of gratitude.* A common response of those called by God was an awareness of their own shortcomings. Isaiah declared to the angelic messenger, "Woe is me, for I am ruined! Because I am a man of unclean lips" (Isa. 6:5). The called often served out of an awareness that they had done nothing to deserve the call. If they were going to be conscripted into God's army, they would serve with a heart of gratitude. They were a blessed few who enjoyed a special anointing and close fellowship with the Creator of the universe. Their attitude was like that of the writer of Hebrews: "Therefore, since we receive a kingdom which cannot be shaken, let us show gratitude, by which we may offer to God an acceptable service with reverence and awe" (Heb. 12:28).

5. *God's will and your own emotions are not linked.* You may have heard someone in ministry say something like this: "I just heard God speak, and I feel good about it." That seems absurd in light of the biblical evidence. I highly doubt Gideon felt good about taking so few men into the battle against the Midianites even though he knew it was God's will (Judg. 7:7 – 8). I'm certain Jonah didn't feel too good about going to Nineveh even though he knew beyond any doubt that it was God's will. Ananias heard God command him to go and lay hands on Saul for his healing, but he was clearly not feeling very good about the assignment (Acts 9:13 – 14). Clearly, just because you don't *feel* good about something doesn't necessarily mean it isn't God's will. Feelings are nice when they complement your convictions, but they should never be the deciding factor in an important decision.

How Many Calls?

Some read through these passages and others like them and come to the realization that there are different kinds of calls. Indeed, there are at least three: a call to salvation, a call to general service, and a call to specific service. Let's take a brief look at each.

1. *Call to conversion.* The concept of a call to salvation has its roots in the doctrine of election. The Greek word *eklektos* is the primary word used for election in the New Testament. It literally means "to pick out, choose." A passage that illustrates this concept is Ephesians 1:4 – 5: "He chose us in Him before the foundation of the world, that we would be holy and blameless before Him. In love He predestined us to adoption as sons through Jesus Christ to Himself, according to the kind intention of His will." In contemporary terms it can be said, "If election is God's sovereign choosing in eternity past, then calling is the actualizing of that fact in history. Calling becomes the initial, temporal saving act of God.... We are not referring to a vocational calling but to a call to salvation."[4]

It stands to reason that one cannot be called to vocational service without first hearing—and subsequently accepting—an initial call to salvation. Therefore, individuals who are trying to find God's will for their lives regarding a vocational call must first be sure that they have responded to Christ's invitation to salvation.

2. *Call to general service.* This type of call naturally extends beyond the foundational call to salvation. The Scriptures teach that all believers should be involved in the work of building up the body of Christ (Eph. 4:11 – 13; 1 Peter 4:10). We have been given salvation for the purpose of making a contribution to the body of Christ. In Ephesians 2:10 we read, "For we are His workmanship, created in Christ Jesus for good works, which God prepared beforehand so that we would walk in them." God intends for every believer to use his or her God-given talents and abilities for the furtherance of the kingdom. These acts of service may include playing the piano for the church choir, directing crafts at a vacation Bible school, or serving as a camp counselor one week during the summer. No act of service is too small, and each helps further the cause of Christ's kingdom.

In essence, everyone who is called to salvation is also called to serve. In a very real sense then, every believer is also a minister, for the Bible does not differentiate between clergy and laity. However, that is not to say that every believer should change his or her career after conversion and enter into full-time ministry. One's career calling is a different issue altogether. This general type of calling views "every legitimate occupation of life in a significant sense as a calling of God."[5]

3. *Call to specific service.* This type of call is what someone entering vocational ministry might expect. It is predicated upon the individual accepting Christ as Savior (i.e., call to salvation) and having begun to serve in some ministry capacity on a volunteer basis (i.e., general call to service). At some point, then, this individual senses God's direct leading toward the vocational career of ministry.

Discerning Your Call

As I said, one's calling is usually a unique personal experience. Some calls are dramatic and some are slow to form. It isn't that one is right and the other is wrong — they're just different. I'm not saying, however, that there aren't ways to know whether one's call is real. God's Word gives us some general indicators, including the following.

Indicator #1: A stirring of the heart. Many times when God wants to raise up a man or woman for a particular task, he stirs the heart of the individual and begins to do a work in the person's spirit in preparation to receive his or her marching orders. Even while a shepherd, David's heart evidenced kingly courage as he faced the overwhelming odds of fighting Goliath (1 Sam. 17). God was preparing his heart for the challenge of shepherding his people while still deeply involved in his daily occupation. This is particularly common for those who enter the ministry as their second career.

Indicator #2: The confirmation of church leaders. The Bible clearly teaches that every believer receives a gift from the Holy Spirit that is intended to be used in ministry (Rom. 12:4–8; 1 Cor. 12:7; 1 Peter 4:10). For those who are entering the ministry with a desire to use that gift in full-time service, it stands to reason that they have identified that giftedness and have tested it in real-life practice. We see that in the way the early church called out men for positions of ministry leadership. Before men were commissioned for full-time service, they had already demonstrated their giftedness in the local church. The calling out was simply the church's way of confirming what they had already seen in practice.

Ever since seven men of "good reputation, full of the Spirit and of wisdom" were chosen to minister to the widows in the church at Jerusalem (Acts 6:3), local church leaders have exercised this most important task of identifying and commissioning qualified ministers based on past experience. Every mission organization I have ever worked with follows this biblical principle and requires the leaders of the candidate's local church to validate and confirm his or her gifts, ministry skills, and character before he or she is accepted.

Indicator #3: Prayer. God confirms his calling on men and women through his voice. God calls and people respond to (or in some cases reject) the voice of God through the spiritual conversation of prayer. Prayer is used to ask God about the nature of the call, the specifics of the destination, the training that will be required, and of course, the timing of the task. Rarely does all the information come at once. Sometimes the details come in small increments, but since it is God's sovereign plan being revealed and not ours, it is important that we wait to hear from him on his timetable and that we learn to discern the difference between what he wants us to do and what we want. More on this will be presented in chapter 19.

Indicator #4: The guidance of a mentor. Mentor relationships take time to develop, but the best ones are marked by one critical component. Mentors are honest with their protégés and speak the truth — even if it sometimes hurts. That's because the mentor knows that he or she has been entrusted by God to prepare this young leader for vocational service. It's a huge responsibility.

Mentors can influence your life long after you move to another city. You know you have a good mentor relationship when you can phone after several years' absence and pick up right where you left off without skipping a beat. Now that mentor is a colleague, and the advice he or she provides is priceless. God can, and often does, speak through the counsel of mentors and colleagues who have known you over many years. This can be one of your best resources for confirming God's call on your life (Prov. 12:15; 15:22).

Indicator #5: The partnership of a spouse. Some may disagree, but I believe that entering into ministry without the full support of your spouse is foolhardy. I've known far too many male pastors who sincerely felt called into God's full-time vocational service only to discover that their wives wanted nothing to do with it. They couldn't see themselves in that lifestyle, and they let it be known that if they had to go down that road they would go kicking and screaming. Some of these pastors went anyway, and the results were devastating. The church never warmed up to the spouse, and conflict was the inevitable result. If you've made a vow to another in marriage, you're now a team and travel as such to wherever God has called you. A divided house cannot stand, so before you respond to God's call, make sure both of you are on the same page and hear his voice together. Be honest. Now is the time to reveal any hesitations and to be willing to wait until both of you hear God's voice.

Whatever the process by which you're convinced God has called you to specific vocational ministry, a word of understanding from a pastor in Nebraska is worth heeding:

> Those called into ministry usually fall into the trap of considering it to be a career rather than a calling. Then, when the troubles come, they break into little pieces (as I did), and some, I fear, don't ever truly recover. Either they're able to find another position through their own efforts, but apart from the pleasure of the King, or they leave ministry entirely for greener pastures.

At the end of this chapter you will find a calling worksheet. Take the time to respond to the items as you contemplate the next stop on your ministry journey. Perhaps in so doing you will avoid the tendency our colleague mentions and go forward convinced of your God-given call to duty. Service to the King of Kings demands nothing less.

Two Critical Questions

While asking ourselves if we are confident of our vocational calling we might overlook other important questions. We have a tendency to think about our gift(s), job descriptions, geography, and whether we will serve in a church or parachurch setting. Regardless of the kind of ministry we pursue, it is essential to have answers to two critical questions: What am I called to *be*? and What am I called to *do*? The right answer to each of these questions will keep us on track for a lifetime.

Question #1: What am I called to be? Many titles have been used to describe those called to serve God as ministry leaders. They include elder, bishop, preacher, teacher, servant, and messenger. The titles presbyter, priest, parson, rector, and minister could also be added to this list. And then there are the metaphors used by the apostle Paul to describe ministry leaders — shepherd, slave, father, nurse, helmsman, ambassador, farmer, builder, soldier, and athlete.

Of all the metaphors that describe the ministry leader, shepherd rises above the rest. After all, it's the picture used to describe the ministry of Jesus as he was sent to seek and to save those who were lost. Knowing how this metaphor is used to describe the role of the local church pastor helps us understand the nature of our calling, because as ministry leaders, we are called to serve God's sheep as shepherds. There are four reasons for this.

First, shepherd is a primary means through which God identifies himself. Jacob refers to God as a shepherd in Genesis 48:15 as he blesses Joseph: "The God before whom my fathers Abraham and Isaac walked, the God who has been my shepherd all my life to this day...." David declares in Psalm 23, "The LORD is my shepherd." Jesus refers to himself as the "good shepherd" (John 10), and the writer of Hebrews calls Jesus the "great Shepherd of the sheep" (Heb. 13:20). It is a role that God uses to describe the manner in which he wants his nature to be revealed. Therefore, as ministry leaders, we are to emulate that role in our service to his sheep.

Second, shepherd is the one biblical metaphor that spans the boundaries of the biblical record. Genesis 4:2 tells us that Abel was a keeper of sheep, and Revelation 7:17 carries these words of encouragement for the coming age when John writes of Jesus, "For the Lamb in the center of the throne shall be their shepherd, and will guide them to springs of the water of life; and God will wipe every tear from their eyes."

Third, shepherd is the one image used most often in describing the work of both Old and New Testament leaders of God's people. Kings (Cyrus — Isa. 44:28), prophets (Moses — Num. 27:17), judges (1 Chron. 17:6), apostles (John 21:15–17), and elders (1 Peter 5:1–3) are designated as shepherds throughout the pages of biblical history. Even in today's larger churches, many pastors see themselves, in spite of the specialization of ministry, as shepherds of God's people. A study of one hundred large church pastors found that over 89 percent saw themselves as shepherd preachers as opposed to teachers, students, or administrators.[6]

Fourth, throughout church history, leaders of the church have looked to Christ the shepherd for inspiration and direction concerning the pastoral calling. Thomas Oden writes:

> No image has influenced the practice of pastoral care more than its chief formative metaphor, the good shepherd caring for the vulnerable flock amid a perilous world.... It is only on the basis of this axial metaphor that the pastor can reflect rightly upon due authorization to ministry and upon *diakonia*. It constitutes an important link in the correlation of Christ's shepherding with contemporary shepherding.[7]

Charles Jefferson adds:

> If the aim of our life is to be Christlike, then we must be like a shepherd. If we are called to fulfill Christ's mission, then our work is that of a shepherd. If we are to be judged by Christ, then the standard of judgment day is to be the standard of a shepherd.... To glorify him we must do a shepherd's work, and to enjoy him forever we must have the shepherd heart.[8]

Regardless of the size or condition of our congregation, we are all called to the same duty—to shepherd the flock under our care. We might look different, but we all do pretty much the same job.

Question #2: What am I called to do? The job description of a pastor is anything but uniform. What one church is looking for in one location may be, and probably will be, quite different from a church in another location. Even pastoral job descriptions in the same denomination vary a great deal. Too many variables go into making a job description for space to allow a detailed discussion at this point, but suffice it to say that factors such as denominational affiliation, size of the congregation, size of the city, and general demographics of the congregation (e.g., education level, socioeconomic class, gender, age, etc.) all contribute to making the *average* job description of a pastor difficult to define. Some time ago a friend sent me a Help Wanted ad he came across while reading the classifieds. It read:

> SHEEPHERDER with minimum of 30 days' experience. Attends sheep grazing on range, herds sheep using trained dogs. Guards flock from predators and from eating poisonous plants. May assist in lambing, docking and shearing. Large flocks with a single-pair herder. Food, housing, tools, supplies and equipment provided. Hours variable but on call 24 hours, 7 days a week. Minimum salary is $650 in WY, NV, AZ, MT, and OR; $650 in CO and ID; $700 for CA and UT.

I have seen a lot of pastoral job descriptions over the years, and this ad reminds me of more than a few. Any pastor who reads this advertisement will agree that there are some similarities between their role as spiritual shepherd and the role of a shepherd of real sheep: long hours, low benefits, and hard work. These circumstances have prompted some pastors to amend their role to that of a rancher rather than a shepherd. Such a distinction allows them to remove themselves from the day-to-day crunch of ministry responsibilities and delegate the "dirty work" of ministry to others who are lower on the ministerial food chain. Obviously, such distinctions are not biblical, and I would caution pastors against using such labels. I like the words of admonition one author wrote in *Leadership Journal*:

I don't think it's wise to stand up and say, "Folks, I don't think I have the gift of shepherding so don't expect me to act like a shepherd. I'm a preacher. So I'm just going to give myself to preaching." Chances are, if you say something like that, your Christmas bonus will include a gift certificate from Allied Van Lines. Instead, you need to find individuals who love doing the things you find difficult.[9]

Shepherds of sheep and shepherds of people are pictured in a number of settings, going about their important work under the watchful care of the Great Shepherd. The biblical vocation of spiritual shepherd includes at least five common responsibilities.

1. *Shepherds feed and sustain their congregations.* As understood by those in the days of Jesus' sojourn in Israel, the shepherd was the one responsible to oversee the feeding and nourishment of the flock. Peter admonished the church elders to "shepherd (*poimaíno*) the flock of God" (1 Peter 5:2). Peter had been given the same admonition from Jesus shortly after his resurrection. The apostle Paul also gave the elders in Ephesus the same charge to "shepherd (*poimaíno*) the church of God" (Acts 20:28).

Biblical shepherds had to labor diligently to secure enough food and water to sustain the flock. Changing weather and seasons, geographical obstacles, and the frequent scarcity of water made the job of filling those woolly bellies a formidable one. It's also important to feed the sheep healthy food. In Psalm 23:2 David rejoiced in God's ability to lead him to *green* pastures. The Hebrew word pictures new, young, tender vegetation. This suggests that our teaching should come from a deep personal study of the Word, not ready-to-use sermons from the Internet. Pastoral work is challenging, requiring our hard work and personal commitment to faithful teaching and preaching.

2. *Shepherds lead and guide their congregations.* The lives of the sheep were dependent on the leadership of the shepherd. He led them to safety and watched over them to ensure their security. It should be no different for the ministry leader today. Today's Christian bookstores are filled with volumes on leadership, management, vision, and a host of other subjects related to this important dimension of a shepherd's role. However, as helpful as many of these resources are, the Bible had much to say about leadership long before any of these popular books.[10]

In the Old Testament we read of God leading the children of Israel in the wilderness. "The LORD was going before them in a pillar of cloud by day to lead them on the way, and in a pillar of fire by night to give them light, that they might travel by day and by night" (Ex. 13:21). Leadership was clearly an issue with God in relation to the responsibilities of the shepherds of his people. His messages through the prophets to the kings, magistrates, and religious leaders of Israel often made mention of their failure to lead the people of God.

3. *Shepherds go looking for lost sheep.* Pastors who are faithful to their calling do not shirk the evangelistic nature of their work. Though they may not be specifically gifted in the work of evangelism, they are still responsible to do the work of an evangelist (2 Tim. 4:5). With a 92 percent increase in the number of unchurched Americans between 1991 and 2004 according to the Barna Research Group, those of us in ministry have plenty of lost sheep to find.[11]

I have never had so many opportunities to go looking for lost sheep as when I served as a pastor. The position gave me countless opportunities for sharing the gospel. In one encounter, my wife returned from an eye examination and told me how her ophthalmologist was considering quitting after being on the job a few short months. The next day I went to his office to thank him for taking such good care of my wife. We struck up a conversation and an eventual friendship. I invited him to attend my church and soon had the joy of watching him and his entire family give their lives to Christ. That's what shepherds do. They go and find the lost and invite them into the fold where the Great Shepherd will take care of their eternal needs.

4. *Shepherds care for the sick and needy.* Healing is mentioned more than two hundred times in the Bible. Shepherds continually keep an eye out for wounds and diseases among their flocks. Caring for the perishing, in contrast to Zechariah 11:16, indicates the attending to, visiting, or looking after those that have been cut off or made desolate.[12] One aspect of caring's broader meaning is "to pass in review," much as the sheep do as the shepherd inspects them each day as they return to the fold for the night. The shepherd looks for signs of parasites, injury, poor nutrition, and any other indications that the sheep are in distress.

Our heritage as shepherds carries a wonderful and challenging call to be there for our people, ready to roll up our sleeves and get involved in their lives as compassionate caregivers. Loving ministers are called to emulate the shepherd who carries the sheep, bearing them up in their time of need (Ps. 28:9; Isa. 40:11). To fulfill this responsibility, we need to know the sheep by being involved in their lives enough to recognize the danger signals and be willing to jump in and invest ourselves in their struggles.

5. *Shepherds guard and protect the congregation.* The words of the psalmist "He makes me lie down ..." from Psalm 23 reflect the presence of a faithful shepherd. The Hebrew word used here means "to stretch oneself out, lie down, lie stretched out."[13] One can visualize the sheep spreading out securely in a pasture of green grass and cool streams. Author Phillip Keller, once a shepherd himself, writes that sheep will behave in this way only if they are free from hunger, free from friction with other sheep, free from flies and pests, and free from fear.[14] We have

seen how the shepherd's roles of feeder, leader, seeker, and healer provide the first three requisite freedoms. The final role of the shepherd is that of guardian and protector of the sheep.

Danger is everywhere these days. Our congregations are being bombarded by false messages and destructive influences daily. As shepherds, we are called to bravely and faithfully stand in protection over God's people. As the shepherds kept "watch over their flock by night" on the night of Jesus' birth (Luke 2:8), so we must keep vigilant watch (Heb. 13:17) when it comes to guarding those given to our charge. We can accomplish this in more obvious ways by providing resources to battle the false doctrines and subtle lure of cults and other philosophies of this world system that seek to make idols of people or their environment. But we must also be attentive to the sneak attacks that Satan employs to devastate our flocks.

The answer to this second question of "What am I called to do?" is provided as simply as this. Shepherds are called to feed, lead, search out, care for, and protect those whom God places in their sphere of influence. Though it is simple to list these things, they often take a lifetime to learn to do well.

Summing It Up

Transitions are great times to revisit one's call, but we should do so periodically even if we aren't changing positions. Reviewing the various confirmations we received and taking the time to reexamine them is healthy for us from time to time. Understanding the process and nature of God's call to ministry will enable us to thrive in the exciting and often dangerous world of pastoral service. No matter what position you now hold or hope to acquire, contemplating your call is worth the time and energy. The following questions are designed to help you review and reestablish both your call to ministry and commitment to faithfully shepherd God's people no matter where this journey you're on takes you.

REVIEWING YOUR CALL TO VOCATIONAL MINISTRY

1. Under what circumstances do you believe God has called you into vocational ministry?

2. Of the five indicators of discerning a vocational call presented in this chapter (i.e., stirring of the heart, confirmation of the church, prayer, guidance of a mentor, and the partnership of one's spouse), which one(s) are you most sure of at this time? Why?

3. Of the five indicators for discerning a vocational call, which one(s) are you most uncertain of at this time? Why?

4. What, if anything, is making you question your call to vocational ministry right now?

REESTABLISHING YOUR CALL TO VOCATIONAL MINISTRY

1. Where are you restless in your current ministry assignment? Why?

2. Where are you finding the most pleasure in your current ministry assignment? Why?

3. How has the Holy Spirit been speaking to you lately about your vocational ministry?

4. What are your mentor's observations about your ministry assignment now?

5. What are your spouse's observations about your ministry assignment now?

TWO CRITICAL QUESTIONS ABOUT YOUR CALL

1. Are you comfortable with the metaphor of a shepherd, or is there another word picture you would prefer to use in describing your current ministry setting? If so, describe it here.

2. As a shepherd, how do you rate the following areas of ministry responsibilities? What might your answers be telling you regarding the nature of your next ministry position?

		Love it—this motivates me	Do okay here—can manage	Struggle with this one	Need others to provide this
AREA OF OVERSIGHT	**Feeding them**				
	Leading them				
	Seeking the lost				
	Caring for them				
	Protecting them				

CHAPTER 2

I HAVE A DREAM

Personal Mission, Vision, and Values

MICHAEL ANTHONY

Where there is no vision, the people perish.
Proverbs 29:18 KJV

Some years ago a survey was conducted to determine how satisfied a cross section of men and women were with their careers. If they scored a 10 on the scale, they saw their work as passionate play. They looked forward to going to work each day and thrived in their career environment. On the opposite side of the scale were those who saw their work as drudgery. They dreaded each thought of work and nearly had to be dragged there each day kicking and screaming. The results revealed that 10 percent saw their work as passionate play, 10 percent saw their work as a living nightmare, and the remaining 80 percent fell within the categories that could best be summarized as neutral. The majority of workers neither loved nor hated their jobs — they simply endured each day. The majority went through the motions each day and returned home when the clock struck 5:00 p.m.[1]

How sad to think that the vast majority of people today have no sense of excitement and vitality about their work. If only 10 percent of all workers across North America are passionate about their chosen careers, what does that say about the quality of their personal lives as well? How can people work at meaningless jobs all day, then go home feeling good about themselves?

Waking from the Dream

Men and women weren't created to live lives of mind-numbing drudgery. God calls us to lives of fulfillment, joy, and meaningful purpose. Pastors enter the ministry expecting their lives to make a difference in the world. They hope to see daily victories as God uses them to recapture paradise lost. However, ministry leaders in our national survey didn't always share such a perspective. In fact, their satisfaction levels mirrored those in the national study mentioned above. In other words, becoming a pastor doesn't guarantee years of employment bliss!

But why is that? Shouldn't we expect to live lives of meaning and purpose if we're serving God? Why is it unusual to hear a pastor say, "I love my job and there isn't anything else in life I'd rather be doing"? In countless interviews we have had with ministry leaders over the years, we have often heard the lament voiced, "I'm too old to change careers now, but if I knew in seminary what I know now, I never would have accepted the call to enter the ministry. It just isn't what I thought it would be."

The reasons for this lament are many and varied, but more often than not, these ministry leaders never really had a deep understanding of their call and what expectations would be placed on those who accepted the invitation to enter a career in ministry. They lacked a healthy understanding of what was expected of them and, as a result, entered into ministry with a certain wanderlust. They thought life would be filled with endless victories and countless transformed lives.

It is interesting to note that there is seldom a relationship between levels of ministry satisfaction and what we would expect. That is, survey after survey confirms what we find nearly impossible to believe. Simply stated, money, reputation, and prestige don't bring happiness. Those at the top of the corporate ladder who surround themselves with the trappings of corporate luxury are rarely the ones who speak of contentment, personal fulfillment, or meaningful existence. More often than not, they're lonely, driven, and insecure people who attained their wealth by taking advantage of others along the way. In their hearts, and often-times in their interpersonal relationships, they are lonely and desperate people in search of peace. The old adage "It's lonely at the top" is true for most of corporate America today. And unfortunately, it's also true for many pastors as well.

So how do you wake up from this nightmare? How do you get beyond the elusive quest for more recognition, compensation, or ego-driven living? Career satisfaction, personal contentment, and meaningful living are not found in a job. They are found in a personal calling. And there's a big difference between the two.

The Anatomy of a Call

We discussed the nature of the call to ministry at length in chapter 1, so we will be brief here. Countless books have been written on the subject. Some view this call as a response to a dramatic dream, vision, or life-changing experience. Some view it as a natural response to one's gifts and talents. A few see it as a decision that is made when all the boxes on a chart are checked. I'm not certain that any of these are right. Sure, some biblical evidence can be presented to illustrate that God called men and women into service through dreams and visions. God called Moses into service by talking through a burning bush, but that was a rare occurrence that hasn't been duplicated since. One person's experience isn't normative for all others.

A call may be different things to different people. As unique as each individual is before God, one's call to ministry is unique as well. For one, it involves an intense search of the Scriptures. For others, it comes as a result of a life-changing experience. They declare, "Oh God, if you just get me through this crisis, I'll become a missionary in Africa." However, for others, it comes over time as they realize that God seems to be nudging them along on a journey. They experience no dramatic turns or sudden catastrophic events, just a slow conviction that grows over time. Each type of call is sure and convincing to the recipient, but much like snowflakes, no two calls are identical.

The Value of Life Mission

Perhaps a better way to look at God's direction for your life is to take a step back and examine the unique configuration of your personality, life experiences, education, and current circumstances. No one element is the sum of who you are, but neither can you deny any one element's importance in shaping you into the person you have become. Together they form a kind of mosaic of who God has made you to be. Flowing out of this unique configuration of traits and circumstances is your life mission. A life mission explains your reason for being, why you live to draw breath, and what sustains your will to survive when you travel life's deep valleys. It gives you strength when the road gets long and tiresome, and it recharges your batteries when you feel weary from long hours of work. This mission shapes your core values and forms the basis for guiding your decision making.

Those who live without a personal mission lack direction, meaning, and purpose. Their lives are characterized by impulsive change and insecurity. They wander about, hoping the decisions they make will pan out in the end and won't come back to haunt them. There is little assurance that decision making is intentional, so life is one endless string of choices based on information gathered at the time but without a sense of certainty that new forthcoming information won't change everything. For people without a personal mission, abiding peace is elusive.

The value of a personal life mission can be illustrated by a trip I took with a group of high school students a few years ago. They had never been on a sailboat, so I rented a thirty-foot Erickson and set out for Catalina Island, about thirty miles off the California coast. We left early in the morning while the fog was thick, but excitement filled the air. Soon after leaving the coastline behind, the guys grew anxious about not being able to see land behind them or in front of them. Without landmarks, they feared being lost at sea. I had them put on blindfolds, and then I spun the boat in circles. Within seconds they were clueless about what direction to travel. I asked them which way I should go to find Catalina, and they had no idea. It was at that point, just when they felt most anxious, that I taught them the value of a compass. Once they learned how to steer the ship according to the right heading, they knew they were safe. Their fears subsided, and they grew confident about which way to go — even though they still couldn't see land. The compass made all the difference.

In a sense, a life mission serves as a compass that points you toward your true north. Important decisions about what direction to travel are made only after consulting this directional reference. It guides you when you are faced with hard questions, such as What college should I attend? What should I major in while at seminary? Should I marry Betty? Should I take advantage of this "once in a life time opportunity" or let it go? A personal life mission can arbitrate these decisions for you.

When we asked the pastors who completed our survey if they had ever taken the time to develop a personal mission statement, they responded with an overwhelming yes. In fact, 79 percent said they had developed such a statement, and 84 percent of those said that it had been useful in making important ministry decisions.

A life mission should reflect your theology about God, your connection to his purposes, and your philosophy about life in general. A life mission is a general statement about your reason for being. It clarifies your focus and provides unwavering conviction about what you feel is most important in life. However, knowing the benefits of a mission and writing one are entirely different.

Although a number of verses could be used to demonstrate a mission statement for the life of Christ, perhaps one of the best would be Isaiah 61:1–2, a passage he read while addressing Jewish leaders in a synagogue:

> *The Spirit of the Lord GOD is upon me,*
> *Because the LORD has anointed me*
> *To bring good news to the afflicted;*
> *He has sent me to bind up the brokenhearted,*
> *To proclaim liberty to captives*
> *And freedom to prisoners;*
> *To proclaim the favorable year of the LORD*
> *And the day of vengeance of our God;*
> *To comfort all who mourn.*

Crafting Your Life Mission Statement

A life mission statement tells the world why God made you. It connects the dots between God's sovereign plan for the universe and the part he created you to play in it. Some examples of a personal life mission statement might include the following four examples:

> Paul Stevenson lives to explore and experience God's creation through passionate relationships with nature, music, art, and drama.

For Paul, life is viewed as a journey of discovery rather than a specific destination. It reflects his emphasis on unique and creative expression. Would it surprise you to learn that Paul is a worship pastor at a church in Southern California?

> Dan Miller lives to serve those throughout the world who are living broken lives and are in need of physical healing and restoration.

It should come as no surprise that Dan is a medical doctor who spends his personal vacation each year serving on medical teams that travel to Third World countries to provide surgical treatment to destitute people who otherwise couldn't afford such services. If Dan had a life motto printed on his business card, it would read "Medicine with a Mission," because Dan wants his medical training and experience to be spent on far more lasting things than new cars and vacation homes.

Some people craft their life mission around their favorite verse of Scripture or Bible story. This passage "says it all" for them. Perhaps more than any other verse, this passage lifts the fog and gives clarity and direction. Sometimes it is a paraphrased version of a passage that restates their mission in a more personal or contemporary way.

> Todd King lives to go into all the world to make disciples of all people whom he personally encounters. He seeks to bring these individuals to a point of spiritual conversion and then journey through life together until he can present them complete in Christ.

Obviously Todd's life mission is based on a blending of the Great Commission in Matthew 28:19–20 and also Colossians 1:28. Todd and his family are serving as missionaries in South Africa as I write this. He is creating a new Christian camp with a desire to find a unique way to evangelize and disciple needy people in that part of the world. He is living out his life mission through his vocation. Below is one final example that shows the relationship that can exist between a life mission and a passage of Scripture.

> Tom Baker's life is a testimony of God's grace and reconciliation. He desires to bring those who are broken and downtrodden into a renewed and restored relationship with God in Christ.

Tom is a Christian marriage counselor living in California. He conducts marriage enrichment seminars at Christian camps and conference centers. He has written several books to help couples in crisis and has an extensive private practice dedicated to helping people whose lives have come apart at the seams and are suffering without hope.

Mission is a general statement about life's meaning and direction. Those in our survey who had taken the time to reflect on the importance of a life mission and had actually written one down said it helped guide them in decision making and allowed them to feel greater confidence in the direction their lives were taking.

Going beyond Mission to Vision

Whereas a mission is a general statement about what you sense is your reason for existence, a vision statement is far more specific in nature. The vision statement builds on the mission to bring about more specificity. It is unique to you.

Pastor Bill Hybels says that "when a church needs a God-honoring, kingdom-advancing, heart-thumping vision, it turns to its leaders. That is why God put in the leader's arsenal the potent offensive weapon called vision."[2] George Barna defines vision as "a clear mental image of a preferable future imparted by God to His chosen servants, based upon an accurate understanding of God, self, and circumstances."[3] Martin Luther King Jr. put it this way: "If a man hasn't discovered something he will die for, he isn't fit to live." Dr. King's personal life vision had a lasting impact on his ministry and also on an entire nation. Others have sought to describe life vision as *foresight.* "It means seeing that which is yet to be and putting a plan together to make it a reality."[4] In other words, vision brings the mission to life. Where the mission statement gives a general sense of purpose, a vision statement is far more precise, detailed, customized, and specific to each person. It provides the audience with the *who, what,* and *how* of its efforts.[5]

Barna provides a set of guidelines to help ministry leaders determine whether what they have is more of a mission statement or a vision statement.[6] With some minor modification, we have taken this same list and modified it to reflect a personal vision rather than a corporate statement. Using the set of questions cited, if you can respond "no" to most of them, then what you have is a statement of mission rather than vision.

Conducting a Life Vision Interview

In Susan Sully's book *The Late Bloomer's Guide to Success at Any Age,* she suggests a helpful approach to developing a life vision statement.[7] Imagine that you are being interviewed by someone you highly regard. This interview is taking

Mission or Vision?

1. If someone contacted you regarding involvement in what seemed like a reasonable ministry opportunity, is the statement specific enough to permit you to have a ministry-oriented reason to reject that opportunity and explain the reasoning for the rejection?

2. Does the statement include information, which, when compared to the vision statement of other individuals, clearly sets you apart in a significant manner?

3. Does the statement identify a target audience whom you hope to impact through your ministry?

4. Is the statement one that points you in a clear and unique direction for the future?

5. Does the statement lead to a precise understanding regarding the strategies and tactics that are permissible for you?

6. Does the statement provide focus for you so that people are excited about being involved in your life?

7. Does the statement prevent you from seeking to be all things to all people?

8. Has anyone around you become excited or engaged in your life's work after being exposed to your statement?

place for a magazine with nationwide circulation or is perhaps even being done by a television talk show host. The individual who is interviewing you has scheduled an appointment, so nothing should disturb the next few hours this exercise will take. Take a drive to a quiet park or nearby lake so you won't be disturbed. Stop by Starbucks on the way and pick up your favorite drink. Now you should be relaxed and ready for the interview. Begin by responding to the following questions. You can respond by answering in your mind or out loud, by writing your answers down on a separate piece of paper, or by writing them down in the space provided. It is best if you make a written record of your responses, because you'll be coming back to them again later.

1. When you look back at your life and all the various experiences that you've had, what would you say were the high points—that is, the moments when you felt most exhilarated and passionate about what you were doing?

2. Describe a time when you felt truly inspired by what you were doing.

3. Describe a moment when you felt you were performing at your personal all-time best. What led you to this peak performance capability, and how often have you experienced it in life?

4. What is it about the situation you cited above that gave you such a deep sense of joy and fulfillment?

5. What would you say was the single most important thing you have ever done in your life to date? Why?

6. What is the biggest challenge you had to overcome in life so far? How did you overcome it?

7. What gave you the motivation to overcome such an obstacle in your life?

8. Most people can look back through the years of their lives and pinpoint a defining moment in their development—something that really shaped the person they eventually became. What was that one defining moment in your life?

9. If you could turn back the hands of time and change the direction your life has taken, what would you be doing differently today?

10. If God appeared to you in a dream as he did to Solomon (1 Kings 3:5–15), what one thing would you ask him to do for you?

Now that you have had a chance to record your thoughts, the next step in the process is to review your responses to the first five questions. These questions asked you to reflect on when life brought you the greatest personal satisfaction. When you read your responses, do you see any common denominators? Do you see a common theme being woven throughout? Are there similarities between your responses even though the situations may have occurred at different times and in different locations? For example, you may see a common thread of helping people in each of your responses. Maybe taking risks is indicative to each as well.

Now take a look at the remaining questions. These questions cause you to examine your response to obstacles, examine your personal motivations, and express your hopes about the future. By taking the time to consider these important issues, you should gain fresh insights about what makes you tick.

Now it's time to put a vision statement together. Remember, the vision statement is far more specific in nature than a mission statement. The vision statement should summarize your personal passions and interests as expressed during your interview. For example, if you find that many of your responses relate to your desire to come to the assistance of those who find themselves in distress, you might consider developing a vision statement around that theme. It might read, "The vision of my ministry is to provide biblically based counseling resources to people who are living in the greater Houston area. I will do this through my private counseling practice, conference workshops, and media productions, such as tapes and videos."

Don't worry if the process seems cumbersome at first. And don't be concerned if your sentences run on. You can edit your statement as you collect your thoughts and sharpen your focus. The important thing is that you are giving words to your dreams, desires, and heart passions.

Getting to the Core of One's Values

The last step in this self-discovery process is to identify your core values by asking yourself what the most important things are in your life. What principles drive your decision making? What issues stir up your deepest convictions? In her job-finding book, *I Don't Know What I Want, but I Know It's Not This*, Julie Jansen provides a checklist of possible core values. She cautions not to mark those core values you think *should* be yours but to honestly mark those that are evidenced in your daily living.[8]

- ❏ Achievement: producing results that are significant; completing them successfully
- ❏ Advancement: consistently moving ahead to new and progressive opportunities
- ❏ Autonomy: ability to choose your own projects and assignments, set your own pace, schedule, and work habits, minimal supervision of your efforts
- ❏ Balance: spending equivalent time and effort on tasks, work, and overall life
- ❏ Belonging to a group: having a sense of being a contributing member of a group
- ❏ Building something: creating or establishing a thing or idea
- ❏ Challenge: involvement with stimulating or demanding tasks or projects
- ❏ Competition: engaging in activities where results are measured frequently and compared to others
- ❏ Creativity: making, inventing, or producing innovative, imaginative, or original things or ideas
- ❏ Doing good: contributing to the betterment of the world
- ❏ Entrepreneurship: organizing, managing, or starting a business or enterprise
- ❏ Equality: having the same capability, quantity, effect, value, or status as others
- ❏ Excitement: involvement with new and dynamic experiences with variety, change, and risk

❏ Fame: possessing extreme visibility, a great reputation, being recognized and renowned

❏ Family happiness: focusing on relationships, time spent with and attention to children, spouse, parents, or relatives

❏ Financial security: pay and benefits that are satisfactory and predictable

❏ Friendships: frequent and caring relationships, camaraderie, and interaction with others

❏ Fun: experiencing pleasure, amusement, and enjoyment

❏ Happiness: feeling or showing pleasure and satisfaction, contentment and well-being, joy and happiness

❏ Harmony: feeling inner calm and tranquility

❏ Health: optimal functioning of body, mind, and spirit

❏ Helping others: giving assistance, support, and aid to others

❏ Independence: self-reliance, freedom from the influence, guidance, and control of others

❏ Integrity: strict personal honesty, firm adherence to a moral code

❏ Leadership: guiding, motivating, or directing others

❏ Learning: acquiring knowledge and satisfying curiosity

❏ Leisure: pursuing non-work-related activities

❏ Personal development: challenging your capabilities, acquiring new skills, and demonstrating abilities

❏ Physical activity: involvement in activities that rely on your body and physical exertion

❏ Recognition: being positively acknowledged by others, being given special notice and attention

❏ Respect: being treated with consideration and fairness

❏ Risk-taking: facing unknown or dangerous challenges or demands

❏ Safety: freedom from danger, risk, or injury

❏ Security: protection from fear, anxiety, or danger, a guarantee of the fulfillment of an agreement

❏ Self-expression: ability to communicate personal ideas, emotions, or feelings

❏ Spirituality: participating in a religious or ecclesiastical belief system

❏ Stability: maintaining an enduring, dependable, and predictable situation

❏ Status: possessing a prestigious position or rank

❏ Teamwork: working closely with others toward common goals, having close working relationships

❏ Wealth: owning a significant quantity of money or possessions

Reviewing this list of core values allows you to explore those life qualities that are important to you. This list is not exhaustive, so feel free to add a few values of your own by writing them below.

Now that you've taken some time to reflect on your personal core values, you should have an inclination about what motivates you in life. This composite list, when pulled together, should allow you to see what it is that makes your life compass point to true north. Take a moment and summarize below the values you checked on the list. If you indicated more than ten, then list only the top ten that are most indicative of your life. Remember, don't indicate the ones you would like to possess or should possess, but just the ones that you can look back through your life experience and see evidence of.

Now take a few moments and reflect on your current ministry position. To the right of each personal core value, check Yes or No to indicate whether or not your current ministry allows you to express this value in some aspect of your job. If you answered No to more than five, you may have some indication as to why you may not be experiencing much ministry satisfaction at the present time. Consider this list of core values when evaluating the ministry position in which you are currently serving and in any new position you may pursue in the future.

TOP TEN CORE VALUES

	Yes	No
1. _____	❏	❏
2. _____	❏	❏
3. _____	❏	❏
4. _____	❏	❏
5. _____	❏	❏
6. _____	❏	❏
7. _____	❏	❏
8. _____	❏	❏
9. _____	❏	❏
10. _____	❏	❏

However, he didn't like speaking in front of people, planning activities, or dealing with budgets and reports. Mark said his greatest fulfillment and joy came from working at home on the computer. Nothing filled Mark's cup of personal happiness more than that. He valued working independently, being creative, giving attention to details, and serving in ministry as a support person.

I explained to Mark that many of the problems he had faced weren't of his own making. He wasn't a failure in life or ministry. He simply lacked a connection between his personal mission, vision, and core values and those of his pastoral ministry. I suggested he think outside the box of traditional church ministry, so we brainstormed ideas about what kinds of jobs would allow him to live out his passions. Today he owns a successful desktop publishing business operating out of his home. He is happily married with children and serving churches in his area as their personal "publisher in residence."

Finding your fit in ministry shouldn't be as complicated as rocket science. But admittedly, it usually isn't as obvious as you would like it to be either. God has provided us with a mind to discern his movements in our lives. Some he calls into pastoral service, while others serve him in the marketplace. Each is critical to reaching his or her world for Christ. Pastors need to take the time to reflect on who God made them to be and only then look for ways to match that unique mosaic with a career. Only then will they find the deep personal fulfillment that God intends for them.

Every pastor should be in that top 10 percent of the population who find deep personal happiness and fulfillment in their jobs. The key to finding that is first coming to an understanding of your personal life mission, vision, and core values. Only then can you begin this journey looking for a career opportunity that will match your uniqueness.

Pulling It All Together

When you bring together the three elements of personal life mission, vision, and values, you will have a good idea of what makes you get out of bed in the morning. Your mission and vision statements, along with your core values, will give anyone who reads them an accurate description of who you are and why you have become the person you are, and a glimpse at where you want to be in the foreseeable future. Here's an example of how they might all come together:

The mission of Dan Smith's life is to reflect God's glory and celebrate His grace and mercy. In order to do this, my vision is to shepherd the congregation of New Faith Community Church as their Minister of Creative Arts and Worship. This will allow me to reflect my core values of worship and creative expression through music, art, drama, and video production.

Now that Dan has taken the time to get inside himself and see what makes him tick, he has a better idea of what kind of job he needs to pursue to remain true to the person whom God created him to be. When a person doesn't take the time to conduct this degree of self-analysis, disaster can be the end result.

Dan sees things differently today than he did when he came to me a few years ago as a desperate young pastor. As soon as he walked into my office, I knew I was in for a painful meeting. In one sense, I had seen it coming years earlier when he was a student in my seminary classes. I'd been following Dan's career over the past few years from a distance. For instance, I knew he had been fired from his first ministry position as a youth pastor within four months of starting and had gone through his second ministry position in about the same time frame. He now came to see me after being terminated from his third pastoral position in three years. He was a broken man in tears.

Dan described his pastoral journey, and from what I knew of him when he was my student, I wasn't surprised. You see, Dan never should have gone into pastoral ministry in the first place. He wanted to be a youth pastor, but the simple truth was that he didn't like people very much. In fact, he was afraid of them. He was overly shy, withdrawn, and nervous around people. These aren't character traits you want to have in a junior high youth pastor! Within months of Dan's coming to each ministry position, the church soon discovered his interpersonal deficits and fired him.

I asked Dan many of the same questions we have highlighted in this chapter. The resulting analysis proved there was absolutely no match between his chosen ministry and his personal mission, vision, or core values. Dan said that God had created him to do ministry and that he wanted to serve in some ministry capacity. However, he didn't like speaking in front of people, planning activities, or dealing with budgets and reports. Dan said his greatest fulfillment and joy came from working at home on the computer. Nothing filled Dan's cup of personal happiness more than that. He valued working independently, being creative, giving attention to details, and serving in ministry as a support person.

I explained to Dan that many of the problems he had faced weren't of his own making. He wasn't a failure in life or ministry. He simply lacked a connection between his personal mission, vision, and core values and those of his pastoral ministry. I suggested he think outside the box of traditional church ministry, so we brainstormed ideas about what kinds of jobs would allow him to live out his passions. Today he owns a successful desktop publishing business operating out of his home. He is happily married with children and serving churches in his area as their personal "publisher in residence."

Finding your fit in ministry shouldn't be as complicated as rocket science. But admittedly, it usually isn't as obvious as you would like it to be either. God has provided us with a mind to discern his movements in our lives. Some he calls into pastoral service, while others serve him in the marketplace. Each is critical to reaching his or her world for Christ. Pastors need to take the time to reflect on whom God made them to be and only then look for ways to match that unique mosaic with a career. Only then will they find the deep personal fulfillment that God intends for them.

Every pastor should be in that top 10 percent of the population who find deep personal happiness and fulfillment in their jobs. The key to finding that is first coming to an understanding of your personal life mission, vision, and core values. Only then can you begin this journey looking for a career opportunity that will match your uniqueness.

CHAPTER 3

ANATOMY OF A CARRY-ON BAG
Gifts, Personality, Talents, and Temperament

MICK BOERSMA

We have gifts that differ according to the grace given to us.
Romans 12:6

Most seasoned travelers have experienced this at least once in their lives: that sinking feeling you get when all others at the baggage claim turnstile have picked up their suitcases and gone on their merry way. You're standing there alone and bewildered, wondering if you're at the right turnstile. You have recognized fellow passengers from your flight and noticed as each one claimed his or her bag and left. There you stand, all alone, with no bag to retrieve. What do you do?

When that happens, you walk over to the counter and explain your problem. A few clicks on the computer keyboard reveal that your suitcase was never taken off the plane. As a result, it went on to some distant land without you. I've had this happen a number of times.

When it happens in the United States, there is a good chance that you will get your bag back within a day. But when it happens in a Third World country, you may never see your suitcase again. That's when you look to the items you've stored away in your carry-on bag—those essential items that suddenly increase in value because they are all you have.

When I was young and a relatively inexperienced traveler, I usually didn't bother packing a carry-on bag. I didn't want to be bogged down with having to haul it around with me through airports. As soon as I had my first "lost suitcase" experience, however, I started packing a carry-on bag with all the items I couldn't live without if my suitcase never made it to my destination with me.

As we travel through life from one ministry to another, we also have to "pack our carry-on bag" with the essential items that will enable us to thrive in our service to Christ. And while on a vacation or business trip we might have to do without some personal items, such as a bathing suit or tube of toothpaste, we can't afford to leave behind the essential items that define who we are. These are things that have taken a lifetime to develop. We can't do without them because they are essential to our ministry at the new destination. These essential items stay with us as our carry-on bag. In case an emergency arises, we will always have them with us.

In this chapter we will go through our carry-on bag and check its contents. We will identify seven items essential for going into ministry.

Carry-on Item #1: My Call to Ministry

We have already visited this subject in chapter 1, but it is worth reiterating the importance of having a sure grip on your personal call to ministry before you head off to the next assignment. Your call is a God-given commission that gives you confidence that you are going where God has given you personal orders to go. It has been confirmed through a stirring of your heart, affirmation of church leaders, thoughtful prayer, counsel of mentoring partners, and your spouse's agreement. As you are laying out items for the trip, make sure you have done your homework in chapter 1 and have a sense of peace and clarity regarding your call.

Carry-on Item #2: My Character

Christian ministry is all about character. A ministry leader must exhibit a spiritual life bearing the marks of maturity required for such service. It's interesting to note that in one recent study, pastors who were most dissatisfied with their spiritual lives were also significantly more likely to doubt their calls.[1] It's crucial that we take stock of our walk with God before moving to a new place. I have known few pastors who left ministry because they were not smart enough, gifted enough, or knowledgeable enough. Sadly, I'm aware of dozens who have lost their ministries due to serious lapses in personal judgment and character.

Most seminaries excel in academic preparation. After all, that's what they are in business to do. However, rarely do these institutions take the time to examine the candidate's character preparation. Fortunately, things are changing. A number of seminaries in North America have now instituted rigorous programmatic elements addressing the character development of students as well. Spiritual disciplines are being emphasized, and students are being held accountable for more than just knowledge gain. Their character is also being examined beneath the looking glass of self-analysis, peer review, and ministry leadership mentoring.

John Cionca, in his helpful book for pastors in career transition, writes of this priority when he reminds pastors that their lives must be above reproach (1 Tim. 3:2).

Pastors are expected to have a great relationship with their spouses and children. Likewise, they should have a healthy relationship with people both inside and outside the church. Their motivation must never be for money or status. Their deportment should be respectable, hospitable, and gentle. Leaders who best emulate these lifestyle qualities are most fit for service. Those who fail the character check, regardless of their desire, should not expect a remunerated ministry position. Whereas inner compulsion drives us toward service, godly character makes us fit for that service.[2]

As you're packing, this would be a good time for your own progress review. It would be wise to seek honest feedback from someone who loves you enough not only to applaud your strengths, but also to point out your areas of weakness. Few of us ever venture this deeply with another human being, but it's crucial for growth. Far better that we uncover and work on deficiencies now than have them destroy us and others along the journey.

Carry-on Item #3: My Spiritual Gifts

In a context in which nearly half of born-again believers are unaware of their gifts, claim they don't have gifts, or don't know what their gifts are,[3] it is probably no surprise to learn that even pastors are not always aware of their own spiritual giftedness. One survey found that 4 percent of senior pastors didn't even think spiritual gifts were biblical![4]

Websites for Spiritual Gifts Indicators

Website	Purpose/Organization
churchgrowth.org	Ephesians Four Ministries, Church Growth Institute
mintools.com	Ministry Tools Resource Center (nondenominational resources)
elmertowns.com	Resource ministry of Dr. Elmer Towns at Liberty University
elca.org	Evangelical Lutheran Church in America, official website resource
uniquelyyou.com	Helps Christians identify their gifts and match them to new ministry opportunities; used by denominational church planting leaders for assessment purposes

When asked, most pastors will tell you that the gifts of teaching and leadership rank at the top of their list of giftedness. Gifts of mercy, hospitality, and service are generally at the bottom of their list. It's not that pastors don't love or care for people, it's just that their giftedness tends to focus more on the proclamation of the gospel and other public manifestations of the shepherd role. However, it's troubling to see that so many don't want or even care about the gifts of service and mercy. It's as if those gifts were discounted as "optional" to the body. That's very unfortunate, because each gift is essential for effective ministry to take place.

Knowing your giftedness will certainly enhance your future service. Below are some ways to sharpen your view of these gifts.

1. *Take a spiritual gifts inventory.* Many are available online, and most are free. Realize that every gifts inventory rises from particular doctrinal assumptions and/or denominational traditions. Taking more than one may help give you a better overall picture of your personal profile.

2. *Review your ministry experience.* Think through the ministerial work you have already been doing, and ask yourself the following questions:

- What sorts of ministries have motivated me and given me a sense of personal fulfillment and satisfaction?
- What areas of pastoral ministry make me run for cover?
- If I could create my ideal pastoral position, what kinds of activities would I put in the job description?

3. *Ask your friends and colleagues for their feedback.* We may think we know our own giftedness better than anyone else, but I've found that it sometimes helps to have an outsider's view of things. Pull aside a trusted friend or colleague and record his or her feedback to the questions below.

My friend/colleague sees these gifts operational in me (ask for examples):

He/she believes I would be best suited for a ministry that involves:

4. *Take a risk and try something new.* Sometimes you never know what you're good at (or bad at) until you take a risk and give it a try. Some of the best discoveries in the world came about after lengthy experimentation. Where would we be if Thomas Edison had quit after a failed experiment? It took thousands of tries

before he ever harnessed the power of electricity. In the same way, you may have a latent talent that has never been discovered because you were too fearful to put it to the test. What is your heart telling you to try? A short-term missions trip? Leading a new program venture at your church or for your denomination? Providing some direction on a board of directors for a local school or camp? Running for public office in your community? Do you want to live the rest of your life with the regret of knowing you were afraid to try?

Carry-on Item #4: My Personality Temperament

Perhaps at one time or another you have shouted out in frustration, "Why can't everyone just be normal like me?" A wise pastor once said there is no such thing as "normal" except as a setting on a clothes dryer. It's true. No one is normal, certainly not normal like everyone else. God created each of us to be unique. God is the master of creative expression in nature, so why wouldn't he be creative in shaping our personalities as well? As ministry leaders, we should delight in the knowledge that our personalities are uniquely our own. But we must also understand that what makes us special can present challenges in our ministry to others.

Because this is true, it is important that we get in touch with our own personalities and temperaments. It is helpful to know if you are an extrovert or introvert, patient or forthright. Such knowledge will go a long way in assessing the kind of ministry you want to enter into on your journey. For instance, if you know that you are by nature a very shy and withdrawn introvert, you would do well not to accept an invitation to become the executive director of a Christian camp that requires a good deal of social interaction for the purposes of fund-raising. It won't be a good fit for you or for the ministry. In the end, both will suffer for the mismatch of your temperament with their ministry needs.

So how do you find out what your unique personality and temperament are? Many tools are available today to assist you in this task. Three excellent tools for this purpose are described below.

1. *The Myers-Briggs Type Indicator (MBTI)*. This instrument was developed in the 1940s by Isabel Briggs Myers and is taken by over two million people worldwide each year. Based on personality-type theory introduced by Carl Jung in the 1920s, it helps respondents become aware of their personality preferences in four areas: (1) extroversion or introversion, (2) sensing or intuition, (3) thinking or feeling, and (4) judging or perceiving.

The MBTI can be taken online at no charge at humanmetrics.com. The Myers-Briggs Foundation (www.myersbriggs.org) advises that people who take the test secure professional feedback, because the basic inventory results provide no individualized interpretation.[5]

2. *The 16 Personality Factors (16PF).* This inventory measures sixteen personality factors that were identified by Raymond Cattell in the 1930s. These factors include the following:

- warmth
- vigilance
- reasoning
- abstractedness
- emotional stability
- privateness
- dominance
- apprehension

- liveliness
- openness to change
- rule-consciousness
- self-reliance
- social boldness
- tension
- perfectionism
- sensitivity

In addition, these factors have been grouped into five global factors: (1) extroversion, (2) anxiety, (3) tough-mindedness/willpower, (4) independence, and (5) self-control.[6] This assessment tool is particularly helpful for people changing career paths. Reports from your personal profile can be purchased that describe how you cope with stressful conditions and interact with others. They also indicate your preferred organizational and leadership roles and work settings, as well as occupational interests. Websites such as www.discoveryourpersonality.com offer a range of services, enabling you to use this instrument in a timely and convenient manner.

3. *The Taylor-Johnson Temperament Analysis (T-JTA).* This inventory is described as a simple measure of personality traits that impact one's personal, interpersonal, scholastic, and vocational abilities. It is helpful as both a diagnostic device and a counseling tool. The brief 180-question test can be administered to individuals, couples, or groups in about thirty minutes. The beauty of this profile is that it works well with adolescents too.[7]

Your score is plotted on a vertical line between two temperament descriptors indicating the degree to which this particular trait is evident in you. Nine traits and their opposites are displayed as follows:

Nervous	Depressive	Active Social	Expressive Responsive	Sympathetic	Subjective	Dominant	Hostile	Self-disciplined
100	100	100	100	100	100	100	100	100
0	0	0	0	0	0	0	0	0
Composed	Light-hearted	Quiet	Inhibited	Indifferent	Objective	Submissive	Tolerant	Impulsive

Training in the administration of this inventory is advised but not mandatory. Care should be taken in understanding the definitions of each temperament before drawing any conclusions. It can be taken online at www.tjta.com or secured in hard copy from several vendors. As with all the inventories mentioned, it is advisable to spend the money and time for professional interpretation of the results. One unique feature of this inventory is that individuals can compare their own personality description with another's *perception* of them. It is used a great deal in premarital and marital counseling settings and has enjoyed extensive use and appreciation for many years.

Carry-on Item #5: My Leadership Competencies

In addition to discovering your personality temperament, you may want to determine your personal leadership style. Since your leadership style will be a reflection of your personality, the two should be looked at in tandem. Three helpful inventories are available to help you assess this item in your carry-on bag. They are the Leadership Style Inventory (LSI) developed by Teleometrics, Inc., the Leadership Style Survey by Norman Shawchuck, and the Develop an Understanding of Your Behavior in Conflict Situations Inventory. These last two inventories are available at www.spiritualgrowthresources.com. A final consideration would be to take the DiSC Classic Profile, which is designed to help you better understand your behavioral style in the workplace. This inventory can be taken online at www.internalchange.com.

Anyone who has ever seen a job description for a typical pastoral position knows all about "great expectations." I have seen hundreds over the years and have yet to find a candidate who measures up on all counts. Organizations today seem to be looking for an infinite number of competencies among the myriad ministry positions available. Knowing your own personal leadership competencies is of infinite value, because you will be applying for a position based on the ministry's perception of what they need. An awareness of your competencies and the church's needs will help both avoid a mismatch.

What are some key leadership competencies expected in the ministry marketplace today? The sidebar on page 58 shows what many church planting organizations are looking for.[8] Not possessing these particular competencies doesn't mean that you aren't a gifted ministry leader, but it does reveal that those who are successful in church planting ministries generally do have these leadership competencies, and there is value in knowing what is needed in such positions.

One professional search firm has catalogued a long list of "unusual characteristics of exceptional leaders" based on many years of interaction and dialogue between pastors searching for ministry positions and churches that are looking for a candidate with the right fit. These include the following:[9]

- Knows self—strengths, weaknesses, what he or she likes to do and not do
- Secure in who he or she is—doesn't compensate for insecurities
- Self-confident—creates positive expectations
- Varied approach—deals with people individually
- Has contagious enthusiasm—casts vision that causes others to enlist
- Authenticity—what you see is who he or she is—transparent and consistent
- Stretches people—believes in people and motivates them to excellence
- Supports people—gives them resources; encourages risk taking; supports them
- Encourages innovation—helps people think outside the box; rewards good ideas
- Keeps learning—challenges self and others to improve
- Understands how organizations work—enables effective teamwork between groups
- "Big picture" perspective—knows organization and culture surrounding it
- Values both "process" and results—can start up and patiently develop a project

Of course, the typical church pastoral position will include expectations related to teaching, preaching, counseling, worship leading, and a host of other ministerial responsibilities that require certain spiritual gifts and training. And though a person can most certainly be an effective leader without having all of the qualities listed above, it becomes immediately apparent that to successfully match a candidate with a position, the job seeker must have a good handle on his or her abilities related to the work. You will need to pack your carry-on bag with knowledge of what you can do—the skills and talents that will help determine a good fit. To help accomplish this, review your work history. As you did before

Key Leadership Competencies

- Visionary leadership skills
- Initiating/gathering skills
- Communication skills
- Evangelistic skills
- Discipling skills
- Equipping and training skills
- Emotional intelligence
- Team-building skills
- Group multiplication skills
- Staff development skills

with your spiritual gifts assessment, reflect on your past ministry and ask yourself the following questions:

What ministry competencies can I honestly identify as being evident in my life? Provide an example of each from your experience.

Competency: _____. I have seen this _____

_____

Competency: _____. I have seen this _____

_____

Competency: _____. I have seen this _____

_____

Competency: _____. I have seen this _____

_____

What ministry competencies can I honestly say are not evident in my life?

Competency: _____

Competency: _____

Competency: _____

Carry-on Item #6: My Ministry Preparation

You will notice that I didn't say educational degree. That's because there is much more to ministry preparation than a seminary degree (which I'll address next). Some of the most qualified men and women who ever served the cause of the kingdom never had a seminary degree. In fact, many of them never attended college—not that a college or graduate degree isn't helpful. Of course, I believe they are, but they aren't the panacea of all preparation. In fact, sometimes the pride that comes with accomplishing a degree can become detrimental to one's ministry. The issue is not the level of education per se but rather the sum of experiences, both formal and informal, that have brought you to this point along your journey.

I once met a pastor who took a job as a funeral director while attending seminary. The job gave him the opportunity to study in a quiet office when business was slow and paid fifty cents an hour more than working at a retail store. Years later when he became a pastor, he had to come alongside people who had recently suffered the death of a loved one. What he learned as a funeral director provided him with a rich background in how to navigate what is a difficult assignment for many pastors.

Someone has said, "Don't let your schooling get in the way of your education." The point I want to make is that along the course of your life you probably have had a variety of experiences that make you unique and special. It may be what you learned while working as a camp staff member years ago or while serving in the military overseas. It may be travels you have taken or a part-time job you had while in college. These experiences provide you with a rich heritage of knowledge that may be transferable to a ministry context. Such preparation is considered a carry-on item, because once you have had the experience, it stays with you wherever you go and is always available when you need to call on it.

Carry-on Item #7: My Educational Preparation

The last item in your carry-on bag is your academic preparation, all the formal learning you have had throughout life—the undergraduate degree you earned in accounting, the graduate degree you received in communications, and so on. You probably have a seminary degree in your bag as well. Whatever degree you have gets carried on with you wherever you travel. That knowledge goes with you wherever you go.

Now take a moment and ask yourself if the degree you have in your carry-on bag is really the right fit for the kind of ministry position you're pursuing. In some cases, you may discover that your degree doesn't fit the job you want. Maybe you want to transition from being a youth pastor to an executive pastor but you don't have any education in financial management, human resources, or strategic planning. You may be a senior pastor who is dreaming of a ministry in Christian school administration. Your seminary degree probably didn't give you much training in educational administration, so you need further education. Now that you have taken an inventory of your carry-on bag and have discovered that you need more education (not necessarily an entire degree), you will need to pursue ongoing education.

Ongoing education is a key to leadership effectiveness. If you want a ministry career in counseling but don't have courses in counseling, you will need to consider going back to school to earn the necessary education. Desire isn't enough; you also need education. Several degree programs and seminars are available to anyone desiring to add to their carry-on bag.

Let's Get Packing

You're on a journey. You may not know where you will end up once the travel is over, but one thing is for sure: you travel with a carry-on bag filled with essential items. Your personal call to ministry, character, spiritual giftedness, personality temperament, leadership competencies, experiences, and educational preparation all contribute to making you the person you are today. The contents of your carry-on bag are critical to your success. You don't want to go into a ministry without a solid understanding of each item's value and the contribution it makes to your ministry effectiveness.

In my own experience, I have seen my carry-on items serve me well as a music minister, youth pastor, senior pastor, carpenter, interim preacher, and seminary professor. Let your carry-on bag take you to new possibilities, but don't be intimidated if you take an inventory and discover that an item or two needs some attention. Be encouraged! Each item can be developed and improved. We all are under construction, and the possibilities for improvement are endless. Take this opportunity to ponder the future and ask God which items in your carry-on bag need to be developed during this stretch of your journey.

CHAPTER 4

HOW TO GET THERE FROM HERE

Drafting the Travel Itinerary

MICHAEL ANTHONY

*To enjoy your work and to accept your lot in life—that is indeed
a gift from God. The person who does that will not need to look
back with sorrow on his past, for God gives him joy.*
Ecclesiastes 5:19–20 TLB

One of the scariest travel experiences I ever had occurred in the remote Masai Mara Game Reserve in southern Kenya. I had decided to surprise my wife for her birthday and give her a present she would never forget. Together with my eighteen-month-old daughter and a missionary couple, we journeyed off to explore the isolated frontier. Exploring a real game reserve is nothing like traveling through the Adventure Kingdom Zoo where well-fed animals are kept behind tall secure fences. No, this was the real thing—man-eating lions, the unpredictable Cape buffalo, herds of elephants, families of leopards, and a host of other animals basking in the warm savannah grass dreaming of eating a human for lunch. Along we came down a lonely road, miles from any living soul.

Hours earlier when we entered the reserve, I had neglected to stop and pick up a map of the area. I had made reservations for a lodge on the far side of the park and had a fairly good idea how to get there. Notice the operative word "fairly." Like most men, I'm not real good at asking for directions. Preferring to wander my way to the location and then claim I knew where I was going all along, I soon had us in the middle of nowhere. I could tell by the condition of the dirt road that no one had traveled this way for many months. There were no signs, guideposts, game wardens, or clues to point us in the right direction. To say we were lost would be a gross understatement.

To make matters worse—far worse—our van got a flat tire. Ever try changing a tire while looking over your shoulder wondering if a lion or leopard was stalking you from behind the nearby brush? I have! It's very disconcerting. Once I replaced the flat tire with the spare, I dropped the van down off the jack, only to hear air escaping from the tire I had just installed. It had a slow leak, and we were in serious trouble! I had a general idea of where we were, but I had no idea how to get where we needed to go. There were mountains, dry riverbeds, and forested jungles between where we were and where we needed to be. Still worse, we were traveling on borrowed time. There was no cell phone reception, no AAA to call, and if the van broke down, we dared not get out and walk. By some miracle of God, we stumbled across a remote lodge and got our tires fixed. It was there that I humbled myself and asked for directions. Apparently I had missed a critical unmarked turn in the road some miles back. It wasn't until we got our bearings that we were able to find our way to the lodge we were looking for.

Perhaps the journey from where you are today and where you want to be seems equally perilous. You have a general idea of where you want to end up, but the path to get there seems to have more bends and turns than you imagined. Maybe your vehicle has an emotional or financial leak, and you find yourself wondering if you'll survive. Will those traveling with you panic and lose confidence in your leadership? Where can you go to get directions? These questions and many more reflect the natural fears and anxieties common among those traveling the road of pastoral career transition.

The process of finding the perfect fit between what you want to do and what a ministry wants to have done is no small feat. There are so many things to consider. Much like a series of stars that form a unique constellation, your spiritual gifts, personality, natural talents, abilities, interests, education, family needs, and a host of other areas all come together to form a package of what you bring to the position.

The other side of the equation is equally complex, for no two churches are the same. Churches vary by size, denomination, geographical setting, age, government, worship style, traditions, and a dozen other factors. That's why choosing a place of ministry service, which is rarely a once-and-forever decision, surpasses many other major life events in terms of potential impact on a person's life.

The process of determining one's unique constellation of career characteristics is not unlike the challenge of complexity and importance we face when we choose a mate. Some pastors are successful in finding a match with a church that is personally satisfying and consistent with their capabilities. For many others, the process of finding that successful match may take years. Every ministry opportunity and the inevitable dilemmas associated with making a move represent a potential plot twist in a life story filled with incipient longings and hopes.[1]

The purpose of this chapter is to guide you in some personal reflection and to provide you with some directions—even if you're the type who isn't inclined to ask for any. You're on a sojourn of career transition, and you're somewhere between where you are today and where you want to be in the not-too-distant future. The question on everyone's mind is, How do I get there from here?

One Size Doesn't Fit All

The first step to answering that question is identifying the kind of ministry you feel God wants you in. Too many pastors come through seminary with the view that serving in a local church is all that will satisfy their ministry longing. They grow up as members of a church, do their seminary internship at a church, and expect to graduate to a job in a local church. Their goal after graduation is to pastor a church, in part, because that's the only kind of ministry they have ever seen or experienced. If that is your concept of ministry, you may have a long journey ahead, because you will limit God's options for your life down to a prescribed place of service. God, however, doesn't confine himself to our parameters.

A good place for you to start on this journey is to ask yourself and God where he wants you to be. What is the goal of your job search? Is it only a local church within your denomination and preferably within a particular state or city? Richard Bolles, author of the bestselling book *What Color Is Your Parachute?* warns pastors not to limit their ministry calling to one place.

> The minute you choose only one possible employer, you'll probably by stymied, because you have absolutely no control over his whims. The problem with most pastors' job searches is that in defining their vocation, they have essentially defined only one employer, namely, the church. There's no way out of the bind without beginning to think, "I can do ministry for God in places other than the parish."[2]

Pastors who limit their concept of God's calling to a particular church in a specific city may be in for a big disappointment. A healthier way to look at the start of this journey is to begin with a career goal that views vocation from a bigger perspective. Ministry can take many forms. The same gifts, talents, interests, and abilities that are used by a solo or senior pastor in a local church may also be demonstrated in the context of a hospital, police, or fire chaplaincy, parachurch ministry, or educational institution. If your goal is ministry, think outside the box and consider ministry positions beyond the limitation of a particular church, denomination, city, or state.

Which Way Do I Go?

You may recall from your childhood reading the Lewis Carroll classic, *Alice in Wonderland*. Along her journey Alice stumbles across the Cheshire Cat. She is lost and in need of direction. Alice asks the cat, "Can you tell me please which way

I ought to go from here?" "That depends a good deal on where you want to go," says the Cat. Alice declares, "I don't much care where," to which the cat responds, "Then it doesn't matter which way you walk." As silly as that dialogue may seem to us today, many pastors approach their search for a new ministry setting in much the same way. They really haven't a clue where to go or how to get there. They haven't taken the time to set realistic goals to guide their future activities. Goals can make all the difference between aimless wandering and purposeful activity.

An interesting study was done among Harvard alumni. Before they had graduated, these alumni—then seniors—had been asked a series of questions, including which ones had taken the time to develop a list of career goals. Years after graduation researchers followed up on this same group of alumni and discovered that the students who had taken the time to develop a list of career goals prior to graduation were experiencing higher levels of income, job satisfaction, and personal fulfillment in both their careers and personal lives. They left school with a plan and began working that plan soon after graduation. Even though life didn't always go according to their expectations, as it seldom does, they were able to keep on track and accomplish their goals by staying focused and pursuing alternative paths to their goals.

The same can be said for those in career transition who prepare career goals. In chapter 2 we asked you to lay out life mission and vision statements. The first is a general understanding of why God brought you into this world, and the second involves more specific ideas of the kind of ministry setting that would provide you with the best opportunities to use your capabilities. In chapter 3 we asked you to evaluate your area(s) of spiritual giftedness, examine important elements of your unique personality and temperament, and explore your natural talents. The final step in this self-assessment process is to identify some goals to get you from where you are today to where you want to be.

> The process you need to follow in order to create your plan is very similar to that used by organizations that are planning change. Strategic planners create a vision statement fairly early on in the process, describing where the organization needs to be in a few years. Then they do something called "gap analysis," measuring and defining the "gap" that lies between where the organization is now and its desired future condition. Once planners define the challenges that must be met, they develop strategies to handle these challenges effectively. These strategies usually take the form of sequential goals and supporting tasks [objectives]. These goals describe major accomplishments that address the challenges identified. The tasks [objectives] refer to smaller steps that are required to accomplish these goals.[3]

Back to the Future

Before we begin laying out an itinerary for your career transition, it will be helpful to take a look at life in the rearview mirror. In other words, before you journey forward, take a moment and look back at those things that prevent you from forward progress. Unless you take the parking brake off, forward momentum will be that much harder. Things that prevent forward progress include the following:

1. *Unhealthy relationships.* Sometimes unhealthy relationships need to be severed or wrapped in protective boundaries before we can move forward. These may include overbearing parents who seem to want to live vicariously through your life. They may have expectations that fit their reality but not yours. Some parents, especially those who are not walking with the Lord, prefer their children to find secure and stable jobs with lucrative salaries that pay into ever-growing retirement accounts. Being a pastor seldom meets those expectations, so they may find some subtle, and not so subtle, ways of getting you to second-guess your call to ministry. They may have discouraged you from attending seminary or marrying someone who shared your "extreme" religious beliefs. They may even have opposed you accepting a ministry in another state where they couldn't be in close contact with (or control of) your family.

For those who have been in ministry for a while, unhealthy relationships may be found in members of the congregation who are wielding an inordinate amount of influence on your life, such as a board member who feels he owns you because of his position or the "E. F. Hutton" of the church who expects you to stop what you're doing and act on his sage advice.

2. *Reality check.* We all have personal weaknesses that reveal themselves at work. An example of this is the youth pastor who has a dynamic evangelistic ministry with young students but can't relate to adults. Parents are viewed as threats to his creative vision and church board members are all grumpy old spoilsports. These weaknesses will hinder his career search, and unless he takes a realistic look at what needs to change, his search will be long and lonely.[4]

3. *Presumptive miracles.* The pastor who sits home all day watching TV and waiting for God to call on the phone to tell him where his next job awaits is most likely going nowhere. God expects us to get involved in the job-finding process by drafting a resume, meeting people, contacting churches, and so on. I have heard of pastors who did none of these things yet did receive a phone call with an offer from a church. Yes, miracles do happen, but miracles are never the norm, and God expects us to use the resources on hand to discover his plan and accomplish his will.

Just as God can miraculously heal cancer today but usually chooses to do it through medicine, he can bring about a job offer in a miraculous fashion but usually chooses to use other people to reveal his plans for your life. Some pastors have said, "God is sovereign, and my new ministry position is up to him. It doesn't matter what I do; he'll bring it to me in his timing. All I have to do is sit here and wait for it." If that's your expectation of how God works today, you may be trying to drive forward with your foot on the brake.

4. *Failure to prepare.* Some pastors find it difficult to find a new position because they fail to take the time to prepare. They will skip the first half of this book and move directly into the chapters dealing with networking, contacting church search committees, and interviewing. They are also the ones who will be out on the street in twenty-four months looking for a new job because the last one didn't fit. They never take the time to do their homework before finding God's place of service. They are quick to jump at the first offer that comes along without giving much thought to whether or not it is the best fit for them or their family. They may not take the time to pray, meditate on the Word, and seek the mind and will of God.

Ready, Aim, Fire!

Now that you have done your homework and developed a mission and vision statement, determined your area(s) of spiritual giftedness, assessed your personal talents, and considered your unique personality and temperament traits, you are ready to draft your travel itinerary. This is the collection of goals and objectives needed to accomplish your career objective. The diagram below indicates where you are on the journey thus far.

STEPS IN THE CAREER TRANSITION PROCESS

Step 1   Draft your mission and vision statements.

⬇

Step 2   Determine your giftedness and assess unique personality, talents, and temperament.

⬇

Step 3   Prepare goals and objectives to accomplish the plan.

⬇

Step 4   Implement the plan.

In the context of a career search, we suggest that you ask yourself, "If God gave me the desires of my heart, what would I want to do?" (see Ps. 37:4). Put that in writing at the top of a sheet of paper. (A sample sheet is located at the end of the chapter for your use.) That becomes your career objective. What you need to do now is develop a set of goals that will get you there. If goals are going to be of value, they need to pass five tests. This is sometimes referred to as the SMART test — that is, each goal must be *specific, measurable, attainable, relevant,* and *trackable.*[5]

Most people struggle with being able to craft a well-thought-out goal statement. That is why some prefer to add some corresponding objectives to each goal to ensure that each one meets and passes the SMART test. For example, you may have as a career objective, "I want to become the senior pastor of my own church." Let's put this to the SMART test to see if it passes.

1. *Is it specific?* No, not really. Other than saying that you want to become a senior pastor, it doesn't give much detail. The more specific you can be in your goal setting the better.

2. *Is it measurable?* I suppose to some degree it is. A year from now you can look back and see if you are the senior pastor of your own church. However, it doesn't state any time line. Do you want to become a senior pastor this year or next?

3. *Is it attainable?* That all depends. Does it take into consideration the requisite experience, education, giftedness, personality, and temperament? For example, I'd love to play professional baseball, but since I never played in high school or college, let alone the fact that I'm already over the age of fifty, that goal just wouldn't be realistic. Goals must be attainable.

4. *Is it relevant?* Again, that's hard to say without knowing more details. However, the purpose of this test is to be sure that you stay focused on the accomplishment of your overall purpose.

5. *Is it trackable?* No, there are no clear and discernible steps to ensure that your activities are keeping you focused on your career objective.

As you write each goal, keep in mind that the overall intent of the SMART test is simply to make each goal as clear, concise, and measurable as possible. When you have all of these goals written out, you will have a strategic plan for moving on to your next ministry position.

A better way to lay out a travel itinerary that will get you from where you are today to where you want to be in the near future is as follows:

Date:

Career:

Objective: Should God give me a clear sense of release from my current ministry position, I would like to pursue a new full-time ministry as a senior pastor in my denomination. Although not a requirement, I would prefer to stay within the boundaries of my district due to personal health and family issues.

Goal 1: I will take a three-day retreat in early January to study Scripture, reflect on my current position, and pray about moving to a different ministry. My spouse and I will also come to an agreement on making this move. If we have a consensus of agreement (God, self, spouse) to move forward, I will begin the steps identified below.

Goal 2: By January 15 I will revise my resume and send it to three friends to get their confidential feedback. Based on their input, I will make recommended changes.

Goal 3: By January 31 I will make contact with the district superintendent and see if he is aware of any pastoral positions open within the Northwest District of our denomination.

Goal 4: By February 10 I will contact three search firms specializing in church leadership positions and inform them of my availability.

Goal 5: By February 15 I will write or call 15 ministry colleagues and request their confidential assistance in helping me identify churches where their need might be a good fit with my capabilities.

Goal 6: By February 15 I will make contact with my seminary's graduate placement office and let them know that I am searching for a new position of service.

Goal 7: By March 15 I will screen a list of potential churches and consult my wife and three trusted colleagues to see if they feel I should make contact with the search committee of each church.

Goal 8: Pending direction from those cited above, I will send a resume to each of the three search committees identified in goal #7.

Goal 9: If a search committee contacts me and requests further information, I will send it to them within forty-eight hours.

Goal 10: Once contacted by the search committee for an interview, I will pray and make a decision about moving the process forward within forty-eight hours.

This list isn't intended to be a complete and exhaustive set of goals, but you get the idea. The purpose of this "travel itinerary" is to map out each step along the way so you will always know where you are in relation to where you want to be. It isn't set in stone, and it is always subject to the movement of God's Spirit and the unforeseen interruptions of life.

Don't Forget Personal Improvement

Once you have taken the time to set your goals, you need to reflect on the actions you will need to take to accomplish them. In many cases, some form of self-improvement will be in order. For many pastors, this is an opportune time to learn a new skill or gain knowledge in an area that will make you more attractive to a ministry looking for a new pastor. In today's highly competitive employment market, there are certain skills and abilities that can give you an edge over other

Areas for Self-Improvement

Writing skills. This means writing clear, coherent, and effective reports and using quantifiable data to support your argument.

Negotiation skills. This means being able to articulate what you want and knowing the trade-offs you will accept to get your priorities met. It also means understanding varying perspectives and devising win-win strategies to bridge conflicts.

People/management skills. You should be able to understand others' points of view, direct projects and teams effectively, manage your emotions, and negotiate office politics with finesse.

Computer literacy. Basic computer skills are a must in this high-tech age. At a minimum, you should know your way around a computer desktop and be able to use word-processing software, a spreadsheet program, and email.

Appreciation. As the workplace becomes more diverse, it is important to be accepting of people from a variety of backgrounds, who may have different perspectives and values.

Public speaking. This means being able to develop a public speech or statement that is persuasive and appealing and gets your point across clearly — then presenting it confidently in front of an audience.

Foreign language skills. Because the number of nonnative English speakers in the U.S. is growing exponentially, you will want to be able to speak their language and understand their culture if you want them to be among your clients or customers.

candidates. In their helpful career guide, *Take Charge of Your Career*, authors Cynthia Ingols and Mary Shapiro suggest a number of areas you may want to consider for self-improvement (see the sidebar on page 70).[6]

Obviously, Ingol and Shapiro's list is directed more to the general public than to pastors seeking a position in a local church. But pastors would do well to add some personal and professional development skills to their list of goals. Such things as honing counseling or staff supervision skills or learning new computer programs to assist you in sermon preparation, accounting, or visual presentations are worth considering. Search committees may ask in their interview what new skills you have been learning lately, so having a few up your sleeve indicates to them that you are current in your field and always looking for new ways to become a better ministry leader.

As you prepare this travel itinerary, don't forget that God wants you to experience a joy-filled and personally enriching ministry. He never promises a ministry free from struggle, hardship, or pain. He does, however, promise to be our resource and guide along the way. As such, there should be a match between the things that bring you the greatest joy in your work and the things that bring you the greatest fulfillment in your personal life.

Charles Broach, director of human resources for Ford Motor Company, puts it this way: "Career goals and personal life goals are inexplicably intertwined. If you can find the right balance that meets both sets of goals, you will be well on your way to a long, productive, and rewarding career. What's more, you will know that you are one of only a small percentage of individuals who are truly fortunate enough to have found that balance and fulfillment."[7]

What makes this journey so challenging for pastors in the twenty-first-century church is the realization that the landscape of our journey is somewhat unpredictable. Ministry is ever changing, and just about the time you think you know the needs of your congregation, society changes and the congregation's needs change along with it. Before you know it, you find yourself struggling to keep abreast of the culture in which your ministry is located. The next chapter will help you identify some of these challenges and provide you with some practical ways to survey the journey.

A LIFE MAP WORKSHEET

Mission Statement: _____

_____

_____

Vision Statement: _____

_____

_____

My Personal Core Values: _____

_____

_____

   1. _____

   2. _____

   3. _____

   4. _____

Career Objective: _____

Goals to Accomplish Include: Date to Accomplish:

   1. _____   _____

   2. _____   _____

   3. _____   _____

   4. _____   _____

   5. _____   _____

CAUTION! TURBULENT WEATHER AHEAD

Changing Expectations of the Twenty-First-Century Church

MICHAEL ANTHONY

Preach the Word; be prepared in season and out of season; correct, rebuke and encourage—with great patience and careful instruction.
2 Timothy 4:2 NIV

Never board an airplane without first checking the weather conditions. I learned this lesson the hard way as I boarded a plane in Travandrum, South India, for what would become the most fear-inducing flight of my life. I thought the monsoon had passed, but unbeknown to me, we were merely in the eye of the storm. All around us were the remnants of what had been a devastating tempest. Rivers were swollen, homes had been washed away in the ensuing floods, and most roads were closed. "That's funny," I commented to my travel companion as we approached the airport, "I don't recall that lake when we arrived." "That's not a lake," he said; "that's the airport runway."

We crammed the Air India Airbus to its maximum occupancy and taxied to the beginning of the runway. With the engines screaming and the body of the plane shaking mercilessly, the pilot let go of the brakes and we rocketed down the runway. Water was cascading onto the windows as we struggled to see the end of the runway. *Will we make it?* we all pondered silently. Prayers in English and Hindi were no doubt being offered throughout the plane.

We soon lifted off, and my heart returned to its natural position in my chest. It wouldn't remain there for long though. Soon after takeoff, the pilot informed us that we were flying through the eye of the monsoon and "it's going to get a little bumpy." He wasn't kidding! I had no idea a plane could withstand such violent shaking. *Surely planes aren't built for this much stress,* I thought. I knew my body wasn't designed to take this kind of stress! I thought my life was over.

For what seemed like an eternity, we flew through one thundercloud after another trying to fight our way to calm skies. When we arrived in Madras some four hours later, I threw myself on the tarmac and swore I'd never fly again. I vowed I'd never travel anywhere without first checking the weather conditions. It was a lesson I nearly paid for with my life.

This chapter is designed to help you travel through some turbulent weather. Maybe it has been a while since you took a trip out of the safety of your current pastorate, and if so, I have some news for you: "It's going to get a little bumpy." We want to present you with a glimpse of the changing face of the North American church. In essence, it isn't your grandmother's church anymore, and if you aren't prepared to make the necessary changes to go along, you'll get swept out the door with the rest of the outdated items. In addition, we want to give you a reality check regarding the changing role of the pastor in today's church. What was once a secure and stable profession has evolved into a thrill ride that rivals the latest roller coaster at your local amusement park.

The Changing Face of the American Church

Bob Dylan's famous song "The Times They Are A-Changin'" couldn't be a more accurate description for the context of the American church today. Everywhere we look we see change.

Pastoring a church a century ago in America seemed idyllic. In hindsight, it probably wasn't, but there is much to be said about living your entire life shepherding the same group of families through life. Being there for the major milestones of life, such as weddings, births, infant dedications, baptisms, confirmation classes, marriages, and funerals allowed the pastor to hold a revered place in society. He was looked upon with honor and given respect wherever he went. When there was a disagreement in the community, the community looked to the pastor for direction. He spoke for God and was rarely challenged. When he preached, people listened. My, how times have changed!

We entered the twentieth century with a passion for the fundamentals of the faith. Sermons were pounded out from pulpits across our land with a fervency that rivaled professional sports events. Preachers were animated, loud, and convincing. Evangelistic zeal sparked new movements, such as Youth For Christ, World Vision, Campus Crusade, and the Navigators. Bible colleges sprang up across mid-America with a mission to reach the forgotten corners of our country. New preachers, fresh out of these Bible schools, planted churches like wheat on the prairies. Pastors were ordained and missionaries were commissioned in local churches virtually every week and sent out to herald the Good News. The gates of hell were shaken, and this new army of God marched out to expand the kingdom of Christ. Soon a harvest of souls would come forth.

The 1960s experienced a new spiritual phenomenon with the advent of the Jesus Movement. Disenfranchised hippies began to rethink their quest for free love. They had come to realize that nothing was free, and the consequences of living such a radical lifestyle were taking their toll on their inner peace. Lacking the kind of peace they were looking for, they discovered the true Prince of Peace and gave their lives to Christ in unprecedented numbers. Having been rejected by the traditional church, they turned instead to those few churches that would let them in. The birth of Calvary Chapels and Vineyard churches had begun. Energized with new songs and spiritual vibrancy, these young believers were convinced that Jesus could change the world, and they set about challenging everyone they met to consider the claims of Christianity. They were bold, in-your-face preachers. They expected God to do miracles in people's lives, and God didn't disappoint them.

In the 1980s the seeker-sensitive model began to impact the focus of the church's ministry. No longer concerned with their own comfort, parishioners grew passionate about making the church a place where non-Christians could come and feel welcome. Philosophies of ministry changed. As a result, worship services where rewritten, allowing spirited choruses, drama, multimedia, and action-oriented sermons to communicate the same gospel message but with newer methods. The days of expositional preaching through the Bible gave way to shorter topical messages focused on practical application. Though criticized as "sermonettes for Christianettes," these messages struck a chord with the masses who had come to reject the church's stale services. They didn't want stained-glass windows, pews, or preachers in impressive robes. They preferred warehouses located in industrial parks, quality nurseries for their children, action-oriented services, and preachers who appeared casual and approachable. Leading churches in this movement offered conferences on how to attract the unsaved in their communities, and soon this model was being replicated in neighborhoods from coast to coast. Risk-taking pastors took new ground and found contemporary methods for communicating a time-honored message of salvation in Christ alone.

As we enter the twenty-first century, we realize that we are products of our environment. Postmodern thought, characterized by relative values with no moral absolutes, cultural pluralism, and a demand for authentic living, have permeated all corners of our society. And the church is no exception. The average American is less inclined to accept the Bible as a source of authority, the pastorate is no different from any other vocational choice, and the media, if anything, has painted the church as being out of touch with society, if not downright corrupt. Ministry is an uphill battle.

Today the emergent church movement is coming of age. Those who attend this growing style seek a return to liturgy characteristic of Orthodox and Catholic traditions. As such, they want to associate with deep and abiding traditions of faith. They prefer somber mood lighting, Gregorian chants, icons and art, and small choirs located in the rear of the auditorium. They also hear messages spoken by pastors wearing shorts and polo shirts while sitting at a bistro table. This has become the ministry vogue. Emergents shun authoritative declarations and respect the views of others—even if they are contrary to what they personally believe. Generally speaking, they don't want to sacrifice decency for doctrine. And while a recent national poll confirms that over 90 percent of Americans still believe in God, the question is, what kind of god do they believe in?

No one knows what the future will hold, but one thing is certain: if the past is any indication of what the future holds, we're in for a wild ride! Those who can't get beyond traditional ways of preaching and reaching will struggle and find it hard to call anything other than what they've been taught "church." Those who meet in industrial parks or have multiple site venues will be held suspect. Who knows what they must think of those ministries that operate solely on the Web and have no formal meeting time, building, or pastoral leadership.

Changes in the way ministry has been done over the past two hundred years have been significant. Even in the past one hundred years we have see monumental change. But in some ways we see reminders that we still face many of the same basic issues, such as population growth, adjustment to change, and an uncertain future. One church growth strategist writes, "The church world in the year 1900, as in 2000, was a world challenged by intense immigration, the multiplication of new churches, changing organizational structure issues and the creation of multitudes of small groups through the Sunday school."[1]

These changes, and the many that are yet to come, will have a significant impact on the way we do ministry, train for it, and reach out to the lost in our communities. God calls us to lead, not react, so it may be difficult for some to accept the changes that are coming. But whether they accept them or not, they will not wait for ministry leaders to adjust. Like it or not, change has been thrust upon us. The question is, Are we ready for it?

The Changing Role of the American Pastorate

As the church struggles to keep up with an ever-changing world, the role of the pastor is changing too. According to seminary professor Eddie Gibbs, "Yesterday's style of leadership will not be adequate for the opening decades of the twenty-first century. The future is too unpredictable for the predetermined parameters once provided by long-term planning."[2] Change comes at such breakneck speed today that by the time a ministry leader gathers consensus, it is already too late to stay ahead of the need. Life in the church becomes one constant game of catch-up.

Watching what other churches are doing is a popular sideline activity for contemporary ministry leaders today. After all, why waste your energy trying to gain a new vision for your ministry if you can easily replicate one that's working in a nearby neighborhood?

> While some leaders mistake opportunity for vision, others borrow their visions. The easiest course of action is often the one taken previously, especially if it was successful.... Churches are remiss to assume that because God once worked mightily in a particular way, he will continue to work in exactly that way. His resources and his methods are innumerable.[3]

Even though these transcontinental visions have become the staple of many a church conference, are they really God's plan for the entire body of Christ in the twenty-first century?

While researching material for this chapter, I came across numerous mind-numbing articles from a broad range of perspectives. Some predicted the end of the church in the twenty-first century due to its ever-increasing irrelevancy. Other authors advocated a formulaic approach, as if a "one-size-fits-all" viewpoint to ministry leadership would be the silver bullet for the twenty-first-century American church. *Twenty-one Laws of This* or *Four Steps to That* sells books and makes for catchy seminar series but doesn't meet the needs of all churches where they are applied.

The purpose of this next section is simply to point out what some may see as already pretty obvious. Ministry leadership is changing. The pastorate that your grandfather enjoyed a hundred years ago is gone forever. Today things have changed, and those who will stand the test of time will have a different set of expectations and job skills. Let's look at a few matters of reality check for twenty-first-century pastors.

Reality check #1: Paradigms of training. Twenty-first-century pastors will need to have a broader range of education and training going into the pastorate than the generation of ministry leaders before them. Gone are the days when a seminary degree was the cure-all for the congregation's problems. Now it's simply the starting point. Life experience has no substitute. That's why second-career pastorates are so valuable to the church today. Those who come into the church after already experiencing a career are well received as being more realistic and down to earth.

Don't misunderstand. I am not denigrating seminary training. Mick and I both teach at one. But we also realize its limitations. A seminary degree is still the foundation upon which church ministry is established; there is no substitute for solid biblical teaching and theological grounding. However, many churches argue that such training is insufficient for pastoral ministry today. In fact, some megachurch leaders argue that they can better prepare a pastor for ministerial leadership at their churches than a seminary. That's wishful thinking, but because of their desire for relevance over against what they see as rote memory, their argument does have some merit for seminary administrators willing to listen.

Topics that don't get enough airtime in our curriculum-packed seminaries today include managing multiple staff ministries, strategic planning, bookkeeping, conflict resolution, marketing, statistical analysis of community demographics, family therapy, and information technology. Since more pastors are terminated over mismanagement than false doctrine, courses in these areas are desperately needed. Pastors should avail themselves of workshops, seminars, and outside training opportunities to keep abreast of issues that impact their ministries' effectiveness.

Reality check #2: Dysfunctional clergy. It isn't just the laity who live messed up lives. The ugly little secret in many churches is that the pastor is just as messed up—though few are willing to admit it. More and more seminary students are coming into seminary (and graduating) with personal dysfunctions. These dysfunctions may be caused by their family of origin or habits established in their childhood or adolescence, or perhaps as a result of our culture. In any case, they don't possess the emotional and relational health they need to lead a congregation of equally unhealthy people. That is why when they come into conflict with someone in their church, they end up becoming a casualty themselves rather than being the source of healing and strength for others.

Ministry leaders of the twenty-first century will face some of the most profound and complex counseling issues they ever dreamed possible. Sometimes without warning, they find themselves embroiled in their own personal pain as well. These wounded healers, as Henry Nouwen calls them, don't have the luxury of taking time off to heal their own personal wounds while they are binding the wounds of others. Contemporary ministry leaders need to go through some intentional counseling as part of their ministry preparation. It's unfortunate that so few actually do.

Reality check #3: Power shift. Twenty-first-century church members have different expectations of their pastors. Due to the proliferation of radio and television ministries in which preachers deliver well-polished and thoroughly researched messages, most church members expect their pastors to stand and deliver in similar fashion every week. They want their church to be on the cutting edge of technology, contemporary trends, and dynamic ministry methods. It doesn't matter that they aren't willing to pay the cost of what it takes to receive such benefits.

This generation of church attendees has grown up on a steady diet of "Have it your way" service-oriented corporate values. Customer-service training in stores and restaurants propagates the mantra that the customer is always right. When this mind-set enters the church, especially one with several hundred members, it is only a matter of time before the train wreck, because it simply isn't possible for all the "customers" to always get their way. The result is conflict and eventual termination of the pastor.

No generation of church members has been so quick to discard ministers as the current one—and this trend shows no sign of letting up. We'll discuss this in greater detail in chapter 10, but for now, suffice it to say that if it seems your congregation is getting harder to please, you're right. Their standards are getting higher, and ministers cannot satisfy the vast array of differing expectations. Ministry is not for the faint of heart.

Reality check #4: Governance. I wrote a book in the early 1990s titled *The Effective Church Board.* I wanted to call it *The Myth of the Effective Church Board,* but the publisher thought it might offend my audience. The truth hurts! When I speak at conferences for pastors or consult with a church board, I inevitably get asked, "What is the best governance model for the church?" Sometimes the question is posed in desperation as though, having struggled with the issue for some time, they are willing to accept whatever answer I supply. If only it were that easy.

I understand why they ask it. In most cases, the church leadership has been embroiled in tensions over power, change, and/or conflict, and they want to establish a source of authority by which they can "solve" the issue. I have worked with churches undergoing a split that were governed by a highly charismatic pastor who seemed to have carte blanche, and I have met with those led by elders, trustees, and deacons. It really doesn't matter what you call the body of leaders that occupies the box at the top of your church's organizational chart; the issue has little to do with titles.

I have met pastors who swear they will never serve at a church led by deacons. Their experience has led them to hold the elder board as the form of governance with the least amount of drama. I have also met pastors from churches governed by elder boards who swear the deacon board is the way to go. Congregational rule, bishops, elders, deacons—it doesn't really matter. You name the flavor, and I can give you examples of failed leadership. On the other hand, I can also sight as many good examples of each. Not the titles, but the hearts of those who hold the titles, are what makes the difference.

My point is that there is simply no First Church of Utopia. If you left your church in disillusionment over the governance model, don't blame the model. The model can bring great joy and happiness, or it can bring great pain and suffering. Remember, God looks at the heart, not a name or title. You should do no less.

Reality check # 5: Keep focused. Churches split and leaders get sacrificed over arguments of methodology. No matter what your method of communication may be in the dawn of the twenty-first century, your message must remain the same. Don't get so hung up arguing over methods of communication that your message is nullified.

In recent years we have seen a virtual explosion of different forms of communication. Churches are using multimedia, drama, multiple venues, and the Internet as the means for delivering the message. Don't let all the hype about method distract you from the essence of your job, which is to communicate Christ as the answer to humankind's greatest need. Simply put, nothing else will do.

Your message is the reason for your existence. At the end of the day, humankind is lonely, guilt ridden, and confused. God's message, spoken through humans, answers humankind's need for each of these conditions. It connects sinful humans to a loving Creator and gives them hope that life can be meaningful. It gives peace as no human invention can. And of course, God's message straightens out the most confused among us by providing a compass for decision making. No matter how badly we have spun our web of sin, God's Word provides freedom and release from bondage. When Jesus asked his disciples if they would abandon him at the end of his earthly ministry, their response was "Lord, to whom shall we go? You have the words of eternal life" (John 6:68). Ministry in the twenty-first century is based on your ability to communicate a timeless message using contemporary methods.

Supreme Court Rulings

- 1962 (*Engel v. Vitale*) Banned nondenominational prayers in schools.
- 1980 (*Stone v. Graham*) Removed the Ten Commandments from school walls.
- 1985 (*Wallace v. Jaffree*) Struck down one minute for period of silence even though 69 percent of Americans supported having prayer in public schools. In 1991 that figure had grown to 78 percent.
- 1987 (*Edwards v. Aguillard*) Censored creationist viewpoints but ruled evolution viewpoints were acceptable.
- 1992 (*Lee v. Weisman*) Barred prayers at all public school graduations.
- Currently, it is illegal for a coach or teacher to share Christ with a student during school hours.

Reality check # 6: Focus on the fundamentals. No, I'm not talking about a certain list of theological fundamentals—although they are important. I'm talking about focusing on the most important target at your church—the family. Many pastors get sidetracked in their ministries due to an overemphasis on a particular age group (e.g., children, youth, college, singles, etc.). You may disagree with me, but I don't believe a strong foundation for long-term viability of the church is found in a dynamic ministry to children, youth, or single adults. Yes, each is critical for building a balanced church, but none of these ministries should be the primary focus. Healthy families should be the focus, and great ministries to children and/or youth are by-products of it.

It doesn't take much to realize that the spiritual foundation of our society continues to be eroded by our legal system. Whereas once we were free to teach biblical values to our children in school, today we are no longer permitted to speak of Christ on campus. Legal challenges have all but forbidden God to step on a school campus. Even our courts are forbidden to show the Ten Commandments in the courtroom lest someone be offended. God has been swept into inconsequential corners of our society.

Ask any public school teacher today, and you will hear a litany of different parental combinations prevalent in their classroom. Children are being raised by grandparents, single parents, stepparents, extended family members, and same-sex partners. Traditional nuclear families have become the minority. Because the family will continue this trend toward fragmentation, twenty-first-century pastoral leaders need to make the family a priority in their churches' ministries.

The purpose of this chapter has been to highlight the ways that twenty-first-century ministry will differ from that which has taken place in the past. Our culture has changed radically, so it stands to reason that our ministry must change to keep pace. We no longer live in an agrarian culture but rather one that is technological in scope and emphasis. Significant events that occur in one part of the world are communicated in seconds to countries on the other side of the planet. We can travel around the world in hours now rather than days. Medical miracles prolong life and ease pain. All around us are vestiges of change, yet many churches still operate as though they were living in the Middle Ages.

Those who lead the church in the twenty-first century must recognize that change requires leadership, not management. No one ever managed an army into victory. It was led by those willing to take risks and assume command. The church needs to be led by men and women who have servant spirits and hearts of courage. It takes strength to be gentle and wisdom to be humble—not easy qualities to emulate but indicative of the Great Shepherd. Our prayer for you as you lead the church in this next era of human history is that you will serve with the courage and confidence that come from the Holy Spirit.

PART 2

WHERE ARE YOU NOW?

CHAPTER 6

PARADISE LOST

Knowing When It's Time to Leave

MICK BOERSMA

In his heart a man plans his course,
but the LORD determines his steps.
Proverbs 16:9 NIV

When I was growing up, our family traveled every summer, usually taking two weeks in August to get away from the rigors of farm life. We often visited relatives in other parts of the country, staying at their homes and enjoying each other's company. The experience was quite pleasant. And I have learned at least one reason why: my parents always knew when it was time to leave. They had a sixth sense that told them when the optimum visiting had taken place and when we would soon become a burden on those we were visiting. The good times had been good, but it was time to pack up and go home.

It's no secret that pastors do a considerable amount of traveling over the course of their careers. While some stay in the same church for many years, even a lifetime, most move along a number of times throughout their ministry. We have spent many hours counseling students and pastors concerning this issue and suggest that before anyone begins thinking about a move, he or she remember a few basic rules of thumb.

1. *It's not easy saying good-bye.* One former student wrote, "There are days when I repeat the mantra 'Never quit on a Monday,' but I've expanded that to include Tuesday as well. Do you think it's too much of a stretch to include Wednesday?" He was in the midst of a leadership struggle and thinking of leaving. But with a newly planted church, a huge investment in the people, and the needs of a growing young family, a move would have been a huge and potentially disastrous undertaking. He stayed, and a rich season of growth and peace came upon the fellowship. Leaving for another church would have circumvented that

blessing. When we asked our pastors if they had ever given serious thought to quitting ministry completely, 44 percent said they had. Being a ministry leader can be very stressful at times. It is an exhausting position that requires a firm call of God on your heart. Anything less and you simply won't last.

2. *If the grass looks greener, it's probably Astroturf.* At best, pastors trade one set of challenges for another whenever they move from one ministry location to another. Do they really think a ministry exists that is free from heartache, pressure, and struggles? If it did, the church wouldn't need them! And while there are often great advantages in moving to another ministry, escape from all difficulties is not one of them.

When we asked our pastors why they wanted to quit, we got a mixed bag of responses. They ranged from losing one's passion for the ministry to personal health issues (see figure 6.1).

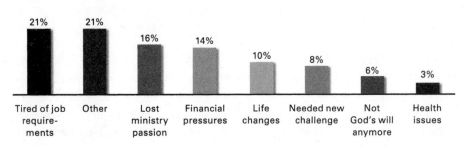

Figure 6.1, Q 24: Why did you consider leaving the ministry?

21%	21%	16%	14%	10%	8%	6%	3%
Tired of job require-ments	Other	Lost ministry passion	Financial pressures	Life changes	Needed new challenge	Not God's will anymore	Health issues

The temptation to "see green" is especially strong today as pastors are exposed to a host of dynamic ministries that appear as oases in the midst of their personal ministry desert. Sociologist Dr. Barry Schwartz observes:

> When people evaluate an experience, they are performing one or more of the following comparisons:
> 1. Comparing the experience to what they hoped it would be
> 2. Comparing the experience to what they expected it to be
> 3. Comparing the experience to other experiences they have had in the recent past
> 4. Comparing the experience to experiences that others have had[1]

Any of these comparisons can lead a pastor to search for that one special ministry that has it all—a place where everything is going well and the future is guaranteed. Pastors have been looking for Camelot Community Church since the dawn of the ages. It doesn't exist on this side of eternity.

3. *The pastoral job description includes pain.* Jesus said it himself, "If anyone would come after me, he must deny himself and take up his cross and follow me" (Mark 8:34 NIV). Every time a cross was used in Jesus' day, it involved hardship and suffering. Paul instructs Timothy, "Keep your head in all situations, endure hardship, do the work of an evangelist, discharge all the duties of your ministry" (2 Tim. 4:5 NIV). We are in a battle for the hearts and minds of people. While considering a move can be a very good thing, we must not forget the "suffering factor" and leave one battle thinking we can avoid the war.

Recent research of five major denominations shows how much the hardship of ministry factors into pastors leaving ministry altogether. Of the seven most common reasons, most are related to the challenge of denying oneself.[2] So if you are thinking of moving along or getting out of ministry entirely (we will deal with that in chapter 10), remember the words of Jesus and his embattled apostle. You can expect a healthy dose of trouble in pastoral work.

4. *Haste makes waste.* It is tempting to make the process of deciding to leave a ministry as uncomplicated as possible. Sometimes we'd like God just to tell us what to do — perhaps give us a kind of mystical experience that will bring peace and clarity. Pastors report that they seek God's direction through four primary means: obedience to his commands, prayer, Scripture, and counsel from mature Christians.[3] Implied in these strategies is a kind of rigor that brings forth a well-reasoned and wise outcome based on thorough research and reflection.

We want to help you with your travel planning here. Any great adventure takes a lot of that, and it is our contention that deciding whether to make the trip at all is worth some serious reflection. We would like to help you review your present ministry situation in six crucial areas using what we call the "six flags of assessment." Each flag is unique, displaying its own array of patterns and colors. Your challenge is to look long and hard at each one, respond to it honestly, and trust the Lord to give you wisdom and peace that only he can provide (James 1:5; Phil. 4:6–7).

Top Reasons Pastors Leave Church Ministry

- Preference for another kind of ministry
- Need to care for children or family
- Conflict in the congregation
- Conflict with denominational leaders
- Feelings of burnout or frustration
- Sexual misconduct
- Divorce or marital problems

The Relationship Flag

Ministry is all about people—loving them, leading them, caring for them. The effective shepherd knows the sheep and does his or her best work in close relationship with others. Pastoral work is also about our relationship with Jesus, the Good Shepherd. When things aren't good with people, the Lord, or both, it is pretty easy to feel the pull of a "better place." But here is where we need to ask ourselves the tough questions: do we really understand the state of our relationships as we consider a change? The following are a number of questions for you to ponder.

Do I have an intimate personal knowledge of people in my ministry? If you have been around for a few years and can't respond positively, you may want to consider investing more time and energy in those around you. Pastors often like to do things on their own, robbing themselves of the benefits of teamwork or relationships. As one put it, "I'm beginning to find that in the areas that I'm strongest, I don't tend to train others and hand off ministry opportunities. I tend to be a sort of one-man-show." It is possible that your ministry style has kept you from developing meaningful relationships with your flock. On the other hand, you may find the people you serve difficult to know. Perhaps in another setting you would find folks easier to relate to and consequently serve more effectively.

How deeply has my ministry invested in people? Fruit needs time to grow, and how long your ministry takes to bear fruit may well depend on the condition of the congregation when you first arrived. One pastor in the northeastern United States began his ministry with an elder board that didn't really understand the gospel. His first task was to help them make sure they knew Jesus Christ as Savior. Seems pretty basic. Jesus did the same thing. He started with men from

Benefits of Ministry Longevity

- Deeper relationships
- Growing heritage of faith with a local church body
- Witness of Christians learning to love one another through difficulties
- Sense of belonging to a larger community outside the church
- "Adoption" of pastor's children by surrogate grandparents, aunts, and uncles
- Consistent educational experience in one district or school
- Potential to establish home ownership (have your own nest)

a wide array of personal and professional backgrounds. Their spiritual transformation didn't happen overnight. Even after several years with him, observing miracles that still amaze us, he would have to say to them: "Do you still not see or understand? Are your hearts hardened? Do you have eyes but fail to see, and ears but fail to hear? And don't you remember? When I broke the five loaves for the five thousand, how many basketfuls of pieces did you pick up?" (Mark 8:17 – 19 NIV). Had Jesus given up on these disciples and chosen a new team, we never would have seen the stunning transformation of these men following the three years' mentorship and subsequent coming of the Holy Spirit.

How healthy are my relationships with other staff and lay leaders? These are primary relationships in any ministry. How they function is a key to long-term effectiveness and ministry satisfaction.[4] Conflicting personalities and differing leadership and management styles (see chapter 3) can create a lot of heat between well-intentioned people working toward the same goal. Issues of philosophy of ministry and vision aside (see The Organization Flag below), liking the people you work with can make or break a ministry. Sometimes staff members connect well but their spouses have problems. These rifts can be caused by inequities in salary, authority, or resources or by differences in personality. Problems with lay leaders can come from not knowing them well enough to accurately determine their heart on issues affecting the ministry you share with them. This may be a time to invest more purposefully in these key people.

How healthy is my relationship with God? More than a few pastors have lost their ministries because of a failure to keep their walk with God fresh, honest, and consistent. We often focus on those who have experienced a moral failure. We should probably be more concerned about those of us who quit or move on because of a slow but sure cooling of our relationship with the God who called us. Our commitment to knowing God's Word, communing with him regularly, and sharing our lives with godly counselors and friends will keep us from leaving a ministry too soon or missing his call to another place.

The Organization Flag

In chapter 2 you reviewed your personal mission, vision, and core values. When people serve in environments that encourage and support these convictions, they tend to be more effective and fulfilled in their work. Since ministry is about people, it necessarily involves organization, planning, and management. Asking yourself the following questions will help you determine if your present setting is still a good fit.

What is the level of agreement that exists between your personal mission, vision, and values and those found in this ministry? You may have fit your ministry well at one time, but now things may have changed. Maybe the new senior pastor is going a different direction—one you aren't so sure about. Perhaps new lay leadership is entertaining a different direction in your area of ministry. Denominational changes may be causing you second thoughts. One pastor's wife wrote regarding a possible new ministry: "All was well and our whole family prepared emotionally and spiritually to go, and at the last minute the door closed regarding a denominational issue that my husband could not compromise." It is possible that the Lord is challenging you to adjust and grow through the changes. It is also possible that the Lord will use this mismatch to cause you to move elsewhere.

Are resources present to carry out the mission and vision of this ministry? Sometimes we just get really tired of not having enough support to do what we are called or expected to do. Youth pastors are charged to hang out with the kids yet without an expense allowance. Preachers, wanting to give solid sermons, struggle to build their libraries. Children's pastors long for enough floor space to provide stimulating ministry settings. Leaving a position over lack of funding should be approached carefully, however. According to one poll, the average born-again Christian gives just under 4 percent of income to the work of the church.[5] Inadequate finances, facilities, and staff can make you wonder if it is time to seek a place with more and better resources for ministry.

What impact is my ministry having on building the kingdom? We sometimes forget the effect our ministries are having on the larger population around us. Organizationally, the church is a visible and crucial part of any neighborhood, providing services to members and nonmembers alike. In pondering a change, it is important to ask yourself how your own ministry has been sewn into the fabric of the area in which you live.

How does the stability of this ministry depend on my continued presence? We should be mindful that people are depending on us. Leaving could be detrimental to the ministry and therefore should be considered carefully. Congregations in the middle of large capital campaigns can ill afford to lose their pastor. In fact, many lending institutions require a contractual agreement that assures stability in the senior leadership. Newly hired associate staff members should have confidence in knowing that the senior pastor who brought them in is not planning to leave the church in the near future. Parents and their teenage children appreciate knowing their youth pastor will be there long enough to see them through those challenging years of junior or senior high school. Foreign missionaries on church support are comforted when the home base is stable. One commented to my wife and me during a furlough, "Of all the churches that support us, yours is the only one with the same pastor since we were here four years ago." Stability is a good thing. Consider carefully the impact your leaving would have, not just on you and yours, but on the ministry and community God has privileged you to serve.

The Family Flag

Whether single or married, kids or no kids, one's immediate family should be at the forefront of our minds when making a decision to leave a ministry. How we care for family qualifies us for ministry in the first place (1 Tim. 3:4–5; Titus 1:6). Providing godly care and leadership is our responsibility, especially during times of transition. We have already seen that high levels of stress in the family can lead to pastors leaving their posts altogether.[6] There is a lot you can do to minimize this stress. We will look at family issues again in chapter 11, but for now we invite you to contemplate the following questions concerning your most precious relationships.

In what ways would staying in this ministry harm my family? There are a number of possibilities here. Educational needs of children can generate concern. Special needs programs may not be available where you live. The school system may not measure up to your personal standards, especially in the higher grades. College may be looming for your children, and a more metropolitan address would allow you to be closer to them.

A subtler issue is the level of emotional hurt resulting from congregational conflict. Sometimes a pastor's wife finds it difficult to continue in a church where her husband has been repeatedly attacked by members and leaders. Church splits, which leave the "warring parties" in the same community, can make staying so awkward and unpleasant that a move may be in order.

In what ways would staying in this ministry help my family? The early years of ministry can be characterized by a sort of wanderlust that beckons young pastors to travel the far reaches of ministry by way of many positions in many places. But families thrive on stability. What kinds of benefits can staying deliver? Check out the sidebar on page 88 for our short list.

What extended family circumstances might affect my ability to stay here? Many pastors find themselves serving some distance from elderly parents. When parents get to the age when they need assistance, it is hard for a loving child to help from across the country. Perhaps you are feeling the need to consider a position closer to your parents' home or are thinking about moving your parents closer to you. In either case, a decision to move along or stay is probably in your future.

How unified is my family concerning a potential move? A wise minister is one who includes his or her spouse (and children if possible) in any decision to move. Astute search committees insist on meeting the pastor's spouse so as to facilitate honest and well-considered decisions from all parties involved.

In marriage husbands and wives are one (Gen. 2:24). Decisions made by one affect the other—in all aspects of life. When both spouses have jobs (common in the majority of pastoral families today),[7] unity in deciding to move is not just advisable but is absolutely necessary. Telling your spouse, "We're moving," without being sensitive to how that impacts her or his life and work will most certainly lead to bitterness and resentment—even toward God. Following the marriage instructions in Ephesians 5 will go a long way in keeping you from disunity during these trying days of decision.

The Congregational Flag

Trying to read a congregation to determine whether or not your "time is up" is risky business. If you go by facial expressions, you'll pack your bags while the postlude is being played. Yet there is value in asking yourself questions about the congregation and observing patterns that might indicate the level of effectiveness you are having as one of their spiritual leaders. Following are four questions that beg an answer as you decide whether it is time to leave.

Am I the right person for the season this ministry is currently in? Most of us are familiar with the pattern suggested by church growth experts. A ministry begins with vision and passion. After a period of solid growth, a plateau is reached. Decline will occur after a while unless vision is renewed. You may be the kind of leader who is gifted to lead the first charge but not effective at helping an established congregation renew its vision. You may be skilled at leading churches through the level places or even during times of decline. You may be finding it a struggle to lead your ministry through its current season.

What is the overall level of support for my leadership in this ministry? Like it or not, we usually first look to attendance numbers or finances to help us determine the answer to this one. People vote with their feet and their checkbooks. When the end is near, congregations can show it by a decline in these areas. One executive minister for a major denomination described it this way: "The conflict begins to reach crisis proportions when the members not only absent themselves from public services, but deliberately withhold contributions to force the issue of conflict more rapidly. Ironically, sometimes contributions are higher after the pastor leaves than they were before he left."[8]

More difficult to quantify are levels of support from elders, staff, and other key leaders. Elders sometimes indicate lack of support by withholding pay raises or benefits. Staff can torpedo your leadership any number of ways, both subtle and overt. Yet it is important not to rush to judgment. All congregations have financial constraints at some time or another. Staff may just be on a different page philosophically and need your help in appreciating the perspective on ministry God has given you. It is important to take note of these issues and honestly assess how things really are. A change in the level of support may not be a sign for your leaving, but it should be a factor in making that decision.

How well do I fit with the prevailing church and community culture? Anyone who has moved from one location to another realizes the impact of cultural change and adjustment. Different neighborhoods within cities can be vastly diverse. In our work with hundreds of seminary graduates in pastoral ministry worldwide, they report that cultural adjustments are huge and exhausting. Pastors who move to unfamiliar areas (especially from suburban to rural) find that two to three years are needed to begin to feel somewhat at home in their new surroundings.

What effect would my leaving (or staying) have on this congregation? As mentioned previously, congregations can be in financial circumstances where loss of their current leadership could jeopardize their economic health (see The Organization Flag above). Ethics would suggest that a pastor consider not leaving a congregation when it is apparent that his or her leadership is key to a building program or other major campaign.

Every day churches experience splits as a result of a pastor leaving under difficult circumstances. While this may be unavoidable at times, it should give any servant leader cause to hesitate and search for solutions to conflicts within the body. As well, leaving a ministry can be discouraging to those left behind. One youth pastor who was concerned that his students would feel betrayed if he left for another position responded to a survey question this way: "Yes, I completely understand this and even fear it. I was hounded by my students when my friend announced his resignation (the third for the church in six months) with the question, 'Are you leaving too?'... I told them that I felt God was still calling me here and that I wouldn't trade them for anyone else just to get out of here."

Of course, staying could be harmful to the congregation. Becoming the object of conflict may signal your departure, either voluntarily or by force. Such a possibility could be due to philosophical or doctrinal differences or because you have lived past your "expiration date" and have become too mentally or physically feeble to carry out your calling—at least in the kind of leadership position you have been accustomed to.

The Emotional Flag

One of the reasons we are counseled not to quit on Mondays is because of the emotional instability we may experience after a particularly difficult Lord's Day. Quitting after an explosive board meeting is another unwise move. Yet there are times when we feel the weight of ministry to such an extent that our emotional health is threatened. When is it time to consider moving to prevent further damage and enable healing? Here are some questions to help you decide for yourself.

What emotional manifestations are causing concern in my family or me? The story of Elijah and his depression is an eye-opener. After seeing God move in majestic ways against powerful forces, he ended up in the wilderness having a pity party (1 Kings 19:14). But three days' rest and some good food brought him back. We all occasionally struggle with depression. When it persists over a long period of time, however, it may indicate trouble in our ministry. For some it may indicate the need for a physician visit to have a chemical analysis of their blood done. An overall weariness may suggest a much-needed vacation, but it may also result from prolonged emotional struggles that have gone unattended. Maybe a new ministry setting will be part of the answer, but only if the root causes are addressed through godly counsel, prayer, and the Word.

To what extent has criticism affected my ability to minister here effectively? One of my lifetime mentors encouraged me to make sure I didn't go into ministry to improve my self-esteem. Doubt in our abilities can be amplified in light of criticism, shaking our confidence and impairing relationships. Even when it's justified, the emotional toll can be devastating. And not just for us—our family gets hurt too. If approval ratings are your measure of value, you're in for a hard life. A constant pounding of criticism can make you incapable of carrying out your ministry. Just like Elijah, you may need a good vacation—or a change of location.

Do I sense that I need a new season—a new adventure? Why? Any work has its share of routine tasks that can become wearisome, even boring. Loss of enthusiasm in a pastoral position happens. One researcher calls it "disenchantment":

> In almost every church there is some element which causes serious doubt as to whether the local congregation is a means of God's purpose and will in the world.... The way decisions are made, the relatively small number of people willing to give time and energy to leadership and ministry activity, the constant pressure on budgets and the consequent effect on salaries, support staff and working conditions all can and do lead to varying forms of disenchantment.[9]

And so a change sounds good. It's not that we want to leave the war as much as we want to fight in a different land—anywhere but here. Maybe we just need a temporary leave to renew ourselves before rejoining the front lines. After that we may be better able to determine if a fresh, new assignment is in order.

Are there compelling personal reasons I should leave this ministry for another? In some cases a moral or ethical failure will compel us to leave our current ministry—or ministry altogether. There may be certain "elder" qualifications we don't feel we are measuring up to, prompting a resignation. Cases we hear often involve minor children who are having significant personal problems or marriages that are struggling. "If anyone does not know how to manage his own family, how can he take care of God's church?" (1 Tim. 3:5 NIV). Honoring this standard may involve a move.

Financial integrity is also an important personal character issue. "If anyone does not provide for his relatives, and especially for his immediate family, he has denied the faith and is worse than an unbeliever" (1 Tim. 5:8 NIV). That verse rings in the ears of pastors whose salaries are just not enough to care for their loved ones. While some reparation is possible where you are (see chapter 20), moving to a ministry that provides a living wage can be a tempting, and appropriate, option. The number of personal issues is potentially limitless, and we trust that these few suggestions will help you surface others that may provide insight as you consider a transition.

The Professional Flag

Most ministers we know don't usually refer to their calling to ministry as a "career." But people do consider ministers to be professionals, and it can be helpful to look at your pastoral service in this light as you contemplate a move. As you travel through the various seasons of life, the landscape changes; circumstances arise that alter your route. It's wise to pay attention to the map and adjust your journey accordingly. Here are some questions that should help you with your travel planning.

Have I given this ministry call a full and honest effort? It takes a long time just to get acquainted with a church family, learn the culture, and become aware of the real needs of people. "People's masks take a few years to fall off," as one pastor put it. Then the real work begins—and it's a challenge!

Paul encouraged Timothy to "be diligent in these matters; give yourself wholly to them, so that everyone may see your progress" (1 Tim. 4:15 NIV). Echoing Proverbs 27:23, "Be sure you know the condition of your flocks, give careful attention to your herds" (NIV), he called the young pastor to a high standard of commitment to the Ephesian believers. You have to ask yourself, "Have I given this ministry a fair shake—have I worked hard at the mission and vision of this place?" Only you can answer the question, but it must be answered honestly if you are to move along with a clear conscience. Saying you have been to the Grand Canyon doesn't mean stopping for two minutes at a lookout and snapping a picture. A real traveler takes time to deeply experience the terrain.

Are my reasons for considering a change in keeping with godly values? One thing we don't want to do as ministers is capitulate to worldly standards of careerism. We don't move to another job just because it's with a bigger company, offers more money, or puts us in the trade magazines as an up-and-coming star. Yet we struggle, as did this pastor:

> On going to a bigger church—I guess it's just something I'm intrigued with. I look at it from three factors. One, here's an opportunity to be in a church that isn't "Baptist." What would that be like? Two, here is an opportunity to have full-time paid staff with a budget to really do youth ministry with. What would that be like? Three, here is an opportunity for me to be stretched and to use my gifts and talents to minister to a larger audience. What would that be like?

This pastor is wanting to honor God's call and be faithful in his ministry, yet the possibilities of a career move are pulling him. Will better pay be the motive—a bigger stage—more notoriety?

You may think it's time to move from an associate to a more "senior" position. This could be true, but only if the reasons don't include the desire to run the ship, get the best paycheck, or receive the esteem that often comes by being top gun. Our motives should reflect that of our Lord Jesus Christ, who responded to James and John's status request by saying, "For even the Son of Man did not come to be served, but to serve" (Mark 10:45 NIV).

What strengths have I developed that would indicate a change in ministry setting? As we traverse the landscape of ministry, we gain new skills, develop gifts, and become seasoned in the administration of different kinds of ministry. We often tell our students that getting older is a good thing—you know yourself better, how God has "bent" you, where you fit, how you can best serve in his kingdom work. All this development makes you more effective in ministry. Often God desires that we put this good stuff to use right where we are. But it can also cause us to wonder if there is another setting where we can better utilize all we have acquired.

Youth pastors may desire to take their developing understanding of older adults into a position that affords service to a more "mature" flock. Still other associates find their careers moving toward administrative ministries. Some senior pastors take on denominational positions. Their experience and knowledge of ministry help them be effective supporters of clergy and church alike. Others are more interested in academic pursuits and utilize their doctoral degrees to go

Seasons of a Pastorate

Years 1–3: Focus of energy is on listening, learning, and loving—the building of relationships—and adjustments being experienced by you and congregation.

Years 4–6: Moving into the most productive years of ministry in this congregation—unless clear signals of major problems, go about work of pastoring.

Years 7–9: Evaluate significance of your leadership in this congregation. Still experiencing growth? Fulfilled and challenged?

Years 10 and beyond: Affirm all is going well. Note how you and congregation are continuing to grow. Identify reasons for continuing beyond twelve years. Determine how long-term ministry will affect congregation.

Seasons of a Ministry Career

Early career entry: Shorter tenure position(s) — finding yourself; learning the ropes; gaining experience; identifying strengths; refining vision, call, and purpose.

Midcareer years: Longer tenure position(s) — more secure, strengths developing, more confidence, well-fitted to context, stability sought (family needs etc.).

The transition years: Securing a "fall" season of ministry, leaving a legacy, dealing with age discrimination, planning retirement options (financial, housing, location, ministry possibilities).

from pulpit to lectern. God's good gifts are to be celebrated and may just signal a change in venue—a new place to see them utilized to their fullest potential.

Does the season of my ministry career suggest that a change is warranted? Each ministry *position* has its own seasons (see the sidebar on page 96).[10] Each ministry *career* has its phases (see the sidebar above). The Career Transition Indicator chart on pages 98 and 99 may help you discover where you are right now.

You may be ready to move to a new location, or it may be time to put the car in the garage and continue to serve faithfully where you are. Like it or not, time marches on—and we need to pay attention to the signs and, in faith, wrestle with the challenging task of seeking God's will.

Tallying the Score

We have developed a helpful Career Transition Indicator test listing the six flags along with their corresponding questions. Based on your personal responses to them, rate each accordingly:

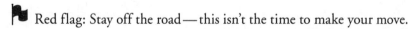 Red flag: Stay off the road—this isn't the time to make your move.

Yellow flag: Proceed with caution—there may be obstacles ahead.

Green flag: The track is clear—you're free to go for a drive.

Add up your flags and see what they might suggest. As we said at the beginning of this chapter, there is no simple way to determine if a move is in order, but you may be able to see a developing pattern that will provide some good visibility in your travels.

CAREER TRANSITION INDICATOR	Stop	Caution	Proceed
The Relationship Flag			
Do I have an intimate personal knowledge of people in my ministry?			
How deeply has my ministry built into the lives of my people?			
How healthy are my relationships with other staff and lay leaders?			
How healthy is my relationship with God?			
The Organization Flag			
What is the level of agreement regarding mission, vision, and philosophy in this ministry?			
Are resources present to carry out the mission and vision of this ministry?			
What impact is my ministry having on the larger community in which I live?			
How does the stability of this ministry depend upon my continued presence?			
The Family Flag			
In what way would staying in this ministry harm my family?			
In what ways would staying in this ministry help my family?			
What extended family circumstances might affect my ability to stay here?			
How unified is my family concerning a potential move?			

CAREER TRANSITION INDICATOR	🏴 Stop	🏳 Caution	🏴 Proceed
The Congregational Flag			
Am I the right person for the season this ministry is currently in?			
What is the overall level of support for my leadership in this ministry?			
How well do I fit with the prevailing church and community culture?			
What impact would my leaving (or staying) have on this congregation?			
The Emotional Flag			
What emotional manifestations are causing concern in my family or me?			
To what extent has criticism affected my ability to minister effectively?			
Is there a sense that I need new chapter—a new adventure? Why?			
The Professional Flag			
Have I given this ministry call a full and honest effort?			
Are my reasons for considering a change in keeping with godly values?			
What strengths have I developed that would indicate a change in ministry setting?			
Does the season of my ministry career suggest a change is warranted?			
Are there compelling personal reasons I should leave this ministry for another?			
Totals (one point for each flag choice)			

CHAPTER 7

MAPPING YOUR COURSE

Developing Your Exit Strategy

MICK BOERSMA

Who is wise and understanding among you? Let them show it by his good life, by deeds done in the humility that comes from wisdom.
James 3:13 NIV

I will never forget my first exit strategy: Get out before they fire me! Let's just say my initial experience at being a youth pastor didn't go so well. *How* to exit did not cross my mind. I just wanted out. My lack of maturity and unsuitability for that particular position conspired against me. And while I did make my getaway, eventually finding a very good fit at another church, the process of leaving that youth job was painful and ill managed.

William Shakespeare wrote, "All the world's a stage, and all the men and women merely players; they have their exits and their entrances."[1] To that I would add, "How you make those exits and entrances makes all the difference." We'll talk about entering your new ministry setting in chapter 21, but now we turn our attention to making the way out of your present place of service as positive and edifying as possible. It may not be easy, but it will be well worth the effort. Wise travelers take the time to carefully chart their courses.

An exit strategy has been defined as "a series of well-defined preplanned steps and options to follow if you are unexpectantly [*sic*] terminated or voluntarily resign."[2] An effective exit route is not only about what to *do*, but also what to *be*. We are in the business of loving people and serving a living God. Our character is as important as our actions. Indeed, one flows from the other. Leaving a place of ministry is not easy, even under the best of circumstances. What must we *be* and *do* in this process to glorify God and preserve the sanctity of the body of Christ?

What to Be: The Question of Character

One pastor from the central United States related that his predecessor's last sermon consisted of a tirade against the elder board, after which he stormed out of the sanctuary, leaving the congregation behind in stunned silence. The new minister spent his first several months convincing this congregation that his character was not like that of "Pastor Previous." Exiting a place where you have served real people who have feelings and with whom you share history is a process requiring great character. This is no time to "get in your last shot" at those who may have made your stay challenging. How can you prevent such debacles as described here? What must you *be* as you anticipate and plan your farewell?

1. *Be close to the Lord.* This should be a given among ministers, but the truth is that we can get caught up in the stresses of moving and lose our grip on God's love and holiness. If you have never lost your temper during a family vacation because of some delay at the airport or botched reservations, you are a better person than most. Keeping your heart close to God in a time of stressful transition has many benefits, few of which we list here.

We keep our focus on God's grace and mercy. Transition is a time of loss, even if you are moving to an exciting new place of service. It's easy to count up all the things you are giving up to serve Christ. But focusing on God's rich blessings can help you keep your perspective. Paul's words in Ephesians 1:7–8 are sufficient to make this point: "In him we have redemption through his blood, the forgiveness of sins, in accordance with the riches of God's grace that he lavished on us" (NIV).

We keep bitterness in check. While many leavings are blessed experiences, you will most likely carry pain from a person who hurt you, a decision by the board that hindered your vision, or a lack of fruit after many seasons of sacrificial labor. Such feelings have to be dealt with properly. We have known ministers whose deep-seated anger has cost them dearly. Cynicism has no place in the work of Christ, yet there are ample opportunities for it to infect our hearts. Staying close to the Lord enables us to follow Paul's exhortation in Philippians 4:8: "Whatever is true, whatever is noble, whatever is right, whatever is pure, whatever is lovely, whatever is admirable—if anything is excellent or praiseworthy—think about such things" (NIV). There are many good things to remember about a ministry. Though we do acknowledge the hard times, we are wise to consider and be thankful for all the wonderful blessings we have experienced in our present position.

We grow in faith and hope. When Christ walked the earth, his presence was an encouragement to those who loved him. Peter was glad to see him during the storm on Galilee. Mary and Martha certainly rejoiced at his coming and raising Lazarus from the dead. Moving is hard for us, but Christ became flesh and journeyed among us so that we might have life (John 1:12–14). And through his redemptive love he became our hope, as Paul asserts in 1 Timothy 1:1: "Paul, an apostle of Christ Jesus by the command of God our Savior and of Christ Jesus our hope" (NIV). A man who knew transitions, Paul found faith and hope in the Lord Jesus. Staying close to him provides this in abundance.

We strengthen and purify our call. Once you have decided to make a move, looking for the next place of service can test your values. In shopping for a new ministry, we can look to considerations that may not reflect God's desires for us. Just because a church is bigger, has more resources, is staffed by people who write books, or is on the cutting edge does not mean that God is calling you to serve there.

Over the years we have noted that ministry positions in economically well-off communities draw hundreds of applicants, while those in poorer areas go begging for candidates. Is God not calling men and women to those who have fewer possessions or less money? Are churches that struggle not worthy of his servants? Staying near the Lord and knowing his heart will keep you invested in his priorities, his values, his burdens.

2. *Be decisive.* If you have determined that moving to another ministry is the right thing to do (see chapter 6), the time will come to follow through on that decision. In the business world resignations are often followed by counteroffers from the company. When I stepped down from a pastorate, the board responded with various offers, hoping to change my mind. I knew, however, that the basic issues that led my wife and me to seek a new position would not be altered in any significant way. It was time to move on. Neither our children nor we would benefit from the uncertainties of negotiation in a ministry we knew was coming to an end.

While it is good for our families to follow through on a difficult decision, it is also beneficial for the ministry we are leaving. When we go back and forth over whether to go or stay, we put a ministry in difficult circumstances. When can they begin the process of grieving our loss? How can they move ahead on finding our replacement? How will the ministry be able to determine a new vision and/or direction? Then there is the perception that people might think we are trying to manipulate the circumstances to our own advantage. In the context of suffering trials (which ministry transitions certainly fit into), James challenges his readers to trust in the Lord for wisdom and not be double-minded, such behavior being a sign of instability in all things (James 1:5–8).

In Psalm 15 David describes the character of one who can dwell in God's sanctuary. This is the kind of person "who keeps his oath even when it hurts" (v. 4 NIV). Leaving God's people is a huge challenge, but once we have determined that it is best for them and us, we demonstrate godly character by sticking with our decision and moving forward.

3. *Be honest.* Decisiveness speaks of honesty, but there are several considerations here that need special mention. Take the case of one West Coast associate pastor who was hired by a senior pastor after a nearly two-year search. Two months after this new associate arrived, the senior pastor resigned. It turns out he had decided over a year before to move on. I still recall the desperate call from this new associate who wondered if his job would be stable once a new senior pastor was hired. If you are the senior minister and know you are leaving, it seems dishonest to operate as if you will be around for a long time. At the very least, hiring new staff should be delayed until your departure is announced.

Then there is the issue of taking time and energy from your current ministry to search for a new one. James Antal, in his insightful book *Considering a New Call*, writes:

> Tension results when one considers that each hour put into revising and updating a profile is an hour not spent in pastoral counseling, sermon preparation, or some other activity that would benefit our current congregations. This tension is not limited to clergy, of course. But the issue of loyalty is so closely linked to service that when we ministers "go a courting" to another congregation, not only do we feel disloyal, many of us feel as though we are betraying our current congregations.[3]

It is never right to rip off one's employer, so we must faithfully maintain our ministries while navigating the waters of transition.

Lastly, there is the question of when to tell your leadership that you will be leaving. When we asked pastors their opinion, we found no consensus (see figure 7.1).

Most have found this a quandary. You are between a rock and a hard place. To say something too early is to invite breaches in confidentiality, potentially making you a lame-duck pastor. Informing the chairperson of the board or your senior minister too late may be read as dishonest or deceptive. One overseas pastor decided to tell his leadership early in the process (nearly a year before his

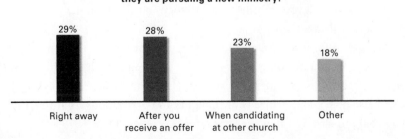

Figure 7.1, Q26: When should a pastor tell their church they are pursuing a new ministry?

Right away	After you receive an offer	When candidating at other church	Other
29%	28%	23%	18%

departure) of his plans to leave the country for additional education. Concerned about their reaction, he writes, "So far, the response has been somewhat surprising. Every person sees this as a perfect fit and has affirmed our decision. Yes, we've had a few tears, but for the most part, people are excited for us. In addition to that, we've had lots of creative thinking about how to keep us involved in the work over here after we relocate back to the States."

While moving from a pastorate to a teaching career may be easier for the church to accept, the concerns about honesty are still very real and pressing. It is suggested that pastors raise the question of "how long I'll be here" with the congregation and keep it an open item of discussion throughout their ministries. When the time to move comes, we will not be deceiving the fellowship by initiating a search, but merely following along in the understanding we have had from the beginning.[4] This may work, but we are not sure typical congregations could handle the sense of impermanence that such an approach could foster. In the end, you have to follow your heart before the Lord. Only with such peace will you be able to move forward in face of what will most certainly be criticism for the method and timing of your announcement (Phil. 4:4–7).

4. *Be gracious.* Retreating armies have been known to destroy everything in their wake. As a result, whole societies have spent years recovering a sense of stability and identity. This kind of behavior should never be seen in God's army. If leaving a job with grace and style is expected in the business world, can anything less be required of us in ministry? Here's a list of dos and don'ts:

Do be thankful. The people and this ministry have given you much. I learned lessons from that first youth pastorate that have benefited me throughout my ministry. Writing personal notes and expressing appreciation face-to-face are fitting ways to show your appreciation. And don't forget to thank those in the community at large for their love and support—the shopkeepers, police officers, and a host of service providers who have blessed you and your family greatly over the years.

Do allow for good-byes. Your people need the chance to express their appreciation. Even when forced to resign, pastors would do well to give the church an opportunity to show their thankfulness for the ministry you have provided. It gives them, you, and your family a time to focus on the good memories and successes that are always there.

Do accept an exit interview. This can be a great help to the ministry you're leaving. This might be something you offer to give to the leadership. If they're open to it, helpful lists of questions are available from various sources.[5] The exercise will also help you organize your thoughts and perceptions regarding ministry as you contemplate your new arena of service.

Do affirm the ministry. This is God's work and deserves your encouragement. Paul's example with the church at Ephesus is helpful here (Acts 20:17–38). While exhorting them to stand firm in the faith, he openly shows his love and affection, allowing them to do the same. Their grief is especially deep because they will not see him again. What a great litmus test of one's leaving. Will our people miss us that much?

Don't publicly vent your anger. It will only hurt feelings and make you look bad. Even if you have been badly mistreated, your place is not to wreak vengeance on the church or its leadership. Any evil done to you is to be returned with good (1 Peter 3:8–9). You can and must be honest with others, but in a spirit of love, not hatred.

Don't air dirty laundry. The congregation doesn't need to know all the details. In most of the cases where we hear there is trouble, the majority of the congregation is unaware of the specifics of the dissension. And in the few times when the whole group has entered into the fray, divisiveness and dissolution has often followed. The leaders of the church are responsible for such decisions, and your interactions with them, be they good or bad, should be left in the boardroom. It is the board's responsibility to inform the congregation.

Don't wallow in self-pity. It only reinforces any negative image of your ministry. This possibility usually occurs when a minister feels badly treated. All this serves to do is conjure up emotional reactions from people and does little to creatively help you find a way to your next place of service. Faithful friends will help you get through this. Make sure you stay close to them (Prov. 27:6).

Don't burn any bridges. You may well need someone's help in the future. It is amazing how small the Christian world really is. You will run into and need the help of many you meet on your ministry road. Cutting off a relationship ungraciously might effectively sever any possibility of future collaboration or mutual assistance. My wife and I could still show up at our old church and enjoy sweet fellowship with those wonderful people—even though our parting involved some pain and misunderstanding. Just remember—you will be spending eternity with these folks. So work hard at making your transition amiable.

Don't encourage division. Unity is still the will of Christ for his church. We are amazed at how casually some pastors will leave their current church and do all they can to persuade some in the congregation to follow them. Church planting of this type is regrettable in most instances and often leads to a bad testimony in the community. You have your reasons for leaving. If they stand the test of chapter 6 and you have God's peace, there is no reason to amass supporters in order to verify your decision. To do so only suggests uncertainty on your part and leads to disunity in the body.

To sum it all up, show class in your exiting. Be like the military chaplains in a 1974 study by Roy M. Oswald.[6] Chaplains with effective closure style

- Were perceived as authentic and genuine
- Remained conscientious about their assignments until the very end
- Tried to consider family, friends, the command structure, their congregations
- Worked to develop an acceptable climate for their successors
- Made themselves available so people could work through their feelings

The research is more than thirty years old, but the findings are as up-to-date as today's newspaper.

What to Do: The Question of Process

The character issues in the above section speak to any situation. We realize, however, that there are many circumstances in which a minister will consider making a transition, just as there are a lot of reasons people travel. Because of this, all the items we list below will have to be personally applied to your situation. They are included, however, because these steps will lead to a smoother and more positive disengagement from your current ministry.

1. *Connect with friends and mentors.* Once you have made the decision to move on, it is best to start by making contacts with trusted colleagues and associates, both in ministry and secular employment. Scanning the job placement sites may be illuminating, but it is too soon to pick out possible matches. You need the wisdom, love, guidance, and collaboration of people who will keep a confidence and help guide you to the next address.

Because chapter 13 is devoted to a more detailed description of this process, we will mention only a few things here. First, make sure you share your decision only with those who have a proven track record of confidentiality. The proverbial cat gets out of the bag pretty quickly in matters like this. Stick to those who can keep a secret, who are careful with what they know and will not let slip the fact that you are looking. The chance that one of your contacts knows someone in your ministry is very high. You may also find contacting your denominational representative risky unless he or she keeps such inquiries between the ears.

Second, include people who have traveled the road you're on. They have experienced the tension of being in one place while looking for another. Perhaps they have struggled with the whole process and can relate to your misgivings, fears, hopes, and dreams. Others may have just completed a transition and can give you a report on the "market," along with tips on what is effective in the job search.

Last, you may want to contract with a professional search firm (see chapter 15). If you do, their approach will require you to update your materials, assess your strengths, and submit to a number of other helpful exercises that will prepare you for the search ahead (see chapter 3 regarding assessments). As you contact various individuals, allow them to help you process and identify the kind of ministry setting that will be a good fit. I will be forever grateful to a dear friend who steered me to our first senior pastorate. His honest and insightful observations and advice brought us to a part of the country and a people unknown to us, yet the result was more than ten years of fruitful, exciting, and challenging ministry.

2. *Take time to carefully assess your options.* Transitions can be desperate times. If you have been fired or forced to resign, you will be tempted to panic and grab for the first opportunity that comes along. Jumping from one bad situation to another is not a good idea. But it is easy to do if you disregard the results of your hard work in chapter 6 and say to yourself, "Well, it's not great, but it's a job." It would be wiser to find a temporary job while you search for the next opportunity than to suffer the consequences of a desperate decision.

One East Coast pastor who resigned his position under *good* circumstances and was living with his wife and kids at his parents' house found himself running out of money. Against common sense, he pursued a church that really didn't fit theologically or philosophically. But the salary would feed his family. He found out later from some friends, after the candidating process fell apart, that the church was "a little weird." Their counsel in light of this near debacle: "Don't rush God and push down all the doors, but wait on him—his timing is perfect."

This pastor resigned before finding a new ministry. While he felt this was the right thing to do, our experience tells us that it is best to make travel plans while still living at your current ministry address. Not being in a position while looking for another may raise questions in the search committee as to the reasons for your unemployment. This can be addressed with a good cover letter (see chapters 12 and 16) but is best avoided if possible.

Bottom line: give yourself time to consider future ministry options in light of your experience, gifts, and leading of the Lord. Taking the first position that comes along might defeat the effort you have put into making sense of all God has done in and through you in the past. Just as you would take time to assess different models of cars before purchasing, you will also want to be astute in the ministry marketplace.

3. *Update your profile.* As you anticipate your next ministry destination, it is critical that you carry with you all the good things God has given you for the trip. You will want to update your resume, revisit theological and philosophy of ministry statements (more in chapter 12), and enhance your credentials in light of your desired goals.

One activity that is very helpful in a time of transition is journaling your thoughts and experiences. There are positive and negative aspects of your current ministry that continue to fashion your approach, and this hard-earned wisdom can be easily lost in the busyness of service. Observations you record now will help in assuring that you reap the most benefit from those years of hard work.

This is also the time to gather a record of your ministry successes. Programs you have created and developed, sermon or teaching series you have delivered, and any special ministry skills you have developed should be identified and put together for presentation to potential ministries. If you make a habit of video-taping your messages or various programs, it will be easy to format DVDs for a search committee. Some pastors who don't routinely record such ministries have found it risky to make a videotape or audiotape. Such activity is usually a dead giveaway that their beloved pastor is looking around!

Learning new things and gaining new skills should be part of every pastor's travel plans. In fact, this part of your exit strategy should be engaged at the very start of your ministry. Many pastors are finding the doctor of ministry degree a wonderful challenge and blessing. It is among several vehicles through which they can improve their profiles while staying in their places of service. And while such a doctorate may enhance the upward mobility of pastors, most simply find such programs effective in advancing their intellectual, spiritual, and pastoral aptitudes.[7]

You will want to enlist your spouse or trusted friend as you collect and prepare these and other profile items. We are often not the best at recognizing our own accomplishments and strengths, so their insight and encouragement go a long way in producing a realistic and helpful presentation of who we are and what we have to offer.

4. *Create a financial plan.* When my wife and I planned a trip to Europe a few years ago, one of our first considerations involved dollars, pounds, and francs. We wanted to go, had a trip itinerary in mind, but needed to determine if we had the financial resources necessary for this adventure. When you are preparing for your transition journey, you shouldn't ignore the financial aspect. What sort of considerations do you have to make?

If you have been terminated, forced to resign, or downsized, determine first if you will receive any severance. In cases of misconduct, don't count on it. But many ministries do provide such payments, and their reasons vary. While sever-ance is not legally required of any business or ministry, some use it to assuage their guilt, others to prevent lawsuits. Many give such payments to affirm their love and support of an appreciated servant. In most cases, severance is given only to those who don't have another ministry waiting for them or have a number of months before the next destination will be reached.

You will also need to consider health insurance. Programs like COBRA pro-vide coverage for up to eighteen months between jobs but are costly. Finding out if the church can and will help cover this cost is important. You may also have some vacation time, study leave, or other benefits coming to you. It doesn't hurt to ask.

If you are seeking a new ministry of your own volition, you will have even more financial matters to consider. Moving expenses add up. In most cases, your new congregation will cover these costs, but don't assume anything. (More about this in chapter 20.) Pastors who decide to leave their current ministries before securing another must consider finding a job to pay the bills and save for moving expenses that may not be covered by the new destination.

One pastor in our survey shared his challenging experiences between pastorates: "I've been employed packing and shipping dried flower arrangements, substitute teaching from first to twelfth grades, assembling parts in a Crosman Airgun factory, working a loading dock for a paperclip factory, packing Styrofoam picnic plates in a plastics factory, selling kites and fruit cups at an outdoor fair, and packing up a mobile army field hospital being delivered to Russia."

Finally, you might ask the church to consider helping with job placement services. Professional search firms can be somewhat costly. In addition, you may need the computer, printer, paper, and postal service of your church. Most are willing to support their pastor in this way. Gratefully accept such help if it is offered.

5. *Secure a good reference.* While this may be one of the trickier tasks in your exit strategy, it is crucial that you receive a positive reference from your current ministry. If you have already announced your resignation, you won't have to worry about confidentiality. If you are leaving under good circumstances, you may be less concerned about getting a positive reference.

Whatever the situation, it is imperative that you obtain a reference from your present ministry. Search committees will wonder why it is missing and will often fill in the blank with something negative. Since their first task is to reduce the large field of applicants to a manageable number, they will "round file" any application that has significant holes in it.

Most certainly you will want a letter from your senior pastor, board chairperson, and/or senior associate under whom you worked. It is within the bounds of decorum to offer to help them with this task. Information about the kind of ministry you are seeking, insight into the sort of setting you believe most suitable for you, and other tips will enable the reference to offer a helpful and insightful recommendation. Even if your current ministry has had negative aspects, these can be turned into positive comments. I have written hundreds of reference letters over the years and have always sought to be straightforward and positive. In areas where students had some deficiencies, I could always find ways to express how they had grown in these areas since beginning their programs. My comments gave the potential ministry a sense that this person was human, after all, but had a heart to grow in Christ and serve him faithfully.

You may also ask people in the congregation for a reference at this point—but only those who are trustworthy to keep a confidence. Again, you run the risk of your search being discovered, so proceed with caution. It is better to relate your travel plans earlier than later, because it is much better to have the fellowship working with you if it is at all possible.

6. *Mend fences.* Running over or bumping into someone in your ministry journey is almost unavoidable. You may say or do something that will drive a wedge between you and individuals or groups. While it is best to tend to these collisions when they occur, sometimes there are lingering effects that prick at your conscience. Invest in rebuilding bridges and repairing roads that have kept you and others apart. This is good advice for anytime in your journey, but it is especially important if you are planning to leave.

Not every breach will be fixable, and some you will not want to touch because of deep hurt. But the word of the Lord through Paul still stands: "Do not repay anyone evil for evil. Be careful to do what is right in the eyes of everybody. If it is possible, as far as it depends on you, live at peace with everyone" (Rom. 12:17–18 NIV). Once again, these are people with whom you will spend eternity. It won't hurt to try and restore your fellowship now so you can enjoy the reunion in days to come.

Once you make your departure public, it is probable some folks will react in a way that causes a strain in your relationship. The grieving process includes reactions of denial, anger, bargaining, depression, and acceptance. You will find people in all these stages when you prepare to leave them. My wife and I saw them all during our good-byes from our first senior pastorate. Having six months to do this before we left the community enabled us to grieve and help our friends to do the same.

7. *Leave your work in good order.* If you have ever taken over a job left in disarray by a predecessor, we need not make a big pitch about this piece of the exit process. Sometimes we are leaving *because* our ministry is in shambles, but under most circumstances we can do a lot to make the future easier for the ministry and the one who will succeed us. Again, this is the Lord's work, and whatever we can do to expedite its effectiveness should be our goal. We offer the following list of items to tend to before you leave:

- Strengthen staff, administrative, and systems support as possible.
- Leave notes regarding the unique and unseen aspects of your job.
- List key resources (counseling services, vendors, camps, contractors, etc.).
- Finish current projects or pass them on to others (training if necessary).

- Communicate the status of all projects to your superior.
- Write a brief history of your personal ministry in this position.
- Leave an organizational chart of your ministry, along with your job expectations (as they really were in daily practice).
- Leave a chart showing time lines in the church calendar for preparing retreats and other activities related to your area of ministry.

These items shared, you have to walk carefully here. Not all congregational leaders will be enthusiastic about your help once you have announced your resignation. Don't take this personally; this just may be their way of dealing with your departure. Under most circumstances, however, your leaders will appreciate anything you can do to smooth the transition for them. After all, no one knows your job better than you, and your assistance here will prove its worth once the dust settles and your replacement is on the scene.

8. *Prepare your family for the move.* Though we will address this more comprehensively in chapter 11, helping your family process a move must be a significant part of your exit strategy. People in all walks of life regularly move during their careers. You can gain a lot of wisdom by talking with those in your ministry or other friends and mentors who have traveled this path before you. The following are a few ideas we think you should include in assisting your family as a transition approaches.

- Start with your spouse—engage in "what if" conversations about moving.
- The two of you together share with your children at the appropriate time and in an appropriate manner.
- Remain positive and faith-based, trusting in God's leading and provision.
- Explore together the new destination (in person or through websites).
- Allow emotions to run their course—listen and be affirming.
- Be decisive—have courage to follow through on your conviction to move.
- Consider job/career issues of spouse (see The Family Flag in chapter 6).
- Consider your children's school circumstances and friendships.

These items will suggest others to you, as each family is unique and requires special attention. This is a challenging time, and your sensitivity will go a long way in making sure the people who move with you will be blessed and encouraged in your new place of service.

9. *Plan a time-out between ministries.* I was raised to appreciate vacations. Most Iowa farmers didn't take time off, but my folks believed it was important to recharge their batteries every once in a while. So every year we took two weeks before the corn harvest to explore the country. Being refreshed, we were ready to tackle the hard work ahead.

We encourage pastors who are moving to a new ministry to negotiate a delay in their start-up at the new location. The process of exiting is physically, spiritually, and emotionally demanding. Starting up a new ministry is just as challenging. Taking some time between these life chapters just makes good sense. Of course, if you have lost your ministry and don't have another waiting for you, a vacation is usually not recommended. Still, if you like to camp or have relatives with a vacation home, a week or two without a paycheck will probably be less expensive than therapy!

Though you may not be able to afford an ocean cruise, just having the luxury of moving to your new location with plenty of time to spare could be vacation enough. My wife and I received our first pastoral call immediately after finishing our education. We spent two weeks resting at her parents' home, then embarked on a three-day "adventure in moving" with a truck and all our possessions. Upon arrival, we had another week before officially starting the ministry there. The first night in the parsonage we dropped into bed, thoroughly exhausted and excited. *One more week off before the clock starts!* we thought. Then the phone rang at 2:00 a.m. — an attempted suicide. "Pastor, could you come to the hospital as soon as possible?" The transition was history. Enter Pastor Mick!

CHAPTER 8

GETTING AWAY FROM IT ALL

Writing Your Letter of Resignation

MICHAEL ANTHONY

He who guards his lips guards his life,
but he who speaks rashly will come to ruin.
Proverbs 13:3 NIV

By the time you sit down at your desk to write out a letter of resignation, your mind is flooded with conflicting thoughts, emotions, and expectations. For some, the circumstances that brought you to this place may be hurtful and discouraging, while for others, it came about as a result of a wonderful opportunity. Some approach this day after months of hard-fought battles perhaps punctuated by one last stand. Others come to this moment with elation as they feel released to pursue new possibilities out on the horizon.

Those who come to this moment after months of tension-filled meetings, long hours of discussions, and enough drama to script a Hollywood movie feel a mixed bag of emotions. On one hand, a certain amount of peace takes hold because you know the long hours of fighting are over. Regardless of who is labeled victor or victim, the end result is that the fighting has climaxed and it is now time to cease and desist. Maybe you have simply agreed to disagree and part ways. That's fine too. At any rate, there is peace in knowing that the conflict is over and all you have left to do is to present your letter and negotiate your departure.

Why Is This So Difficult?

Drafting a letter of resignation is harder than you think. Some do it quickly with one simple, curt sentence. Take, for example, President Richard Nixon's letter of resignation addressed to Secretary of State Henry Kissinger on August 9, 1974. It consisted of fifteen words: "Dear Mr. Secretary, I hereby resign the

Office of the President of the United States."[1] Others use the opportunity to review their past accomplishments and express personal feelings and projections about the future. An example of this approach would be the letter of resignation drafted by Attorney General John Ashcroft to President George W. Bush on November 2, 2004. It is composed of five handwritten pages.[2]

Format and style vary a great deal depending on a number of factors that will be discussed in this chapter. Suffice it to say that if you are struggling with how to say good-bye to your ministry, you aren't alone. Many others struggle with the same issues you're facing. As a general rule, keep it simple and say as little as possible. However, with that said, there are a few elements that must be included in your letter. We'll detail those below so that your letter has all the essentials in it.

Why Do I Feel This Way?

Some approach this moment with feelings of apprehension and fear. You have come to the realization that this ministry is no longer the right place for you, but you aren't sure yet what the future holds. You're thinking, *When will God open the door to the next chapter of my life, and how will I get there from here? How long will I have to wait before I get my next marching orders, and what do I do until then? Will my severance package be enough to get me through? Where will I live in the meantime? What about my kids' schooling? And what about my wife's job? Does this mean a move for her too?* Questions will flow from your mind, but have patience, for the answers may be slow in coming.

For those who have been forced to resign either by ultimatum or by personal resolve, don't be surprised if you are also having feelings of anger, bitterness, or resentment. You drive across town to run some errands and pull into the parking lot of the grocery store and can't remember even getting into the car, let alone driving across town. You sit staring out into space with thoughts that can't be repeated except to your most trusted friends. Sometimes you just need a safe person to "let it all out" to without fear of being misunderstood. The danger comes in letting these unfiltered emotions enter into the content of your letter.

Some ministry leaders who approach this exercise have received some exhilarating news about a new opportunity God has brought their way, and they can't wait to cut their ties, pull up their moorings, and be on their way. Communicating these feelings can be equally damaging because it gives the impression to those who receive your news that you have simply endured your time with them and can't wait to get on to something more meaningful and fulfilling. And even if that's true, it doesn't need to be said.

So don't be surprised if you sit down at your desk to write your letter of resignation and find yourself sifting through a strange mixture of feelings that are swirling around in your head and heart. All of that is perfectly normal. However, it is important as you approach this assignment that you craft a resignation letter that is God honoring and doesn't do damage—either to your reputation or to the ministry you're leaving.

Although you may be hard pressed to find a book on writing resignation letters, if you enter the topic using the Yahoo.com search engine, you'll find more than 2.5 million items of information available. Some sites offer suggestions and helpful insights. Some even provide templates where all you have to do is enter your name and date and the program prints your letter for you. We have done the searching and surveying for you and have provided below what we believe is the most helpful information to guide you through this next step in the career transition journey as it applies to the context of a local church ministry.

Considerations before Resigning

Although you already may have written your resignation letter in your mind weeks ago, you will want to take a minute and answer some fundamental questions before you actually sit down and put pen to paper. First and foremost is knowing whether or not this is God's will for your life and his ministry. Conflict may be God's plan for you or the church right now in order to bring about his purposes. Leaving in the middle of it will only postpone what he wants to accomplish. We suggest you take a few days to fast and pray about your decision before you make your intentions public.

In addition, take the time to bring others into your circle of confidential trust. This must include your spouse, but you may also want to consider a pastoral colleague at another church or a few trusted spiritual leaders at your church. Get their input and feedback as well. Sometimes we lose perspective and need to get the counsel of others who are not as close to the situation at hand. Share with them your thought processes leading up to your conclusions and see if they agree that your decision is the best course of action. You may not agree with their conclusions, but go into the meeting with an open mind to hear God speak through others you trust and respect.

If, after you have taken the two preceding steps, you still feel resignation is the best course of action, review the considerations by Sarah Breinig in her excellent article "How to Resign with Style and Get an Awesome Reference."[3] She recommends that you consider the following issues (some of which we have modified to fit the ministry context).

- Take a few minutes to clear your mind and get a reality check. Take an honest look at all the reasons you want to leave this ministry before you actually write your letter of resignation. If you conclude that this is the best course of action, then stick to it and don't deviate from your course of action.

- What will you do if the church board presents you with a counteroffer? You shouldn't resign in order to force their hand to provide one, because it might not come. However, it is not uncommon for a church board to panic and fear what your departure may do to the church, so they will present a counteroffer to entice you to stay. Keep in mind that this may just be a way to keep you longer until a replacement is found or they can make themselves look better before word of your resignation surfaces.

- If you have already accepted an offer from a different ministry and you are presented with an enticing counteroffer by your current church, it is unethical for you to accept a counteroffer and retract the acceptance that has already been rendered to the new ministry. Eventually, word will get out about what you have done, and this will do serious damage to your personal and professional reputation.

- What are the policies of the ministry regarding resignations? Some ministries have written policies that govern the conduct of those who have presented their resignations. In some cases, it requires an immediate departure. If this is the case, have you prepared for it by removing your personal items from your office and by cleaning up your files from your church computer? It might be good to find out how past resignations were handled and not give advance notice of your impending decision.

- What are the compensation policies of your church? In some cases, you may automatically forfeit some benefits after you resign. You may lose such things as severance pay, holiday entitlements, insurance benefits, and retirement accounts. Some of these are protected by state and federal statutes, but you will want to know what is and isn't protected before you write your letter. Did you sign a contract when you came to the ministry? If so, review it to see what you agreed to when you came.

- If you are leaving for reasons that may require legal counsel, consider your steps carefully prior to writing your letter or signing any documents. Issues involving discrimination, harassment, safety, and fraud are best handled with the advice of an attorney. Let this professional guide your steps and help you control the timetable of your departure.

The Resignation Meeting

Many ministry leaders prefer to preface their resignation letter by having a meeting with their immediate supervisor. Who this person is depends on the governance structure of your church. In some churches it will be the board chairperson. In others it may be the district superintendent, overseer, bishop, or some other church government figure. For associate staff members, it may be the senior pastor or executive pastor of the church. If you choose to go to your immediate supervisor, the advice given by Kauser Kanji in his article "How to Resign with Style and Dignity" offers some helpful suggestions.[4] Again, we have made a few modifications to make the advice applicable to a ministry context.

- Work out in advance what you want to say prior to scheduling the meeting. Don't deviate from your plan. Your supervisor will want to know as much information as possible, but refuse the temptation to divulge more than you need to. Remember, your reason for calling the meeting is to inform him or her of your intention to resign.
- Keep the tone of the meeting positive. You never know when your career path may cross this person's again, so don't let it spiral into a negative atmosphere. A word said in haste can circle around and come back to sting you years later when you can least afford it.
- Don't be surprised if your supervisor has a reaction to the news. It may be a sigh of relief because the stress of conflict is over (you may not even have been aware of it), or it may be a response of shock or dismay. If your supervisor gets confrontational, resist the temptation to defend and accuse. Simply stick to your prepared comments. This is not the time to speak extemporaneously.
- Keep your composure at all costs. Your supervisor may no longer see you as a team player and unleash feelings of betrayal. As before, stick to your prepared comments and don't let someone else control the agenda of this meeting. Speak in a soft deliberate tone with measured speech and regulate your breathing.
- Leave the meeting on a positive note and be as cooperative as possible. Emphasize that you will work together with the church to transition your position as smoothly as possible. Reassure your supervisor that you are willing to complete any outstanding assignments to the best of your ability. He or she will remember both the first and last things you say long after the meeting has taken place.

Once you have taken these steps and given some serious attention to prayer and the counsel of others in your life whom you trust and respect, if you still feel that a resignation is in order, it is time to draft your letter. The following sections will help you organize your material.

How Much Is Too Much?

Once you sit down to write your letter, you may be wondering if you should take this opportunity to blast the chairperson of the board for not leading the congregation through the latest season of the church's life with enough forethought and insight. You may want to take this final opportunity to let someone have it who opposed you these recent months or years. If you are really feeling angry, you may even consider taking this opportunity to expose the secret sin of someone in your congregation who was instrumental in your departure. Such actions would be like throwing a hand grenade into an angry crowd to exact that last moment of revenge. Don't do it! Take the advice of Luke Skywalker, who advises, "Never give in to the dark side." If you do, you may be denying God his timetable for bringing out into the light things that have been hidden for too long. Remember, God is the one who will balance the scales—not you!

When it comes time to write your letter of resignation, you should plan on it being no longer than one page. You may have much that you would like to say, but it can wait for another time and a more appropriate venue. Your official letter of resignation will be kept in your personnel file as a permanent record of your employment at the church. It may be read by people decades later, and words that were written in a moment of anger or frustration may come back to embarrass you when you can least afford it.

Remember, the less said the better. In essence, your letter is simply going to state that you are departing and that you trust that God will continue to have his hand on the ministry in the years ahead. Anything more than that can be covered in meetings behind closed doors while in negotiations with the appropriate people. This is not the time to declare victory or cast blame on those who opposed your efforts. As a general guideline, if you can't limit what you have to say to one page, you are saying too much.

Three Essential Elements

Three things must be included in any letter of resignation: (1) the date you are giving notice, (2) notification to your supervisor that you are resigning, and (3) the date of your departure. Your resignation letter may be as short as one sentence. Just date the letter and write, "This letter is to notify you of my desire to resign the office of senior pastor effective on [date]."

If you don't feel the need to be as guarded, you may want to include a few more optional items, such as a paragraph describing the context of your ministry over the season you were at the church: "Over the nine years that I have served as your senior pastor, we have been fortunate to experience God's blessings as we have witnessed a significant increase in church attendance. It has been my privilege to baptize many of these individuals and see them become contributing members of our church. I will always look back with gratitude for the partnership we have enjoyed together."

You may also include a paragraph thanking the church for their support and encouragement, especially during any difficult times you or your family had over the season you were there: "I want to express my sincere appreciation for all the support that you have shown my family these past years, especially during the year when my wife was undergoing cancer treatments. Your kindness and generosity will always be remembered."

We have provided two sample letters of resignation at the end of this chapter to help you gather your thoughts and express your feelings in a positive manner. "Depending on the nature and length of your relationship with the ministry a resignation letter will vary in length and warmth. If you aren't sure about how much to say, play it safe and maintain a precise, professional but friendly tone to the letter. Do not over-elaborate unless you feel you have to."[5]

Drafting the Letter

Beyond providing your dates of resignation and departure, your letter should accomplish the following objectives.

1. *Lead off clearly.* The first sentence of the letter should declare your intentions. Lead off with a sentence that gives clear and unequivocal direction. You don't want the reader to get to the end of the letter and not know what you are saying. Pastors are renowned for their flowery speech. They are masters of verbal eloquence. But now is not the time to demonstrate your command of the English language. If there is ever a time to be direct, it's now. Something such as "I am writing to inform you of my desire to resign ..." is more wordy than is necessary. Don't hedge the issue or skirt around the obvious. The word *resign* needs to be in the first sentence. Don't use words or phrases that gloss over your intention, such as *transition, ease out of,* or *step aside.* Although you may know what you mean and intend, your reader may not, and this is not the time to confuse or bewilder.

2. *Set a positive tone.* You can set an upbeat tone for your departure by making a few positive comments about your employment at the ministry over your term of service. The old adage "If you don't have anything nice to say, don't say anything" is absolutely right. Even in the most negative ministry context, something positive can be said about something or someone. You may have to dig deep to find it, but lead off with this thought so as to set a positive tone.

3. *Remember that your resignation letter is not a soapbox.* If you're leaving in the middle of a significant conflict, resist the temptation to blast those you feel have mistreated you. Don't turn this letter into a diatribe of venomous outburst. Do not single out individuals who have hurt you or members of your family. Don't make general negative statements about your job description or the conditions of your employment either.

4. *State your reasons for leaving if you can frame them in a positive manner.* For example, you may be leaving to advance your education and return to seminary. You may also be moving to the mission field or another field of ministry service that does not threaten the church's collective self-image. If you are departing for

what may be viewed as a significant move up the ministry ladder (e.g., larger church, college presidency, denominational leadership, etc.), it doesn't need to be identified. Simply indicate that God has given you direction to pursue another ministry venture. Anything more could be interpreted by some as arrogance or your having used them as a stepping stone for something bigger and better.

5. *Express some degree of appreciation and gratitude for their partnership in the ministry you have experienced together.* Even if the position wasn't all that you hoped it would be, it is still a noble act to affirm their efforts and cooperation. Let them know that you have appreciated the opportunity to serve as their pastor and that you are thankful for the time you have had together.

6. *Incorporate a ministry review.* If you are ending on a positive note, you may want to take this opportunity to review your accomplishments over your term of service. Maybe a brief highlight of major accomplishments would be helpful to celebrate what God did under your care. However, be careful not to word this in a way that seems like bragging. Choose your words carefully and use terms such as *we* or *our* rather than *I* or *my*. Remember, this church isn't your ministry; it's God's, and you simply served as a steward of it for a brief season of time.

7. *Do not ask for special favors or considerations in your resignation letter.* If you have a positive relationship with your supervisor, you can request a reference when you speak with him in private (although you may want to wait until after news of your departure has settled in).[6]

8. *Proofread your letter.* It is generally a good idea to have someone you trust read your letter before you deliver it to your supervisor. Remember, once you hand it over, there is no going back.

The Exit Interview

At some point in the process, and generally after the resignation has been submitted and accepted, you will probably be invited to a meeting where you will have the opportunity to share your concluding thoughts. This exit interview is designed to give the ministry a glimpse into what changes need to be considered in the interim period that lies ahead. Let the supervisor lead the discussion and control the agenda. If you are asked for your perspective or opinion, provide it; otherwise, keep your thoughts private. Here are some issues that should be included in the interview:

1. *Start on a positive note.* The tone of your speech is important and provides a basis for open communication. If you start out by being defensive or accusatory, the meeting may degrade before anything productive takes place. Remember, the battle is over (if conflict was present prior to your resignation), and there is no need to open old wounds. Begin by expressing appreciation for the years of service together and for your opportunity to partner with them.

2. *Review any final compensation package details that have been amended since your preresignation meeting (if you had one).* Be sure everyone is in agreement in terms of expectations. If the person leading the meeting doesn't bring it up, you will need to take the initiative by starting the conversation something like this: "I just want to clarify the details of my departure to be sure we're all on the same page. My understanding is that ... [review the details if necessary]." If there are no further changes to the agreement, you can skip this or ask up front, "Are you aware of any changes to my departure agreement since we last spoke?" If not, move on.

The Resignation in Review

1. Make certain that you want to leave your ministry before putting pen to paper. Once submitted, your letter probably won't be rescinded.
2. Consider all your options before you write and submit your resignation. Is there any other creative solution to leaving? What will you do if your supervisor offers you a counteroffer? Are you open to making changes, or is this final?
3. Consider your words, because this document becomes part of your permanent personnel record. Print it on church stationery using professional style. Don't handwrite it.
4. Make sure you include the three essentials: date of notification, statement of resignation, and date of departure.
5. If applicable, express your appreciation for the time of service that you had at the church. Think of something nice to say to set a positive tone.
6. Never use this letter to lash out or accuse someone. This is not the time or place for name-calling or "setting the record straight."
7. Do not provide extended details about where you are going, why you are leaving, how much you will be getting paid, etc.
8. Inform them of your desire to cooperate in a smooth transition process.
9. Sign the letter with an appropriate closing, such as "Sincerely" or "In his service."
10. Begin preparing your thoughts for an exit interview where details of your departure or severance package will be worked out (if this wasn't done in a preresignation meeting) and any other issues that need to be discussed prior to your departure.

3. *Bring up any outstanding commitments or obligations you have made on behalf of the church.* For example, have you signed any contracts obligating the church for future engagements (e.g., guest speakers, musicians, camp reservations, etc.). If so, be sure that you let them know where the contracts are for their reference. I once worked at a church where, just days before taking the church youth to camp, we discovered that the former pastor had not sent in the required deposit, so the camp had given away the reservations to another camp. The parents and youth went ballistic. Such details should have been covered in the exit interview, but no one asked, and the pastor didn't reveal his mistake. Someone needs to ask the question, "Are there any obligations you've made to anyone that we need to be made aware of or any obligations you should have made that as yet have not been made?"

4. *Keep the details of why you're leaving to yourself.* You might be tempted to use the exit interview to vent, but hold your tongue. "If you really do need to get some things off your chest then talk proactively and strategically, instead of griping about how terribly you've been treated. Turn your complaints into positive suggestions for changes."[7] You never know when your words might come back to sting you.

5. *Offer to stay around long enough to help facilitate a smooth transition.* Some pastors prefer to give two weeks' notice and depart as soon as possible. If they have vacation time coming, they use it immediately and depart the next day. Such arrangements are seen as vindictive and counterproductive to your reputation. You should offer a minimum of a month's notice but be willing to negotiate longer if it is feasible (this may depend on the nature of your resignation, family issues, conditions of any future employment offers, etc.).

I know of a senior pastor who gave his church a one-year notice (it was his way of securing a long overdue sabbatical on church expense). In the long run, it was destructive to the church because he mentally withdrew and became a lame-duck leader (e.g., stopped attending staff meetings, elder board meetings, etc.) and took a backseat to decision making. The leadership vacuum that ensued was highly destructive to the church, and it eventually went through a split. Two weeks is too short and one year is too long. A month is generally sufficient.

6. *Depart above board.* I know of a youth pastor who spent all of his church budget on books, music CDs, and other ministry resources in the last weeks of his ministry at a local church and then left with all of these resources in the moving van. Don't upgrade your personal computer or pay in advance for journal subscriptions in the last month of your employment. Be above reproach in the way you handle finances, computer passwords, and other sensitive information. Don't make copies of confidential information from the church database for future reference.

Writing and submitting a resignation from your ministry can be a highly emotional experience for you, your family, and for those involved at the church, especially in church leadership. Be prepared to experience the whole gamut of possibilities from elation and joy to grief and anger. You may not experience some of these emotions at the time of your resignation, but they may sneak up on you weeks or months later. Don't be afraid to talk about them to your spouse or a supportive friend. You are leaving a place that was the recipient of your passion, skills, and gifts. It is natural to have mixed feelings about it.

Final Thoughts and Reflections

The important part of this stage of your career journey is to finish well and above reproach. Don't let your final days provide your enemies (if you have any) with fodder to be used against you. Get everything in writing to eliminate any misunderstandings, and above all, remember that you are a steward of God's church and that you have a responsibility to God to leave in as responsible and spiritually mature manner as possible.

Years ago I served as an associate pastor at a local church. I resigned and went to serve a much larger church a few miles away. A couple of years later, the megachurch suffered a major financial setback and had to lay off a dozen staff members. I was devastated by the news of my impending severance. The former church contacted me and asked me to return. I went back and enjoyed another fruitful season of service with them. That never would have happened if I had burned my bridges and left with ill feelings. When I resigned from the church, I certainly had no intention of returning. However, the experience I gained at the larger church proved invaluable to the smaller one years later. The goodwill that had taken place during the resignation process allowed an open door of opportunity years later.

SAMPLE LETTER OF RESIGNATION
(Short and to the Point)

Date
Supervisor's name
Name of church
Address of church
Dear [supervisor's name]:
I am writing to inform you of my decision to resign as the senior pastor of [name of church] effective [date].
Sincerely,
[Signature]
[your name]
Senior Pastor

SAMPLE LETTER OF RESIGNATION

(When Leaving on Good Terms)

Date
Supervisor's name
Name of church
Address of church
Dear [supervisor's name]:

As you know from my previous conversations with you, I have been giving this next season of my life a good bit of consideration. God has been stirring my heart about new possibilities, and I believe I am sensing his call to assume a new ministry role. After much prayer and counsel, I have now come to a decision that it is time for me to move ahead to where God is leading.

For this reason, I am writing you to inform you of my decision to resign my position as senior pastor at [name of church] effective [date]. I want you to know what a privilege it has been for me to serve [name of church] as your senior pastor for the past [enter number] years. Who would have thought so many years ago that we would have seen the hand of God move in so many wonderful ways? Indeed, it has been a joy for me to partner with the many members of [name of church] in this joyous season, and I am confident that God will continue to richly bless your influence in our community in the years ahead.

Though this may come as a disappointment to some, please know that I am willing to provide any assistance necessary to provide for a smooth transition.

In the partnership of his service,
Signature
[your name]
Senior Pastor

CHAPTER 9

GETTING YOUR TRAVEL DOCUMENTS IN ORDER

Considering Insurance, Medical, and Retirement Needs

MICHAEL ANTHONY

"For which one of you, when he wants to build a tower, does not first sit down and calculate the cost to see if he has enough to complete it? Otherwise, when he has laid a foundation and is not able to finish, all who observe it begin to ridicule him."
Luke 14:28–30

We hadn't even made it out of the airport of Ghana, West Africa, when we discovered my friend's passport had been stolen. *Wow, they were fast!* I thought. Whoever stole it made off with a valuable travel document. An American passport could fetch a good price on the black market in some foreign countries. The more immediate problem for us now was trying to figure out how we were going to get a new passport and the appropriate visas during the five days we were planning to be there.

We visited the U.S. embassy on Monday and made arrangements to secure a new passport. It took a couple of days, and we were pretty happy to have our hands on a new document that would get us out of the country. The next big problem was trying to secure the visas for the next countries on our itinerary. It would be no small feat. Embassy officials at the various consulates made it obvious that a large bribe was going to be necessary for us to get the appropriate visa stamps within three days. We didn't pay bribes, but I learned the old adage "The squeaky wheel gets the grease" works in other countries as well. During that week we learned the value of travel documents.

In much the same way, you and your family have embarked on a journey that entails risk and adventure. This is a venture of faith, believing that God has led you into this ministry expedition. No one ever said it would be easy, and everyone you have talked to has probably warned you that you would face days of testing. There are, however, things you can do to make the journey a little less stressful for you and your family.

One of the ways you can prepare for this season of career transition is to be sure that your travel documents are in order—insurance, health plans, and retirement considerations. Other than negotiating financial compensation, these topics are the next most important for consideration when making a career transition. Getting the details right on these important matters is critical to your happiness and peace of mind.

Legal Protections

Before moving on to this topic, it is important to know that there are several safeguards available to you under federal and state laws. These statues vary a great deal, so providing you with a comprehensive list of everything that may apply in your particular situation is beyond the bounds of this limited resource. However, a good place to start your search of protections is the U.S. Department of Labor.

Congress has been active over the past few years making sure severed employees receive certain protections and provisions. Even though you work as a member of the clergy, in most cases you are still covered under the terms and conditions of these statutes. These legislative actions address the need for continuing pay and benefits while you are between jobs. Most people just need a little help while they are between jobs, and that is what these laws are designed to provide. That is, they help to close the gap between what you have saved up and what you need to make ends meet. They aren't designed to pay *all* your bills while you're unemployed. Four major compensation programs are unemployment compensation, COBRA, ERISA, and HIPPA.

Unemployment Compensation

Some form of unemployment compensation program has been enacted in all fifty states and the District of Columbia. Benefits are limited to employees, but that term may include persons labeled as "independent contractors" if applicable requirements are met. Some ministers refer to themselves with this designation, but the IRS has been limiting its use in recent years.

Most states limit who qualifies for unemployment compensation by setting eligibility requirements. For example, some states require an individual to have paid into the system for a minimum number of months before he or she can receive benefits after termination of employment. "The base period is defined in most states to include the first four calendar quarters of the last five full quarters before the claim filing. Most also require the employee to be employed for a minimum time during that period, typically at least two of the calendar quarters during the base period."[1]

In your case as a pastor, unemployment compensation is generally only a factor if you were terminated. If you accept another church position and you have a few months' gap between appointments, this coverage is not available to you.

People are disqualified from receiving unemployment compensation if they are terminated for misconduct. In addition, people who voluntarily resign also forfeit their rights to benefits if they resign without *good cause*. In most states, the individual who resigns with *good cause* is still ineligible unless he or she is able to prove the good cause is attributable to the employer or in some way connected to the work.[2] In those states, a purely personal reason, such as, "I just didn't feel it was God's will for me to stay," will not be deemed sufficient justification for eligibility. That is why you need to carefully think through whether or not you want to voluntarily resign your position if the church isn't offering you a severance package that includes benefits such as financial severance, medical, health, and/or retirement coverage. Keep in mind that you may not be eligible to receive unemployment benefits if you never paid into the program while you were employed as a pastor at the church.

COBRA

During the mid-1980s America was awash in corporate downsizing and mergers. The end result was a virtual wave of unemployed workers. This eventually put

Disqualification from Unemployment Compensation

Conduct that will get you disqualified from receiving unemployment benefits includes, but is not limited to, the following:
- Frequent absences
- Repeatedly arriving late for work
- Willful insubordination
- Failure to discharge your duties
- Refusal to accept a similar position if yours was eliminated
- Certain inappropriate behavior
- Unacceptable appearance

a strain on the national health-care system as uninsured former employees and their family members needed critical health-care services. As a result, in 1985 Congress passed the Consolidated Omnibus Budget Reconciliation Act (COBRA), which took the needs of these unemployed workers into consideration.

This legislation requires most employers to allow severed employees and their dependents to remain on the company's group health insurance policy even though they are no longer employed by the company. This provision expires after eighteen months for the employee and their dependents. For those in extenuating circumstances, such as a widow, widower, divorced spouse, or dependent children, the provision is extended for a period of thirty-six months (see sidebar below).[3] During this time the employee must pay the company 102 percent of the quarterly or monthly premium.

Organizations with fewer than twenty employees are exempt from this requirement. However, for purposes of COBRA, independent contractors, which is how some ministers classify themselves, are included in the total count of employees. In addition, "certain church plans also are not subject to COBRA. The IRS has concluded that a plan for employees of an institute of higher learning under church auspices was a church plan, and that plan was accordingly not subject to COBRA."[4] There are a number of time constraints regarding deadlines for notification, so consult the plan administrator to secure the exact timetable for required notifications.

HIPAA

For many years one of the greatest fears among displaced workers was losing their health insurance coverage while transferring between policies with a preexisting condition. Many health insurance providers would not accept new

Terms of COBRA Coverage

- Up to eighteen months for covered employees, as well as their spouses and their dependents, when workers otherwise would lose coverage because of a termination or reduction of hours.
- Up to twenty-nine months for employees who are determined to have been disabled at any time during the first sixty days of COBRA coverage; applies as well to the disabled employee's non-disabled qualified beneficiaries.
- Up to thirty-six months for spouses and dependents facing a loss of employer-provided coverage due to an employee's death, a divorce or legal separation, or certain other "qualifying events."

employees into the policy coverage if they had expensive preexisting conditions. The Health Insurance Portability and Accountability Act (HIPAA) made changing health insurance plans more accessible for those with preexisting conditions. HIPAA limits exclusions for preexisting conditions and prohibits discrimination on the basis of an employee's health status. It also gives employees rights to purchase individual coverage if they have no group health insurance available or if they have exhausted their COBRA provisions.[5]

ERISA

Another federal protection that may safeguard your transition is the Employee Retirement Income Security Act (ERISA). Section 510 of this legislation provides employees who are in private pension plans with certain protections and provisions. Although some pastors are not in private pension plans per se, this plan also regulates certain employee health benefit plans as well. The provisions of a severance agreement that includes health and medical benefits could be considered an "employee welfare benefit plan" and may therefore be under the jurisdiction of ERISA regulations. This act is in existence, among other things, to establish fair employer-employee pension-type plans and is far-reaching and exhaustive in its scope. It would be worth your time to explore the provisions of this federal statute as it applies to your particular case prior to beginning any health, medical, and/or insurance benefit negotiations.[6]

Insurance Coverage

Types of insurance often provided to an employee during his or her term of employment include medical, dental, disability, and life. There are other possibilities, but in our experience, these are the ones that are most prevalent when dealing with members of the clergy. When you depart from your current ministry location, be sure that plans are in effect for maintaining your insurance needs. Nothing can wipe you out of personal savings faster than being in a medical crisis without insurance coverage.

For this reason, it is essential that you discuss your needs with the plan administrator who is representing your church. Since the terms and conditions of this coverage may depend on whether you are leaving on your own accord (e.g., voluntary resignation) or under a forced departure (e.g., resignation under duress, layoff, or forced termination), each will be discussed separately.

Voluntary Departure

In the event that you have resigned from your church and are leaving under good terms, you may be able to negotiate a reasonable departure package with your church. It is not uncommon for churches to keep your various insurance policies in force for a reasonable length of time after your departure as an act of goodwill. If you have enjoyed a prosperous ministry with them, they may include this as part of their departure gift to you and your family.

This span of time will include what you will need between ministry locations. For example, you may be leaving your current church at the end of May but not starting your new ministry until mid-August (after an extended family vacation and time to settle into your new house). That two-month span needs to be bridged, and your coverage must remain in force. Identify your needs with whoever is representing your church board and get in writing their agreement to continue your coverage. Do not, under any circumstances, simply accept a verbal agreement without some form of written confirmation. At the very least, email the details of your conversation and make a copy of their response for your file. You don't want to get into an "I said, He said" disagreement months after you have left.

Involuntary Departure

In the event that you are negotiating your departure with the governing board, this is the time to think before you act. While it may be tempting to simply throw your keys on the desk and walk out, remember that your family is counting on your mature leadership and resist the temptation to simply quit. It is far more difficult to negotiate a severance package after you have already left. To do so is to play into their hands. You have given them everything they could dream of and received nothing for it in return.

If the governing board has requested your resignation and you feel this is the appropriate time to comply, don't agree to anything until you request a meeting with the board's representative (preferably once everyone's passions have settled). At this meeting you will want to address the details and conditions of your departure. Financial severance will no doubt be at the top of your list, but it should not be the only thing discussed. In fact, it may even be a lesser consideration compared to your insurance needs.

If you or a member of your family has a preexisting medical condition, it is critical that you keep your insurance policy in effect during the term of your unemployment. Although the federal government has made provisions for you to do this through a COBRA policy (see above, pages 127–129), now is the opportune time to request that the church maintain your policies for whatever length of time you feel you will need before you find another pastorate. Remember that the average length of time it took pastors in our survey to find a new position was three months, and nearly 20 percent needed more than six months to find another pastorate. So just to play it safe, add a few months to the amount of time you think you'll need.

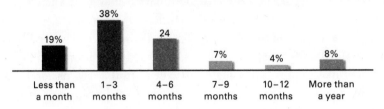

Figure 9.1, Q11: How long did it take you to secure your current position from the initial contact until the job was offered to you?

If the season leading up to your departure has been particularly emotional, you may find the governing board quite generous in what they are willing to offer you during these negotiations. (In their view, a generous package makes it easier for you to go quietly and not stir up a ruckus.) Ask for all of your insurance policies (e.g., health, medical, dental, etc.) to remain in effect for at least six months (if that is what you feel you'll need) after your last day of employment. Be sure to explain that you expect the church to cover the cost of the premiums and that you will not have the amount deducted from any monetary settlement. You don't want them to confuse this continuation of coverage with COBRA. You are not asking for COBRA to take effect at your departure; you are asking that they maintain your insurance policies during your employment absence.

In the event that you haven't found another job by the end of the period you established, at that time you have the legal right to initiate the COBRA provisions. If the church covered your entire family before, make sure they cover your entire family now, and don't let them take this opportunity to reduce your benefits. Finding out that they have done so while in the waiting room at the hospital would be an inopportune time for such a discovery! Since each state has its own version of a labor law, wage law, worker safety act, and other employee compensation protections, you should consult local authorities in your area before signing any documents that will be legally binding.[7]

If your church's policyholder doesn't allow you to receive continuing coverage after your departure and you don't want to start your COBRA provisions, discuss the possibility of the church keeping you on under a "continuing consultancies" title. This title is common practice in corporate America and allows the severed employee to meet the legal requirements of remaining in the organization as an "in-house ex officio" employee even though he or she no longer darkens the door of the establishment. "A departing employee might be called an in-house consultant in name only for a few months following his or her last day to receive life insurance during recuperation from heart surgery or to qualify for early retirement under a retirement or pension plan. In these instances, continuing agreements are quite easy to negotiate, for little is expected of the severed executive."[8]

Retirement

Pastors who are part of a larger denomination may have their retirement vested in their denomination's pension plan. Pastors who are independent may have a retirement plan that is tied to a 403(b). Perhaps it is managed by a firm specializing in securities, bonds, annuities, and the like. Pastors who are middle aged or older may find it increasingly difficult to find a new pastoral position. Many ministries are looking for younger ministry leaders in their early forties who have completed their seminary training and have a dozen years of experience under their belts. For this reason, older candidates find it increasingly important to negotiate the continuance of their pension or retirement premiums.

> Increasingly common, also, is a measure called "bridging to retirement," by which an employee's period of salary continuation during severance is not paid out on a full-time basis but is instead stretched out through smaller payments to reach a minimum retirement age or period of service.... By this method, employment is "bridged" to the necessary attainment of service or age.[9]

While you are between ministry appointments, you should try to make ongoing payments to your pension or retirement fund. If your finances do not allow for such payments at the time, contact your plan administrator (corporate office) and explain that you are between jobs and hope to resume making payments in the near future.

In some cases, you may be tempted to withdraw your retirement savings from the company that is managing it on your behalf. Although many companies do not allow you to do this, some will allow you to withdraw the fund once you meet prescribed conditions. Being unemployed is generally one of these conditions. They will probably ask the church to send them a letter verifying that you are no longer under their employment. However, please be aware that you will face a significant tax penalty when these funds are withdrawn.

The firm that is managing the funds will be required to deduct a minimum amount to cover the payment of taxes and penalty for early withdrawal. Don't be lulled into thinking that the amount they take out is enough. In many cases, it is merely the down payment. At the end of the year when you have your federal and state taxes calculated, don't be surprised if you have to pay even more taxes to the IRS. It is always wise to take some of the original withdrawal and stash it away for the tax man next April. Otherwise, you'll be forced to pay taxes out of funds you no longer possess—a sure formula for marital stress and anxiety. When your checking account runs dry and you have cash in savings to pay your taxes, it is very hard not to tap those funds for the immediate need. Take it from me, I've known some pastors who did, and life wasn't pretty on April 15!

If you are close to turning sixty-two years old, the earliest you can begin to claim Social Security, you may want to negotiate a smaller amount of severance to be paid out over a longer period of time so as to tide you over until you can file for Social Security benefits and Medicare. The same may hold true for those waiting to file for pension benefits from their denomination's provider.

For most pastors who are about to face retirement, making a smooth transition from one ministry to another may take its toll on your personal emotional health. Anxiety about being able to find another position later in life, possible health complications for yourself or a family member, and the anxieties about housing and health-care costs after retirement can contribute to anxious moments during your pastoral transition.

The spouse of the minister should have a counselor, support group, or trusted friend with whom he or she can share feelings and vent personal anxieties. Being between jobs is challenging for both the pastor and his or her family. Never underestimate the importance of having both marriage partners on the same page in terms of personal savings, health insurance, and retirement options during this season of transition.

Not enough can be said about the importance of retirement planning. Most pastors from earlier generations did very little of it, and we are seeing the results of their careless planning. Some have had to beg their denominations for support while others go about burdening family members and friends. It all could have been avoided if seeds of prevention had been planted earlier in the pastor's career.

You need to do some careful planning to be sure you are able to pay your retirement premiums. Once you stop making the payments, it is a lot harder to start up again. If a period of unemployment goes longer than you anticipate, you will probably have significant bills to pay, and it is nearly impossible to send money to a retirement account while the creditors are calling on your phone or the repossessor is hooking up your car out in the driveway.

Do You Have Your Travel Document Prepared?

As the verse at the beginning of this chapter cautions, you need to consider the cost before making a move. Part of that cost is being able to keep your head above water financially before you step out over the side of the boat and start walking by faith. There is a reasonable balance between making preparations and living on faith. Our roles as a ministry leader, spouse, and parent call us to do both.

Looking at the financial storms around you can really rock your boat — and those in it. Now is the time to prepare for the move by making sure you have some money saved up (most financial planners recommend having enough for three months of expenses in savings) and you have made the necessary arrangements to keep your health and medical insurance policies in effect. If at all possible, try not to raid your retirement account, and don't panic if the search process takes longer than you thought. It usually does!

My hope is that this chapter has provided you with the necessary insights for skillfully planning your ministry transition. Knowing how long you may have to go between jobs will help you budget your funds accordingly. However, since most pastors report their job search goes on longer than they thought it would, it is imperative that you spend wisely during the months when you are without income. If the church decides to send you a lump sum severance check, resist the temptation to splurge on a family vacation or second honeymoon until the contract with your next church has been signed. To spend prematurely is to court disaster. Be a good steward and protect the emotional well-being of your family by being a careful provider during your months between jobs.

PART 3

WHERE DO YOU WANT TO BE?

CHAPTER 10

ASKING YOURSELF THE TOUGH QUESTIONS

Hanging Up the Collar

MICHAEL ANTHONY

Weeping may last for the night,
But a shout of joy comes in the morning.
Psalm 30:5

I once served on the pastoral staff of a very large church in Southern California. When I was candidating, several of my friends warned me not to go. They had heard rumors about it being a "pastor-eating" church and didn't want me to get hurt. I was pretty confident that my experience would be different than that of others before me, so when the church issued me a call to join their staff, I gladly accepted. During the interview process, I was told by the senior pastor that if for some reason the job I was being hired for didn't work out, he would find another area for me because he was "so happy to have someone with my qualifications on their pastoral staff." In my naïveté, I believed him.

Pink Slips and Pain

After less than a year of successful ministry, I took a three-month leave of absence to teach on the mission field. I met with the senior pastor in his office a few days before I left. He was supportive and encouraging of my overseas assignment. He gave no hint of dissatisfaction with my performance.

Within days of my arrival overseas, I received a fax telling me that I was being laid off due to financial struggles at the church. Actually, about eight other pastors were also being terminated for the same reason. It was a devastating blow! My wife and I had a newborn child, and we had recently purchased a new home. Communication in those days was done by letter and fax. Over the next three months, we exchanged letters to see what, if anything, could be worked out. I had reluctantly begun my journey between ministry positions.

I was flooded with conflicting emotions. I wanted to trust God and believe that nothing could happen to me outside his will. But deep in my soul, where not even my wife was invited to explore, I experienced anger, rage, depression, grief, and embarrassment. I don't know how I managed to keep my mind on teaching with so much going on behind the scenes. Days were filled with anxiety and fear. Sleep was elusive. I knew what the Bible taught about worry and having faith in God, but I was failing this test miserably. I felt responsible for the needs of my young family yet felt things were out of control. Complicating matters, I was unable to do much about my circumstances because of my remote location.

I reviewed all the mental checklists and asked myself a hundred questions. *Was it really God's will for me to go to this church, or was it pride on my part for wanting to be associated with such a large ministry? Did God intend for me to go through this test, or was the church out of his will? If I was out of God's will, where did I miss the signs? Were finances the real reason I was being let go, or was there another reason? Maybe I don't have what it takes to do church ministry and I should consider another option.* Questions flooded my mind as I reflected on what the future might hold. I reassessed my concept of God's calling a great deal during those lonely months.

Misery Loves Company

I have come to realize over the years that I wasn't alone in my pain. My experience is repeated perhaps a thousand times each month across North America. It has been that way for decades, and it shows no sign of letting up. Thirty years ago John Norval of Notre Dame claimed that one out of every four Catholic priests and one out of every eight Protestant ministers quit the ministry each year.[1] About fourteen years ago, church researcher George Barna reported that the number of Protestant pastors who quit the ministry had increased to one in six.[2] That equates to fifty thousand pastors each year hanging up their collars and walking away from what they once felt was God's call on their lives.[3] By contrast, in our more recent survey of pastors we discovered that 26 percent had been forced out of their churches. Forty-four percent said that they had given serious consideration to quitting ministry altogether. What pain those numbers represent!

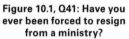

Figure 10.1, Q41: Have you ever been forced to resign from a ministry?

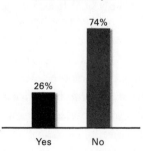

74%

26%

Yes   No

And it isn't just the pastor who is devastated by the news of having to leave a ministry. The family is thrown into turmoil as well. John LaRue, in a series of articles on forced termination (defined as being fired or severely pressured to resign) among the clergy, reports that 75 percent of those who were terminated had to move out of the area. Furthermore, 66 percent said that their children had to change schools and 64 percent said that their spouses had to change jobs. Is it any wonder that 20 percent of terminated pastors need an average of six months of professional counseling[4] and 10 percent suffer a major illness within the first year after being forced out?[5]

Blessings Out of Suffering

It should come as no surprise to those who have studied Romans 8:28 and James 1:2–4 that God can bring about tremendous growth from personal suffering. God has a strange way of transforming tears into joy. In LaRue's survey, he discovered that "two-thirds of ousted pastors report that their faith and prayer life improved because of their trying experiences. On the home front, the majority say their ability to be a loving spouse and caring parent was enhanced. Even though a third of all pastors forced out had not yet returned to local church ministry, nearly half said their ordeal encouraged their sense of call to the pastorate."[6]

I have known pastors who initially went into an emotional tailspin as they tried to discover God's purpose in their termination. In almost every case, after a season of personal reflection, and in some cases intense counseling, the pastor returned to ministry stronger and with a deeper conviction of God's call on his or her life. These pastors returned with more focus and a deeper sense of what God had for them in the next ministry that he provided. Likewise, LaRue comments, "When pastors are finally called to another church, the vast majority (85%) find the new situation to be easier. In fact, over six in ten (63%) discover the new parish to be much easier to handle than the one they had left."[7]

In their book *It Only Hurts on Monday*, Gary McIntosh and Robert Edmondson record the results of their survey of pastors and their former churches regarding why the minister resigned. It is interesting to note the differences in perspective between the churches and the pastors.[8] (See sidebar on page 140.)

In the next few pages I address two different kinds of departures. First, knowing when it is time to leave your ministry at a particular church and, second, knowing when it is time to leave the ministry altogether. The second is a far more challenging soul search.

Forced Terminations

Perhaps nothing causes a pastor to want to throw in the towel and walk away from ministry altogether as much as going through a forced termination from a church. It leaves the pastor feeling like a failure regardless of who is at fault. In many cases, the causes that led up to the pastor's decision to quit ministry altogether were already present in the congregation before the pastor accepted the call to go to the church in the first place. Overzealous members of the congregation or the church board can undermine a minister's effectiveness. Political games and

Contributing Causes of Pastoral Resignations

Contributing Causes	According to Pastors	According to Churches
Resistance to pastoral leadership	63%	67%
Unwritten expectations of the pastor	47%	43%
Resistance to change	43%	50%
Corporate spiritual defeat	43%	33%
Burnout	40%	43%
Conflict with the decision-making body	40%	37%
Disagreement over church polity	33%	17%
Salary issues	30%	13%
Personal loneliness	30%	27%
Doubt about call to ministry	27%	30%
Personal spiritual defeat	27%	27%
Lack of pastoral accountability	23%	23%
Disagreement over theology	17%	20%
Inadequate education	17%	13%
Unwritten expectations of the pastor's family	10%	27%
Inability to meet unwritten job description	10%	0%

power plays within the congregation, church board, or denominational office can threaten a pastor's ministry even before he or she arrives on the scene. It is only a matter of time before things blow up—often leaving the minister feeling as if it was his or her fault even when nothing could have prevented the conflict from surfacing. It was just unfortunate timing that occurred under a particular pastor's watch. It would have happened anyway, but that's little consolation to the one packing up his or her office.

The forced termination of pastors has been occurring with growing frequency.[9] The reasons are many and varied, but in a number of cases, it can be traced to a growing expectation on the part of the church that the pastor is accountable for the condition of the congregation. Put another way, if the sheep aren't healthy, happy, and multiplying, there must be something wrong with the shepherd. Given that train of reasoning, if the congregation isn't growing and experiencing visible effects of God's presence among them, it is time to seek another shepherd who can secure such blessings.

Let's face it: It is pretty tough to compete with the constant diet of radio and television pastors who eloquently preach on the airwaves of America. But that doesn't stop the average church member from wanting their favorite radio or television pastor as their own. When the message they hear on Sunday morning doesn't measure up to their standards, it's time for a change. It matters very little that these ministry leaders aren't available to counsel them when they face

Forced Terminations among Clergy

According to a national survey, more than one in five ministers has been fired or forced to resign. Among the findings:
- Nearly 23 percent had been fired or forced to resign.
- 34 percent said their predecessor had been forced out.

Among those who said they had been forced out:
- 62 percent said the church that terminated them had done the same thing to at least one other minister.
- 43 percent said a faction in the church pushed them out; 71 percent of those indicated the faction numbered ten or fewer.
- Only 20 percent said the real reason for their leaving was made known to the entire congregation.
- 52 percent said they didn't ask adequate questions about the church before accepting the job.

serious problems or need their presence at their hospital bedside. Americans are addicted to a "customer service" mentality; we are used to getting what we want. The end result of these expectations is that pastors get cast aside each week in churches across North America because church members are looking for the "new and improved model."

Pastors themselves grow disillusioned too. They answered God's call and entered into a profession that they thought would bring meaningful purpose and deep personal fulfillment. What they found were unrealistic expectations. Hundreds of pastors are forced out of their churches each week, and many never return to ministry again. They throw in the towel and figure there must be an easier way to make a living. What is even more disheartening is the realization that there is very little a pastor who has been terminated can do, since in almost every case that is brought to trial the courts choose not to enter into wrongful termination suits due to what they perceive as constitutional protection of the church's actions.[10]

But there is hope for pastors who have been terminated. A growing number of ministries have sprung up to assist those who are joining the ranks of the terminated clergy. Dr. Charles Chandler has begun the Ministering to Ministers Foundation to assist pastors who are navigating this difficult career hurdle. He suggests five options that are available to pastors who have been terminated from their church ministries.[11]

1. *Do nothing.* Even if you have legal rights that have been violated, you always have the choice of taking no action, leaving as gracefully as possible.
2. *Negotiate.* Here you seek help in the transition out to ease the impact or, in the rare case, to resolve the problems that led to the termination.
3. *Mediate.* This is a form of negotiated settlement of your rights where each side works through a third person to settle the differences.
4. *Arbitrate.* This form of resolution uses an agreed-upon third party to proclaim the rights and obligations of the contestants.
5. *Litigate.* While this option may seem repugnant initially, if there are clear violations of contract or of constitutionally protected rights, this approach should be considered. Since most cases are settled, the probabilities are high the case will resolve long before trial.

What some denominations are doing is putting forward a statement of understanding that sets out in advance the expectations of each party with the hope that a forced termination will not be necessary. An example of such a document is provided below. It comes from the American Baptist denomination and was adopted at their annual convention in 2003.

The *CONGREGATION* should include in the covenant a clear explanation of compensation and benefits, expectations of work hours and time off for family and self, a commitment to provide continuing education opportunities for the clergy, and a description of the responsibilities the clergy is expected to fulfill. In addition, the covenant should describe how the clergy is to be evaluated and what process shall be followed if the clergy is to be commended or if disappointments or grievances arise with the clergy's fulfillment of responsibilities. A clear statement of the help and resources that would be employed in the event of conflict is essential. Furthermore, the covenant should commit the congregation to a stated code of ethics in dealing with the pastor. The ethical code should include a commitment to honesty, compassion, clarity, open dialogue, gender sensitivity, confidentiality, forgiveness, support, affirmation, spiritual growth, justice, and civility.

The *CLERGY* should include in the covenant an acceptance of the compensation, benefits, work expectations, time off, continuing education provisions, and responsibilities as agreed upon. In addition, the clergy should state a commitment to follow the process established for addressing disappointments and grievances with the congregation, including the willingness to work with the help and resources requested by the congregation. Lastly, the clergy should commit to follow a stated code of ethics in ministering to the congregation. The ethical code should include a commitment to honesty, compassion, clarity, open dialogue, gender sensitivity, confidentiality, forgiveness, support, affirmation, spiritual growth, justice, sexual morality, and civility.[12]

There may be very little a pastor can do once forced out of his or her church ministry. Many pastors begin the career journey looking for a new church while some enter into counseling due to the heavy strain that such an act creates on the minister and his or her family. Some quit the ministry altogether due to the disappointment and pain.

Hanging Up the Collar for Good

Pastors who choose to drop out of the ministry altogether must deal with a host of issues. Several excellent ministries exist to assist the pastor and the family as they deal with the trauma that a forced termination creates. (A sampling of these ministries is displayed in the sidebar on page 144.) Those who are currently going through such upheaval are encouraged to contact these ministries and avail themselves of their resources. Some of the issues that come to the surface due to a forced termination are best dealt with in the context of professional counseling.

In such cases, the assistance of a trained counselor is needed to help the pastor deal with issues that perhaps should have been uncovered prior to entering the ministry in the first place.

Some of the topics for discussion with a counselor may include problems stemming back to one's family of origin, the need for setting up relationship boundaries with those around you, your concept of sexuality, your understanding of personal intimacy and how it affects those around you, personality characteristics, emotional stability, destructive work habits, your leadership style, your financial habits, parenting patterns, and care of your physical needs. This list is by no means all-inclusive, but exploring some of the topics herein may reveal deeply rooted issues that need to be addressed prior to your entering a new ministry. And in a few rare cases, they may give a pastor reason to consider the possibility that the ministry is not his or her best vocational choice at all.

People deal with pain in a variety of ways. Coping mechanisms that work for one may not be effective for another. Some are constructive and helpful while others may contribute to the formation of destructive patterns and lead to fur-

Ministries Focused on Helping Pastors in Crisis

LeaderCare (Southern Baptist Convention). Brooks Faulkner, senior manager, (888) 789-1911.

CareNet (Central Congress of American Rabbis). Rabbi Matthew Michaels of Houston's Congregation Emanu El, regional chair, (713) 629-5771.

The Church of Refuge. (Southern Baptist Convention). A program in Texas offering terminated pastors and their families rent-free homes for up to one year. Sonny Spurger, (214) 828-5169.[13]

Ministering to Ministers Foundation (interdenominational). Rev. Dr. Bill Turner, pastor of South Main Baptist Church, board member, (713) 529-4167. Dr. Charles H. Chandler, executive director, (800) 320-6463.

WoundedShepherds.com. An online community for former pastors and their families, featuring a chat room, message board, and confidential prayer requests.

Saint Barnabas Center. Inpatient treatment center in Wisconsin with extensive experience helping pastors who have reached a crisis or breakdown point in their lives.

ther difficulties. Overeating, excessive alcohol consumption, sexual addictions, and anger are a few of the ways people cope with the trauma of losing their jobs. Depression is also a common side effect. Depression can reveal itself in different ways. Barney Self, a licensed therapist and LeaderCare counselor, presents some danger signs a pastor should look for while going through an involuntary termination. They include the following:

1. Patterns of disrupted sleep. You either want to sleep all the time or can't get a good night's sleep.
2. Weight loss or gain of ten pounds within a month. You use food to deal with depression and gain weight, or you look at food and aren't hungry.
3. Inability to concentrate. You read a chapter of a book, but if somebody gave you a test, you couldn't say what you had just read.
4. Crying spells. These symptoms aren't gender-specific. In fact, this can be worse for men who have John Wayne mentalities and think they should be able to handle it.
5. Lethargy. You know you have something to do, but you just can't get it done.
6. Hopelessness. You feel doomed.
7. Pervasive sadness. You feel overwhelmingly sad, down, negative, and morose.
8. Inability to enjoy usual activities, including hobbies, fun activities, and intimacy with a spouse.[14]

Pastor Brooks Faulkner, in his book *Forced Termination: Redemptive Options for Ministers and Churches*, provides valuable insight for pastors suffering from depression as a result of a forced termination.

> As a minister, you have heard, "I just can't do anything about my depression." We did not believe it then. We must not believe it now that it is happening to us. We can do something about depression. By doing nothing, we are allowing depression to control our behavior. We must take some preventative maintenance steps to avoid having depression take control of our behavior.[15]

When pastors feel that they are exhibiting the symptoms of depression, they should seek out the assistance of someone they trust to provide guidance and support. It isn't an easy detour during this career journey, but for some it's a necessary consideration.

Exploring the Secrets Places of Our Heart

You may be dealing with deeply rooted issues that you have never taken the time to bring to the surface for resolution. Failing to do so will contribute to your high blood pressure, anger, depression, eating and sleep disorders, and stress levels.

In her excellent book *Clergy Stress: The Hidden Conflicts in Ministry*, Mary Anne Coate identifies nine themes that she feels are germane to the production of stress and strain in ministers. She believes that ministers need to explore each of these themes to discover what damaging effect they may create or have created in the life of the minister. A healthy pastor is one who has taken the time to consider the implications of these themes on his or her life and ministry.[16]

- *Goodness and perfection.* Ministers can be driven to perfectionism by unhealthy expectations. Perfectionism may be a form of neurosis whereby the minister gives grace to everyone but himself.
- *Dependence.* Most ministers have difficulty allowing themselves to be dependent on anyone else for their needs. This stems from a lack of trust in others, perhaps because they have experienced betrayal at some point in their past.
- *Self-esteem.* If the minister is suffering from poor self-esteem, it may result in unhealthy relationships between the minister and his or her congregants.
- *Guilt.* Our fallen nature is never fully put to death, and the result is a realization that we are sinful individuals. Where there is sin, there is also a sense of guilt. Ministers struggle with it as much, perhaps even more, than congregants.
- *Rivalries, jealousy, and envy.* Ministry is highly competitive and creates opportunities for boasting, prideful behaviors, and envy over the accomplishments of others.
- *Power.* The adage that power corrupts is as true as the ages. Ministers are spiritual leaders, and where there is leadership, there is the temptation of abusing one's privilege and power.
- *Authority and parent-child models.* When a minister hasn't fully resolved issues that were created in his or her family of origin, dysfunctional patterns can manifest themselves in ministry settings.
- *Sexuality.* One of our most powerful human drives, our sexuality is capable of providing great happiness or causing us great trouble. When sex is engaged in outside of marriage, it can leave a wake of destruction for a minister.
- *Loneliness.* Decision making sets ministers apart from those they are leading. This isolation can cause seclusion and stress. Ministers know all too well the truth of the dictum "We can be lonelier with other people than anywhere else."

Some of these deeply rooted issues may need to come out into the light for examination and thoughtful reflection. They may not be pleasant to discuss with a trusted friend or counselor, but denying them once they are discovered only invites more problems in the future.

When well-established dysfunction is allowed to remain entrenched, unhealthy patterns linger and recurrence is inevitable. If the minister is unwilling to accept the reality of his condition and put forth the necessary determination to resolve the issues, then it would be better to quit the ministry altogether than to go through the destructive patterns again. Given the severity of such consequences, a minister would do well to reconsider his call to ministry.

Knowing Your Enemy

Every good pastor begins a counseling session with some form of assessment. It usually begins with a statement such as, "Tell me how things are going." It allows the individual an opportunity to come clean, perhaps for the first time, by providing the climate for honest reflection and expression. Trained counselors also know that unless an individual is honest with his or her condition and circumstances, little, if anything, can be done to bring the person to a place of healing. In the same way, for pastors who are reading these words, hope is always available, even in the darkest hours, but it needs to begin with assessing your current condition.

If you find yourself in a place where quitting the ministry is a viable option, take a few minutes to ascertain the root of your problem. It could be one of three causes or a combination of them: spiritual opposition, conflict with those in your ministry, and/or sources within you. Knowing your enemy has much to do with developing a strategy for moving forward from here.

Spiritual Opposition

One dimension of our struggles is spiritual in nature. The apostle Paul writes, "For our struggle is not against flesh and blood, but against the rulers, against the powers, against the world forces of this darkness, against the spiritual forces of wickedness in the heavenly places" (Eph. 6:12). Satan would love nothing more than to defeat us and cause us to run in shame. His powers are great, but God's children possess a far greater power. "Greater is He who is in you than he who is in the world" (1 John 4:4).

If the source of your opposition is spiritual in nature, then fighting it with human resources is futile. What you need is a sharpening of your spiritual weaponry by praying, meditating on God's Word, fasting, and praising God joyfully. Reach deep into your spiritual resources and exercise your faith muscles, asking God for his victory. Repeat the words of Winston Churchill, who once said to a group of graduating students, "Never give up, never give up, never, never, never give up!" Don't quit the ministry unless God gives you permission. Anything less would be to desert the ranks of God's army. Going AWOL never brought peace to Jonah, and it won't bring peace to you either.

Conflict from within Your Ministry

Probably the greatest reason for pastors quitting the ministry comes from the pressures associated with conflict in the church. This opposition may be from a disgruntled member, a small faction, or a governing board. Regardless of the source, stop and ask yourself if there is a kernel of truth in their criticism. If, after some honest reflection, you feel there is room for compromise, meet with the source of your opposition and make peace. Perhaps a compromise is the best course of action to take. This may be a case where you are right but winning the battle will cause you to lose the war.

You may have already tried that route, and the individual or group that is in opposition to you has no desire to find a peaceful solution. Then certainly the next step would be to bring in a third party arbiter to help mediate the conflict. There are a number of good nonprofit agencies available for such purposes.

Realistically speaking, not all such efforts end in peace. In some cases, the only reasonable thing to do is wait them out, pray them out, or pack your bags and look for a ministry that allows you and your family more of a stress-free environment. Leave the opposition party in God's hands, knowing that nothing is hidden from his eyes and that he is more than able to balance the scales of injustice in his timing.

Sources from Within

This has been a difficult chapter to write, and no doubt for some it has been difficult to read. It may be entirely possible that the reason you are considering hanging up your ministerial collar and quitting your current church position, or perhaps even your vocational calling altogether, is entirely your own doing. Your strong-willed leadership style, personal emotional dysfunction, or any of the other possibilities discussed in this chapter have created a climate in which healthy ministry just isn't possible. Moving to another location without dealing with the problem will only mean that you will have it with you when you unpack your bags at your next church. Eventually, the toll that such moves will take on your emotional or physical health, not to mention your spouse and children, may eventually lead to a complete breakdown.

You may need some serious intervention either with a trusted colleague or a licensed counselor. Only then will you be able to examine objectively the cause of your desire to leave. For some, with a few months of valuable counseling, you will receive the emotional, relational, and spiritual equilibrium that is necessary for life in the pastorate.

For others, however, you may come to the conclusion that a career in the pastorate is not for you. In nearly twenty-five years of training pastors for the ministry, I have never tried to talk someone into becoming a pastor. The only person who should enter the ministry is someone who is so convinced of God's call on his or her life that nothing else will satisfy. My general rule is, "If there is anything else you can see yourself doing other than the ministry, then you should be doing it."

It has been my desire in this chapter to present you with some constructive thoughts on why you should or shouldn't hang up your collar and leave your ministry. For some, leaving may be the best course of action. For others, God is calling you to stand your ground and allow him to fight your battle for you. Only you can determine which course of action God is calling you to take. Much like the initial call to ministry that God placed on your life, you need to search your heart and have the courage and conviction to follow God's plan for your life regardless of what others may be saying. However, you must also recognize that "without consultation, plans are frustrated, but with many counselors they succeed" (Prov. 15:22). May God grant you wisdom to discern his path for your life.

CHAPTER 11

DRAGGING YOUR FAMILY TO THE MAGIC KINGDOM

Addressing Family Issues That Can't Be Ignored

MICK BOERSMA

Each of you should look not only to your own interests,
but also to the interests of others.
Philippians 2:4 NIV

My wife and I have annual passes to the "Happiest Place on Earth." When the mood strikes, we jump in the car, catch the carpool lane for seven minutes directly into the Disney parking lot, hop on the tram, and cruise through the gate for a few hours of people watching, dinner, and a show. It's a nice way to enjoy a balmy night in Southern California. Since we are empty nesters now, it is easy for us just to pick up and drive to the park. That certainly isn't the case for those with kids.

We see families as they arrive. Strollers the size of VW Bugs and piles of clothes to handle the change in temperature once the sun goes down. It's not surprising that so many people have SUVs—it takes a truck to haul all that gear for a family outing. Of course, the fun is only starting. There's trying not to lose anyone among the throngs and the constant cries of "Mommy, I want to go on Dumbo" or "Let's do Indiana Jones again" (for the fourth time) or "I'm hungry" (for $7 burgers)—and it just keeps getting better. Sure, there's lots of excitement along the family adventure but not without a lot of effort!

If you have a family and are considering a ministry move, you know there are a lot of issues that will arise as your travel plans are being made. We asked the pastors in our survey what they saw as the hardest adjustment for their spouse and/or children related to their last move. This open-ended question garnered a variety of responses. The impact on relationships was mentioned by the great majority, along with several other key issues we will also address in this chapter. As you look ahead to a move, approaching these issues honestly and effectively is critical. If you don't, you may end up traveling alone. As one pastor put it, "The move almost led to my wife and I getting a divorce."

Your Family Issues Checklist

A number of items need to be on your family issues checklist. Neglecting to give attention to any one of them can quickly suck the joy out of life. Our intention is to provide you with this list so you will make sure not to forget anything along the way.

Immediate Family

You may be ministering in an area geographically close to parents, aunts, uncles, and cousins. If you're on good terms with these family members, it may be hard to say good-bye. If you're far away, you may desire to move closer to "home." There are many considerations here, but we mention a few that are often repeated in our conversations with pastors around the country.

Middle-aged pastors are being challenged by the needs of their aging parents. Wanting to honor their parents (Ex. 20:12), some feel it necessary either to relocate nearby or to move their parents closer to their place of service. If your ministry is stable, the latter is more possible, but many take the route of moving closer to parents. This decision may delay finding another ministry position or lead you to consider a job in something other than full-time ministry, at least for a season.

Younger married pastors often leave their parental homeland in the early stages of their careers. But when children start coming along, the desire to have their offspring grow up around grandparents and cousins becomes very strong. We know of one pastor who moved his family to Michigan just to be close to parents during this season of their family life. He is still seeking a place of ministry but believes they made the right decision.

Still others cite a desire to be around immediate family so they can continue to be witnesses for Jesus Christ to unsaved family members. While electronic media has certainly made it easier to keep in touch with loved ones, there is something powerful in being with another person in the flesh. The opportunity to live, love, and share life with another in close proximity is a treasure and may be a consideration as you plan your future.

Friends

In our survey, leaving old friends and finding new ones was cited as the biggest challenge during a move. It takes time to develop deep and meaningful relationships, and a move means sacrificing hard-won connections and having to reinvest in new ones. Of course, this is true in any profession, but ministers tend to have their primary relationships within the church. Making a move often cuts them off from these, especially if the parting was under difficult circumstances.

For this reason, some say you shouldn't have close friends in the church you serve. While this is understandable, my wife and I chose to go deep with our people. Yes, there was pain when we left (and there were difficulties), but they remain some of our dearest friends some thirty years later. When the folks in the church were our problem, we had an outside network of friends and family for counsel, a listening ear, and a more neutral perspective.

Perhaps a combination of friends within and outside the church is the best approach. One pastor's wife found the isolated small-town pastorate to be a big issue with her. She was used to getting together with girlfriends for encouragement and support. The solution was not to isolate herself from the church women, but to add a weekly trip to a larger town forty miles away where she joined a women's Bible study in a larger congregation. She didn't tell them she was a pastor's wife at first, and she found the fellowship a great place to grow spiritually and share her more personal struggles.

Your Marriage

Career changes, especially those that involve a move, can have a profound impact on a marriage. One writer put it this way: "A new ministry frequently means new responsibilities and pressures. It may require more time at the office, and thus less time at home. Or the new congregation may not want to give you as much privacy as you now have. Even things such as a climate change can affect the hobbies you share."[1] Because discussing potential career moves with one's spouse is so important, we have devoted significant space to it later in this chapter.

Spiritual Well-Being

Sometimes we consider a move because staying would jeopardize the spiritual health of ourselves and our families (remember the Family Flag in chapter 6). One pastor reported how his daughter nearly lost her faith due to the youth pastor undermining her dad's ministry and effectively leading to his termination. So as you look to a new position, it is important to consider the changes such a move will have on your family's spiritual life.

If you have kids, they may experience different kinds of children's or youth ministries from place to place. Some pastors reported the difficulty of leaving a church with a great youth program to go to a church with little or no ministry for kids. This was especially noted among church planters. One pastor friend of ours actually received permission from his board to have his three sons attend the youth group in a larger church in town so they would have fellowship with other teens. Valuing his kids' faith as a high priority allowed them to preserve their walk with the Lord and enjoy friendships with others their own age.

You will also want to make sure your spouse has the opportunity to exercise his or her ministry within the new context. While it is not absolutely necessary for them to work with you in the church itself, finding a place to belong in the new congregation is essential for the long-term health of your ministry. Ministry couples need to share a sense of call to ministry, and that includes pursuing meaningful service in the place God has appointed for them. Making sure there is potential for this is critical.

Finally, it is important to find ways to nurture your own spiritual growth in this new location as well. Don't just assume it will all work out. This needs to be an intentional focus on your part. We asked pastors how making a pastoral transition impacted their personal walk with God, and most reported that it strengthened not only their walk, but that of their entire family. One pastor noted, "It saved it. Had I not become a Lutheran, I would have tossed out personal experience with that of the community I left." You never know what a pastoral transition might lead to.

Jobs

Many wives of pastors have jobs other than being a wife and homemaker. More recent estimates put the number at around 60 percent.[2] Therefore, in the majority of cases, the decision to move can involve two careers, not just one. Whose career takes priority in these cases? It is not an easy call. One recent seminary graduate reported not seeking ministry positions outside a certain area because his wife wanted to pursue her career by finishing her master's degree at a particular university. He hasn't found work and may not find any until they can broaden their search area two years from now. Another pastor moved to where a great job offer awaited his spouse. The good income she receives is helping him do creative and interesting things, making for an exciting ministry for both of them. Open communication about role expectations is essential to avoid conflict in such situations.

Making a move from pastoral ministry to another form of service also presents challenges. My wife loved being a pastor's wife. When we decided that I would pursue my doctoral degree and a teaching career, it meant she would have to dust off her teaching credentials and hit the classroom. For the next six years, she graciously served our family in this capacity but longed for a ministry alongside her husband. By God's grace we were able to create a ministry to our Talbot alumni that has given her a place to shepherd pastors and their spouses. She paid a big price for this transition. And you can be sure we discussed it and prayed about it as we considered a move.

Education

As you would expect, the pastors in our survey noted how important the issue of education was in light of considering a career move—and not just the pastor's education, but the educational tracks their family members were on as well. For example, one pastor in our study told us he postponed his search for one year while his daughter completed her senior year in high school. He took a job in the private sector during that year. He was determined not to sacrifice his daughter's senior year to pursue a new career opportunity.

Perhaps you personally want to pursue a higher degree. While Web-based programs are plentiful, if your plans call for a residency type program, you will want to take that into consideration as you look around at the possibilities. Packing up your family while you pursue graduate education is no small feat. Consider the cost to you and each of your family members.

The question of schooling for your children must be a part of your travel planning (also see chapter 18). Do you have a child with special needs? Will he or she have access to necessary specialized educational opportunities? Do you home-school? Will the congregation look approvingly upon this educational option? This could present a problem if there are public school teachers on the church's governing board or if the church sponsors a Christian school itself. Such factors need to be explored prior to accepting an invitation. Never assume you will have the freedom to do as you like. Although the search committee may express this to you verbally, the members of the governing board may have a different opinion—one that should not be overlooked.

Does the church have unwritten expectations concerning the education of your children? My wife and I decided to send our daughters to Christian schools. That doesn't sound like too big a deal until you realize that the superintendent of the public school system considered us his home church and the chairman of our deacon board was the president of the local school board. Naturally, there were many public school teachers in our church as well. While it took some skilled diplomacy and a lot of God's grace, we managed to navigate what could have been a difficult challenge. We were intentional about what we felt was in the best interest of our children yet gracious with those who may have had other expectations.

Health Care

Needless to say, health care is a critical concern for families living in the United States today. All across America people are delaying retirement and spouses are going back to work to provide for the high cost of insurance premiums. But it's not just the insurance people care about. It's important to build relationships and trust with particular health-care providers, such as pharmacists, family doctors, and medical specialists. Once you have a great health-care support network, it's hard to give it up. This is especially true if particular health issues have challenged your family. Having a doctor who knows the health history of you and your loved ones and has built a relationship over the years is not a blessing to take lightly. You will want to include this in your investigations as you consider a potential move.

Housing

It's just wood and plaster, but a house is where a family experiences home. Early in our marriage, I learned that women look at a house differently than men do. I'd moved nine times in eleven years during college and seminary and had no emotional attachment to the rooms I rented. Once married, however, I realized that to my wife, our home was her nest. Though not one to covet a palace on the beach, she considers the house we live in to be a special place where family lives, loves, and grows together. Leaving one house for another is not just a matter of calling the moving van anymore!

When considering a move, realize that your spouse will miss the place you call home. And so will your kids. Ours get upset if we even talk about selling our place and buying another. These are walls that, if they could talk, would share a host of stories about the joys, trials, and blessings of the Boersma family. We will look at the topic of housing again in chapter 18, but for now, just remember that your home is important to your family, and therefore you need to consider the impact moving will have on them.

Culture

Several of the pastors in our survey indicated that the change in culture was a real eye-opener for them once they moved. A few even mentioned that weather was something they were unprepared for, especially those who went from the U.S. Southwest to the Midwest. While people are people, there are significant differences in these places, and only a fool thinks they aren't important.

Ask anyone who has ever moved from California to become a pastor in the South, and he or she will tell you that there is a big cultural difference. Likewise, those coming to California from Kansas will soon comment as Dorothy did, "We aren't in Kansas anymore." Don't underestimate the importance of cultural differences (such as entertainment preferences, taste in foods, dress, or politics).

Finances

Finances are not last on the list because we feel they are the least important. In fact, one study of pastors' families showed that finances were among the top three problems they faced, along with lack of personal friends and inadequate time with one another.[3] Considering a new ministry that represents a cut in pay will have an effect on your spouse and children. One pastor's wife confided that because of a smaller salary she had to redefine the meaning of "need." Moving from the city to a rural setting helped, however. People in the new location, she realized, did not "need" as many things as city dwellers considered important. They even found their children becoming less materialistic as they played with other kids who didn't seem to "need" as much stuff either.

A lack of money challenges us to consider our expectations and view of the things of this world. Yes, we are not to be conformed to the world system (Rom. 12:2) nor to love money (1 Tim. 6:10). Yet we are also responsible to provide for our own families and prove ourselves fitting leaders of Christ's church (1 Tim. 5:8). Therein lies the tension. The struggle over finances must be engaged by the family in a purposeful and Christ-honoring way. Our experience has been that God has provided for us faithfully over thirty-plus years of marriage and ministry. He has been very creative at times and has called us to hard work. And the bills continue to get paid.

A Route to Your Destination

You most likely knew about the issues in this book before you opened the cover. But seeing them all together has probably left you wondering how in the world you are supposed to address so many needs. In the remaining pages of this chapter, we will suggest four exercises that will help you not only in your transition, but in your entire life of ministry.

But before we go there, know this: none of the following tactics will have their desired effect if your spouse and family do not trust you. It took awhile before my wife realized that I would never take her anywhere or do anything that would put her in personal danger of any kind. Through the years we have built a relationship that truly desires the best for the other, a growing experience of what is so beautifully described in Ephesians 5. So, as you encounter these suggestions, realize that your loved ones will follow you to the ends of the earth only if they are confident you love them and would never do anything to harm them.

Step 1: Communicate. Figure 11.1 shows where our respondents found help in their transition journeys. We think it is significant that sharing with a spouse ranked first among the choices. Healthy communication within a family unit is essential to working through a potential move. Only you know if the channels between you, your spouse, and your children are open. (See the sidebar on page 158 of family therapist Virginia Satir's "five freedoms" that promote free-flowing communication in functional families.)[4]

If you're not a good listener already, you will need to become one, allowing your loved ones to honestly process the move with you. Resist the urge to fix every response and answer all their questions and alleviate all their fears.

Discuss honestly the reasons you think a move would be a good idea. Of course, the ages of your children will determine the extent to which you share your decision-making process, but you will want to involve them in some way so they can work through the changes with you. We sat down our eight-year-old twin daughters and shared the basic reasons for our move (without the more heartbreaking details) and the advantages it would bring them. They went to their bedroom, talked awhile, and came back into the living room and declared, "It will be okay."

If you and your spouse are at peace about the move, chances are your children will get there too. Or, put negatively, as one pastor did, "If Daddy is sad, the whole family is sad." Such is the impact of parents' solidarity and attitude in times like these.

Step 2: Emote. One of the freedoms identified by Satir (see sidebar, page 158) relates to the expression of personal feelings. It is easy to stuff our emotions in a brave attempt to put a positive spin on what often is a negative circumstance. We all need time for closure, time to wrestle with the prospect of leaving the known for the unknown. Time to struggle with the grieving process of denial, anger, bargaining, depression, and acceptance. Of course, everyone grieves differently, but the process must be allowed to happen. Some in our survey reported that it took them six to twelve months to "get over" the trauma associated with the move. One pastor's wife said it took her seven years!

While most pastors in our survey reported great outcomes from their moves, they did realize the stress it put on themselves and their families. They counseled not to expect your kids to be thrilled and positive about everything involved in the move. Don't be surprised if their anger is directed at you or even at God. Consider family counseling. One family decided to help their kids adjust to their new surroundings by letting each one bring along a good friend for the first two weeks. They had someone they knew to share the adventure with, and once their friends went back home, they were able to move on with new friendships in the making. It worked so well the first time, they have done it every move since.

Figure 11.1, Q 17: When you faced a decision about making a career move, which of the following resources were the most helpful to you?

All of this emoting takes time and sensitivity. I know from personal experience. In my junior year in high school, in the dead of winter, my father asked if I'd like to move to the West Coast. He and Mom said we could wait another year until I graduated, or we could move that summer. They gave me a few days to think it over. I said yes that evening. But I cried as I contemplated leaving friends I'd known since those nostalgic days in the church nursery. They waited for me. They talked it out with me. It was the best move of my life, and I've always appreciated the fact that they took my feelings into consideration.

Step 3: Revisit. As with all life transitions, this is a great time to take stock of some important commitments in your life. The following are a few you dare not ignore.

Your mission. Revisit your mission as a family in service to Christ. This means going through the focus of chapters 1 and 2, but now as a family. What has God called you together to do for his glory? What gifts have you been able to share with the body of Christ in this place? How have you determined to sacrifice your lives together for the sake of others, enduring the hardships in order to follow his call? One major study learned this from its respondents: "Pastors' comments indicate that the more clearly the call is discerned by the pastor and the more thoroughly the decision is processed by the family, the higher the level of support for ministry and the less likely the family is to be harshly surprised by the realities of ministry."[5]

Your history. Every family has great stories to tell, and this is a good time to open the family album and take some comfort. The pastors in our survey found their transitions to be very challenging but often mentioned the faithfulness and mercy of God in caring for their every need. The children of Israel were encouraged to share their history through various feasts and celebrations. Psalm 136

Five Freedoms of Functional Families

1. The freedom to see and hear [perceive] what is here and now rather than what was, will be, or should be.
2. The freedom to think what one thinks rather than what one should think.
3. The freedom to feel what one feels rather than what one should feel.
4. The freedom to want [desire] and to choose what one wants rather than what one should want.
5. The freedom to imagine one's own self-actualization rather than playing a rigid role or always playing it safe.

traces God's goodness to them on one of history's greatest transitions, the march to the Promised Land. In Psalm 145 God's people are exhorted, "One generation will commend your works to another; they will tell of your mighty acts" (v. 4 NIV).

In our family's move from the Seattle area to Southern California, I invoked the story of God's faithfulness to the Van Rennes family. My maternal grandfather immigrated with his wife and nine children. They had few possessions, little money, and the hope of a new life in America. We would be fine moving from north to south, because the same God who loved Jacobus Bernardus Hendrikus Van Rennes would be there for us too.

Your priorities. Earlier I mentioned the issue of your marriage. If there are problems between you and your spouse, a move will only magnify them. Now is the time to take stock of your relationship and make any adjustments necessary. My wife and I spend many hours with couples who are finding ministry a tough place to grow a marriage and family. Unhealthy patterns need to be caught and changed—now, not later. One pastor came up with the following list of questions he vowed to ask his wife every year.[6] They may provide a template for examining the present nature of your marriage.

1. What can I do to cause you to feel more loved and cherished?
2. How can I best demonstrate my appreciation for you, your ideas, and your role as my wife?
3. What can I do to assure you that I hear and understand your heart's desires?
4. What can I do to make you feel absolutely secure?
5. What can I do to ensure that you have confidence and joy in our future direction?
6. What attribute or practice would you like to see me develop or improve?
7. What attribute would you most like to develop in yourself, and how may I help you in the best possible way?
8. Is there some accomplishment in my life that would bring joy to your heart?
9. What would indicate to you my desire to be more like Christ?
10. What mutual goal(s) would you like to see us accomplish together?

You may also want to rethink how you minister to your children. Many excellent resources are available for pastors' families, giving specific ways to enrich the lives of your children and enable them to thrive as ministers' kids. And don't forget to help them through the trials of a move. Sadly, a few of our survey respondents indicated that their pastoral transitions left their spouses and kids angry, resentful, and most unfortunate of all, skeptical of God's grace and the church. Much can be done to prevent this tragic result.

Your trust in God. Perhaps you remember those early days when, sensing God's call, you were ready to give away all your possessions and trek to the ends of the earth to proclaim the gospel. New beginnings are exciting, but the middle of the race can be a real drag. We lose our enthusiasm, and sometimes we even lose our belief that God is still there beside us. The pastors in our survey reported that they found the Lord to be a faithful companion in the transitions. One pastor wrote this about how a move impacted his walk with God: "I put far more faith in him than in myself, or my ability to keep people happy. I'm saved by the same grace that saves everyone else, and I avail myself of it at every opportunity. I know that my ministry here is at the pleasure of the King—he can move me on at any time. Until then, I'm committed."

Transitions are incredible faith-building times. They are difficult, sometimes scary, and always interesting. That they produce more maturity in us should not be surprising, for trials are the avenue to continuing maturity (James 1). Being convinced that God is trustworthy forms the bedrock for our ministry with others.

Step 4: Rejoice. Far and away the comments from our survey showed pastors being blessed and families growing closer together through their transitions. They found themselves praying more as a family, valuing one another in new ways, and growing in their understanding of one another's needs and aspirations. Even though some reported very difficult circumstances, they consistently found evidence of the loving hand of God.

They also reported making new friends, enjoying expanded opportunities, and gaining a larger perspective on the work of God. Some even indicated a newfound ability to forgive at a deeper level and move on to once again trust their hearts to strangers. Others added these thoughts:

> We're closer because we left all of our friends behind and only have each other.... I'm happier, so that affects the family (less stress).

> Strengthened my dependence ... allowed me to be used more greatly.

> It was bonding for me and my wife to pray and seek God's will together; and sweet for us both to clearly sense the same leading for our future.

> God blessed my two transitions as my wife and kids found new roles, friendships, and connections in the church.

> The kids were involved in the decision process and are intentional about sharing in the ministry here, more than in our last place, where they had no choice.

> We all struggled with the uncertainty and leaving good friends behind. The move made us closer to each other.

The move has caused great stress and pain but also deep joy and fellowship with God. There have been some very hard days, and even months, but God is good and sweet.

Are We There Yet?

As my wife and I stroll around Disneyland, we meet lots of out-of-town families. It's fun to hear about where they live and what they do for a living. And they often volunteer stories about their trip to the Magic Kingdom. We pity those who had to drive long distances with small children or cram themselves into the cheap seats for a five-hour flight. Yet they show no resentment for these and a host of other pressures. All they see is the wonder in their children's eyes. The tensions of the journey are all but forgotten in light of the bounty that awaits them inside the magical gates.

You are in the midst of your journey now, but the day will come when your family asks, "Are we there yet?" and you'll be able to say, "Yes, we're here." Perhaps God will see that sparkle in your eyes when you realize he has brought you safely to a new place of blessing and opportunity.

CHAPTER 12

UPDATING YOUR PASSPORT

Revising Your Resume

MICK BOERSMA

"Who are you? Give us an answer to take back to those who sent us.
What do you say about yourself?"
John 1:22 NIV

"Next!" It was my turn. The customs agent glanced my way as I approached the counter. "Passport, please." Handing over the most precious document any international traveler possesses, I waited anxiously as she passed it through the electronic "don't let this guy in" detector. I was at Schipol Airport, Amsterdam, and even though my last name was Boersma, the only way I was going to get into the country of my ancestors was if that agent said I could. My identity would have to match, the information would have to be absolutely correct, and my homeland and Holland would have to be on friendly terms. "Enjoy your stay, Mr. Boersma. You must have many relatives here with a name like that." She smiled, and I was on my way.

Each year millions of passports are issued to U.S. citizens anticipating travel abroad.[1] Some of these are renewals; many are first-time applications. In either case, details must be completely accurate, verifiable, and consistent with the identity of the holder. There are many resources on the Web and locally (any post office) where one can go to start the process of securing a valid passport.

Your main travel document as a pastor on a career journey is your resume — your passport to interviews with potential local church or parachurch organizations. It too needs to reflect accurately your pastoral identity so that those considering "letting you in" can make a well-informed decision concerning the suitability of joining one another in the journey of service to Christ. And there are myriad resources on the Internet and at job placement centers in most seminaries that provide excellent help in creating a first-class set of documents for embarking on a pastoral search. In this chapter we will share the collective wisdom available so you can faithfully and effectively present yourself to the "customs officers" you meet along the way. Before we begin, here are a few words of advice to guide you.

Don't just dust off your old resume. You have changed, and your ministry skills have grown through expanded pastoral experiences. Your view of ministry has undergone refinement. You have a clearer sense of the kind of ministry you are called to and best gifted to fulfill. After ten years passports must be renewed and new photos are required. It is the only way to help keep your identity up to date and useful to those desiring to grant you access to their world.

Dare to be personal. Secular resumes are normally constructed with a minimum of personal information. That's fine if you are applying for an engineering job. Your personal life is your own business. But in the world of ministry, what you do is who you are. Search committees appreciate getting a glimpse of your character and personality through your resume materials. One search committee chairperson said, "Resumes that caught our attention were those that not only expressed the academic and ministry experience of the applicant but also reflected something of his personality and philosophy of ministry."[2] We'll show you how to build such a resume.

Always be honest. The process of creating a resume offers many opportunities to "fudge the numbers." While it is neither honorable nor advisable to understate your qualities and accomplishments, it is dishonest to paint a picture of yourself that bears little resemblance to who you really are. Remember, passports must

Top Five Purposes of a Resume

To present yourself as you wish to be perceived; to make a first impression

To inform the search committee of your abilities, history, and other personal and work-related information

To persuade the search committee that your qualifications are worthy of carrying you to the interview stage in the candidating process

To serve the search committee by helping them find the best match — provides a chance to demonstrate your pastoral side

To celebrate all the good things God has given to you and done through you

accurately identify the holder. The last thing you want to do is lead a church to believe you are something or someone you aren't. If you create a false identity, you will have to live with it. Far better to be graciously straightforward and trust God to provide a ministry that appreciates who you really are — warts and all.

The Cover Letter

Everyone knows how crucial a good introduction is to an effective sermon. Among other things, it serves to convince the listener that what follows is important and applicable to his or her life in Christ. In sending your resume to prospective ministries, the manner in which it is introduced is equally significant. Remember, you never get a second chance to make a first impression, and your cover letter is the first impression the prospective ministry will receive of you. In the best of all worlds, you would have a well-known and respected person who knows you *and* the leadership of the search committee hand deliver your documents. This "dream sequence" is not often possible, however. A good cover letter from you can be a tremendous help.

Effective letters are basically made up of the following three parts.

The opening. This includes the salutation. Do not use "To Whom It May Concern"; it sounds too much like "To Whoever Cares," which is not really a great way to start things off. Address your letter to the appropriate contact person. Usually a name is provided in job placement listings.

In the first paragraph, briefly introduce yourself and convey the means by which you discovered the open position (website, seminary placement office, friend, denominational source). Knowing this helps to validate your identity in the committee members' minds.

The pitch. This term may sound manipulative, but it accurately conveys the purpose of the midsection of your cover letter. The object here is to show that you are serious about this position and believe you are qualified to fill it. Citing just one or two highlights of your giftedness and experience will help set the stage for a positive look at the resume that lies beneath. This is your way of showing sincere interest in the ministry and a confidence (not arrogance) that there is solid potential for a good fit.

This is also the place to explain anything on your resume that you think might give rise to some questions. As a new seminary graduate, I had been in three ministries in the four years of my M.Div. program. Rather than let the reader assume I was unable to hold down a job, I shared my plan as a student to try a few different areas of service (music, youth, and associate pastor positions) to discover the best fit. Doing so turned a potential negative into a positive. My seeking a senior pastorate was the result of a concerted effort at self-assessment, based on solid experience. I got the position.

The call to action. In the final paragraph, let the addressee know that you are thankful for the opportunity to present yourself as a possible candidate and are looking forward to further interaction in the near future. We often suggest to our students and alumni that a phone call to the church after about two weeks is appropriate. The purpose is to make sure they have received your materials and to offer any additional information. It's a nice way of letting them know you are seriously interested without being pushy.

Close your letter with something like "Yours in Christ" or "Looking forward to your response." "Sincerely yours" is just too cold. Keep things personal. At the end of the chapter, we provide you with a sample letter that you can modify for your purposes.

The Resume

Before you start to construct a resume, you will find it helpful to recall the purposes of such a document (see the sidebar on page 163).

There are many ways to organize your resume. In the years that we have helped pastors with their job searches, we have seen creativity and personal preferences reflected in many ways. We give tips regarding various style points at the end of this chapter, but first we want to lead you through a sequence that will serve as a template for producing a top-rate resume that will faithfully and effectively represent your case for consideration to any ministry opening. Making separate files or documents for each section will be helpful. Work on them until you are happy with the results, then paste them together into a final document. You will find a sample resume at the end of this chapter and may want to refer to it as we move through the process.[3]

Personal Contact Information

Name. Most people have more than one first name or use a nickname. List the name you use in everyday life. My legal name is Micheal, but I've never used it except for legal documents. I use "Mick" on my resume because that is what I want the prospective ministry to call me. We suggest you use bold type and make your name a size or two larger than the other information in this section.

Address. Include your mailing address (if possible, avoid post office boxes, as these can convey a sense of transience). You will want to include your home phone and/or cell phone numbers. Make sure you have an answering device for all phone numbers. Your email address should be listed, along with a fax number, if you have one. Should you have a personal or family webpage, you might consider listing that also. If you are confident it will serve the search committee in a positive way, then go ahead.

Ministry Objective

Some believe this is unnecessary, but it seems that if you have a fairly clear sense of *what* you want to do, *where* you would like to do it, and *under what circumstances* you would prefer to serve, such information can only help in making your case for a position that fits these parameters. For instance, if you like to create and administer programs, have a desire to work with youth, and are most comfortable in an evangelical church in a suburban setting, your ministry objective could read: "To create and administer an innovative program for junior high and high school youth in an evangelical suburban church." Do not use a complete sentence here. Keep your objective simple, short, and focused. A statement such as, "To pastor a church of any size anywhere" can come off sounding desperate, naive, or even arrogant. If you are open to any possibility, it is best not to include an objective.

Having a ministry objective will help you organize your entire resume. Deciding what information to include will be easier as you determine whether it supports your main objective. And to keep your resume at two to three pages in length, you will need help making such decisions.

Finally, a well-written ministry objective will assist you in determining what ministry positions to apply for. Flooding the mail with resumes is not effective and can even anger some search committees. These are busy people who don't appreciate wasting time on candidates who don't come close to their requirements. You should be open to God's leading in any case, but if he has given you a sense of "fit" for some type of ministry, you should allow such information to guide you in your journey.

The Mission-Vision Statement

Some pastors have developed a personal mission or vision statement. In chapter 2 we helped you with this. While you could include such a statement in your cover letter as a way to reveal your personal uniqueness, it may be placed here as well. Whatever you do, keep it concise. Using complete sentences here is suggested, as it will make your statement more personal.

Education

The placement of this information depends on where you are in your ministry career. If you have recently finished a degree, this could be the right place to enter it on your resume. If you are a seasoned veteran, it would be better to list your experience first and place education next. It is advisable to lead with your strengths, and if you are relatively inexperienced but have a newly minted degree from a great school, listing your educational accomplishments now is a good move.

Make sure degrees are listed from most to least recent. Include the degree, name of the school, and date of graduation from each. Undergraduate degrees should be indicated, but not high school. Listing your major emphasis may help you make your case. If, however, your undergraduate degree has no bearing on ministry, you may just want to list it as a B.A. or B.S. and leave it at that.

Then there's the question of seminars and workshops. This is where your ministry objective helps you out. Listing everything you have ever attended may irritate the search committee. Some seminars may represent philosophies of ministry that are controversial, and while you may not subscribe to their positions, it may appear that you do and cause a committee to "round file" your materials. Itemizing seminars that make you appear more fit for the position could be influential as the search committee deliberates. Use your judgment here, but keep these listings to a minimum.

Ministry Experience

You may express your work experience in a number of ways. Some people use a *functional* approach, emphasizing major skills and abilities they have developed over time in various venues. People changing focus in their ministries like this style because it highlights abilities that are transferable from one context to another. It is often used by older graduating seminarians who are moving from the secular marketplace to a pastoral setting. As well, it is helpful if you have been out of the job market for a while and have no current ministry position.

The *chronological* approach is most commonly used in ministry resumes (see sample at end of chapter), especially by those who are in a current position and looking to move on to a similar type of ministry in another setting. As with your education section, positions should be listed from most to least recent. Internships may be included if you are a recent graduate or have limited experience. However, seasoned pastors usually stick to paid positions only. There are various ways to list these. You can focus on the position title or the location. Either way, be consistent. List each entry and include the dates of service. After that, itemize your duties and accomplishments. For instance:

First Church of Our Savior — Stone Mountain, TX — 1998 to present
Pastor to single adults
- create and facilitate fellowship and outreach strategies
- teach Sunday single adult fellowship
- administer 30K budget and staff of 10 volunteers

Entries in this case are in the present tense because this ministry is still ongoing. All previous positions should be described in past tense, helping the reviewer to realize this is work already accomplished. On the next page are a few tips for this section of your resume.

Other Work Experience

If you have secular work experience, it is wise to include that information in your resume. In particular, you should highlight the responsibilities you had that relate to the kinds of skills necessary for the ministry position being sought. Such information will indicate that you can relate to the world your laity lives in every day. Keep this section short, for you are not applying for a like position. All rules for the section above apply here as well.

Philosophy of Ministry

Depending on how you expressed your personal mission-vision statement, you may not need to include a section on your philosophy of ministry. We do hear from committees, however, that they really appreciate applicants' views on ministry, particularly on the kind of work being advertised. Whether or not you include this in your resume, you will need to provide it sooner or later. Most churches send candidates long questionnaires with queries about doctrinal and philosophical issues. Similar questions are a normal part of ordination councils and denominational membership applications.

A philosophy of ministry is what we would call your "pastoral fingerprint." We each have a unique view of ministry. For instance, sharing the gospel is something we agree upon as important in our work. But deciding how to carry it out causes much disagreement, even strife. Are we believer-oriented or seeker-driven in our view of Sunday morning worship? Is preaching the gospel enough, or do

Making Your Ministry Experience Help You

- *Use action words.* Tell what you do — titles alone don't describe your actual work. Verbs are helpful. Check a thesaurus if you need help.
- *Use bullet points.* They are clean, to the point, and take up less space.
- *Use numbers sparingly.* The impression you give will create expectations. If you say, "Our youth group grew from 50 to 200 in one year," are you saying that will happen in the new setting, guaranteed? Find other ways to express growth.
- *Consolidate.* If you have served in one place but changed positions there, put all under the single heading of that one ministry to emphasize longevity even though positions have changed.

we also feed the hungry and house the homeless in our evangelistic endeavors? Providing a short synopsis of how you view a particular kind of ministry can be very helpful for you and those determining your fitness for their ministry position. One candidate looking for a pastorate put it this way:

> These are the four foundations I seek to constantly remind myself of and base ministry upon:
> The goal of ministry: Christian maturity in love
> The mission of ministry: evangelism
> The tools of ministry: God's Word and prayer
> The source of ministry: genuine spirituality

He added brief paragraphs to each item that included Scripture references. The effect was to provide a more accurate pastoral identity to those who might consider him.

Personal Information

Because ministerial resumes should be a bit more personal than business resumes, if you have space left, you may want to include a short testimony. List your spouse and kids if you are so blessed. Mention your hobbies and interests. Being an avid sportsman could warm the hearts of a search committee where such activity is cherished as a part of the local culture. Of course, you will want to be careful what you list here, making sure you don't "shoot yourself in the foot."

Do not list your height, weight, ethnic origin, or other more personal items. These are unnecessary and would only serve to distract the committee from focusing on your ministerial qualifications. One of my former students was looking for a pastoral position while still single. By not disclosing his marital status on his resume, he had the chance to talk with a committee member before divulging that detail. In the end, the church called him, even though they would have preferred a married man. Sometimes less is more.

References

Opinions vary as to whether personal references should be included in one's resume. Some believe "Available upon request" is enough. We think it is helpful to provide at least a few initial names on the document. Search committees *will* request them, so why not provide a few to start? You may be helping yourself, as committees may use a phone call to these individuals to determine if they want to take you to the next level. They would rather talk to someone else about you than interact with you personally during the initial stages. Direct contact with you might be too uncomfortable, as it could imply a level of commitment on their part that is unintended and hard to back away from.

You may want to consider providing a few names from this list:

- a current colleague in your present ministry (see discussion in chapter 7)
- a former seminary professor (if a more recent graduate)
- a longtime personal friend
- a minister friend serving in a similar position to the one you are seeking
- a former pastor under whom you were discipled
- a coworker or boss (if moving from marketplace to ministry)
- a civic leader who knows you and your ministry to the community
- an individual who knows you *and* the ministry to which you are applying

Of course, you will want to secure the permission of the people you use as references and fill them in on the nature of your job search, letting them know a call from a search committee could occur. Also, as you list them on your resume, include accurate contact information and a short phrase indicating their relationship to you (e.g., Dr. John Doe, seminary professor). Finally, you will want to create a master list of all your references for use when requested. Let others help you identify who these people might be. We can sometimes overlook great possibilities.

Miscellaneous Items

In addition to the above categories, you may desire to list various professional organizations and affiliations. These could be added to your education or ministry experience sections or listed in a separate category. As well, you may hold licenses, ordination, and/or certifications that are important in light of your desired position. Honors and awards often can be listed in appropriate places as well. What you do with such information depends on your own intuition and knowledge of the ministry to which you are applying. If you believe it will help serve the interests of yourself and the ministry in question, it is probably worth including.

Matters of Style

Now that you have worked through the various categories and determined what to include and how to express your content, we need to address a few issues related to style.

Photographs. Most job consultants will say, "No way." What if the employer doesn't like the fact that you're not wearing a tie or has a thing against creative hair colors? You could put yourself out of the running before the race even starts. On the other hand, we have heard from some ministry search committees that they appreciate a picture of the candidate. Again, it makes the process more personal and helps them "visualize" the possibilities. If you choose to include a photo, (1) make sure the picture is of professional quality, and (2) include your spouse if you are married. A photo can be printed on the resume itself and should appear on the first page in an upper corner. It should be relatively small (passport photo size).

Web friendliness. Make sure your cover letter and resume can be sent via email. Many church and parachurch ministries prefer receiving documents in this fashion. Format them as a PDF file so they cannot be altered and can easily be forwarded to committee members and printed.

Paper. For hard copies, use a heavy bond (25#) so they can be passed along without damage. And unless you want to give the search committee a good laugh (before they round file your stuff), stay away from vivid colors. Off-white or light gray shades look more professional.

Design. Allow for enough white space so the reader has places to rest the eye. Resumes that fill the page without adequate spacing can be confusing. Stay with a readable font (Times, Palatino, etc.) and use at least 10-point type. A lot of search committee members are midlifers who need reading glasses (but may be in denial). Be kind to them—keep the text readable.

However you construct your documents, be consistent. Make it easy for the reader to identify and follow the content. Don't get too creative. We have seen resumes that were so "over the top" that it was hard to focus on the information. With all the creative fonts and other possibilities afforded by software these days, it is tempting to be cute. Don't do it. Stay with the basics and do them well.

Accuracy. Incorrect spelling and grammar are unacceptable. Your cover letter and resume create a first impression. How you approach this task of preparing your resume is a reflection of how you conduct your ministry. Enlist others to proofread your documents. Set them aside for a few days and go over them again. You may be surprised at what you missed.

Buzz words. Use them sparingly if at all. Don't assume your reader knows what you mean by "seeker-driven." Even though such a term is commonplace in some circles, it may be a mystery in others. Use plain English and time-tested terminology.

Length. As we mentioned, a ministry resume can be two to three pages in length. Committees need good information and are willing to receive a few pages if that is what it takes. You won't have to crowd the page, and you will have space to include some of the helpful categories listed above that facilitate a fair presentation of your gifts, abilities, and experience.

The Doctrinal Statement

As you finalize your cover letter and resume, it might be a good idea to take another look at that doctrinal statement you affirmed once upon a time. Such a statement does the following:

- Provides a concise and clear statement of your core beliefs
- Establishes a means of checking the accuracy of your teaching ministry
- Protects you and your flock from error
- Helps establish fellowship among believers, and
- Assures a good theological "fit" as you interview for ministry opportunities

If you are part of a confessional denomination, you may want to revisit your doctrinal positions (Augsburg Confession, Westminster Confession, etc.) and see if any of these core beliefs have undergone adjustment. You may be more or less specific on some issues. Do not underestimate the importance of such detail. One new pastor thought he could "get along" in a denomination whose views of local church leadership differed from his. A year later he found himself on the road again, deeply hurt from the experience. Invest some time in this important document and recommit yourself to the truth it upholds.

Summing It All Up

As you travel to unknown places, a well-constructed cover letter and resume will give you identity, confidence, and a much better chance of being "let in" for that crucial face-to-face interview. Take time with this. Be yourself. Show your servant's heart as you help yourself and others plan for the future.

Having a colleague review your resume before you put it into circulation is generally a good idea. The last thing you want to do is get fifty copies of your resume printed on expensive paper and then discover a misspelled word or poor word choice. Another set of eyes reading it over could make all the difference in getting you to the next step on your career journey—a call from the search committee.

SAMPLE COVER LETTER

Date
Mr. Timothy Searcher, Chair
Third Church of Deadwood
1111 Fourth Avenue
Deadwood, AZ 00000

Dear Mr. Searcher,

Currently I am the pastor to singles at First Church of Our Savior in Stone Mountain, Texas. A mutual acquaintance of ours, Mrs. Alice Peterson, advised me of your open position for a pastor to adults at Third Church. I have carefully examined the ministry profile she provided and am sending my resume to you for consideration.

After seven years of challenging and fruitful singles ministry here at First Church, I have sensed a growing desire to minister to the broader context of the local congregation. Serving men and women of all ages and life circumstances has become a deep desire of mine, and I believe the position you describe represents a wonderful opportunity to pursue this service to Christ. You will note on my resume a wide array of ministerial experiences, all critical to adult ministry. I love teaching, leading, and building team ministries. I am comfortable with budget responsibilities and have found administration a growing area of enjoyment and effectiveness. My wife and I like to serve as a team and have developed a number of seminars and ministries for single and married adults. I trust you will find the following materials reflective of the strengths and perspectives you are seeking for this position.

Thank you for considering me as a potential candidate. I will look forward to speaking with you in the near future. May God grant you all grace and wisdom in this most important task of securing effective leadership.

Yours in Christ,

Signature
John Doe, M.Div.
Pastor to Singles
First Church of Our Savior
encl.: Resume

SAMPLE RESUME

John Doe
2222 Busy Lane • Stone Mountain, TX 00000
Home phone: (555) 555-5555 • Email: jdoe@xxxxx.com

Ministry Objective

To create and administer an innovative program for adults in an evangelical suburban church.

Education

Great Theological Seminary: M.Div. in Pastoral Studies, 1998
Iowa State University: B.A. in Music, 1994

Ministry Experience

First Church of Our Savior   Stone Mountain, TX   1998 to present
Pastor to single adults

- Create and facilitate fellowship and outreach strategies for singles
- Teach Sunday single adult fellowship
- Administer 30K budget and staff of 10 volunteers
- Develop and lead overseas adult mission projects
- Administer sacraments and preach as requested by senior pastor
- Serve as senior staff elder on church board
- Counsel single and married adults in relational, marital, and family issues
- Train and lead ministry teams for local community service projects
- Develop and teach singles and marriage seminars

Seminary Ridge Bible Church   Coldwater, MI   1994 to 1998
Youth pastor — part-time — (junior and senior high)

- Taught at weekly Sunday morning youth service
- Created and trained worship teams for youth service
- Developed and planned series of annual summer and winter retreats
- Trained youth for local church and community service projects
- Established parent advisory group
- Provided counseling resources for youth
- Planned and facilitated campus outreach events at local high schools

Other Work Experience

Greater Iowa Adult Learning Center   Ames, IA   1991 to 1994
Music instructor — part-time

- Arranged weekly vocal and instrumental classes for adult learners
- Taught lessons in brass instruments
- Conducted annual Christmas concert for local community
- Coordinated programs with local school and community leaders

Philosophy of Ministry

I have come to embrace the following as crucial to effective and Christ-honoring ministry:

- A growing intimacy with my Lord Jesus Christ
- A deepening love for family and friends
- A desire to make people the priority over programs
- A commitment to the rigors of fruitful process
- A grounding of ministry in the grace of God
- A desire to help God's people enjoy lives of victory in Jesus Christ

Personal

Raised in a wonderful Christian home, I was led to Christ at an early age. As college progressed, I sensed God's call to full-time ministry. He blessed me with my wife, Jane, in 1996 and gave us twin daughters in 1999. I enjoy reading historical fiction, woodworking, and participating in musical groups. Our family enjoys camping and exploring the great outdoors.

References

Rev. Alan Speaker (senior pastor of First Church of Our Savior)
    3333 Busier Lane   Home phone: (555) 555-5555
    Stone Mountain, TX 00000   Email: alans@xxxxx.com

Ms. Cheryl Teacher (volunteer in singles ministry at First Church of Our Savior)
    4444 Balanced Street   Home phone: (555) 555-5555
    Stone Mountain, TX 00000   Email: cherylt@xxxxx.com

Dr. Theo Lecturer (seminary professor and longtime friend)
    5555 Academic Circle   Home phone: (555) 555-5555
    Grand Rapids, MI 00000   Email: doctheo@xxxxx.com

CHAPTER 13

COMMUNICATING YOUR TRAVEL PLANS

Networking with Friends and Colleagues

MICK BOERSMA

If one falls down,
his friend can help him up.
But pity the man who falls
and has no one to help him up!
Ecclesiastes 4:10 NIV

Traveling to a place you have never been before is exciting and scary. Our first trip to Europe was both. Where to stay? What to see? How to get from here to there? All these questions and more seemed daunting as we began to plan our itinerary. But as we reached out to a network of friends and colleagues around the world through emails and phone calls, we found the answers we needed, and our travel planning was no longer overwhelming. Our friends helped make London, Amsterdam, Brussels, and Paris wonderful experiences to last a lifetime.

At this point in your journey, you have decided to consider a new place of ministry. Your resume has been updated, and you are eager to see what's out there. The temptation is to make a list of your contacts and send them your resume, along with a request to help you identify job possibilities. While this is certainly a good idea, it doesn't really define what effective networking is all about. As Katharine Hansen writes in her excellent book *A Foot in the Door*, "Networking doesn't mean asking everyone you run into if he or she knows where the job openings are. It means establishing relationships so that you can enlist support and comfortably ask for ideas, advice, and referrals to those with hiring power."[1]

Putting your name out to any number of casual acquaintances or strangers will get you little, if anything. As with most things, it's quality, not quantity that makes the difference. We need to take a closer look at our networking before we go out there and work it. In this chapter we will focus on this task, identify the great benefits of working hard on relationships, and show you how to build a life-long and growing network that will not only enhance your job search but enrich your ministry wherever you serve.

Why You Need to Be a Network Builder

If you are like a lot of ministers, you are realizing right now that you don't have a very good network to utilize in your job search. Many serve in places where ongoing contact with others familiar with the ministry world is difficult due to location, lack of denominational connection, absence of other staff, or failure to invest in meaningful connections over the long haul. Your "net" is out there but may need some "work." And the investment is well worth it. Let's consider a number of benefits of building and maintaining a solid network.

You're not alone. As we counsel students and alumni, they often mention their relief in knowing they aren't the only one dealing with a certain fear, failure, or dilemma. Having friends here and there who love you and know your circumstances is a wonderful gift. Local ministerial groups, alumni friends, and many others can combine to give you a safety net of encouragement and resources.

Pastors, especially senior and solo, are often loners and not surprisingly report loneliness as a problem they and their spouses face. As the son of an Iowa farmer, I grew up to be independent and carried that independence right into the pastorate. It took several years for me to realize the blessing of having a network. My first ministry would have been more effective had I worked harder at networking. Studies have shown that such arrangements are descriptive of pastors who are more satisfied with ministry than those without such support.[2]

You're not anonymous. We don't have to tell you that for every open ministry position there are quite a few applicants. One Colorado search chairman told of their committee receiving 450 resumes. It's a buyer's market and has been for some years. How do you stand out among the flood of job seekers? Churches are looking for the right person, not just anybody who can fill the position. They are interested in character and the right chemistry, and they will wait until they find it.

Therefore, having network buddies who really know you is a powerful asset in the job search. You become real, not just another name on a resume. I was once pastoring in a small town in rural Washington, yet I was chosen to join the faculty of Talbot School of Theology in 1986. How did that happen? It came about through networking.

I was just one of hundreds of guys who would have loved this job. Yes, the Lord had his hand in it the whole way. But he used one of my former professors to set the process in motion. I regularly called Dr. Glenn O'Neal during those eleven years, sharing problems, seeking advice, and passing along victories. He brought my prayer requests to the faculty meetings.

When in 1985 I sensed God's call to further my education, I flew down to Southern California to look for work and housing. As part of that trip, the faculty met with me, whereupon I shared my desire for teaching. Upon my return to Washington, the phone rang. One of the faculty asked if I would be willing to teach one class, since I'd be moving down there anyway. That first year back found me building houses in the daytime and teaching a course in the evening. The following year I was hired full-time. No doctoral degree, no seminary teaching experience, no books written. But there was Dr. O'Neal, a wise, trusted, and gracious friend who raised my name up to his colleagues. Networking made all the difference.

You're not limited. Even though we live in a global era, we live and work in a relatively confined context. Ministry demands make it that way. So when we start looking for a new destination, our frames of reference can keep us from even knowing about great possibilities in other geographical, denominational, or ministerial settings. When you are part of a healthy network, though, you do have access to a greater field of choices.

From 65 to 75 percent of all jobs are never advertised.[3] We are finding that churches increasingly desire that their positions not be posted on a website, but rather that they receive a few good names to pursue. So there are great opportunities out there you will find only through networking. Our study, as we saw earlier, shows how effective this can be for the job seeker.

Figure 13.1, Q11: How did you find your current ministry?

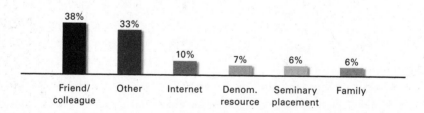

If we consider denominational and family resources in terms of people, not job sites, it becomes clear that well over half of the pastors in the survey found their jobs through network relationships.

One West Coast pastor was seeking a particular kind of worship-teaching ministry for several months. He was beginning to wonder if such a job even existed. Then a friend living in Pennsylvania called him. It seemed his church, a very healthy and growing congregation of 2,500, was looking for someone to lead a ministry of this sort. Now he lives in a beautiful city north of Philadelphia, enjoying a rich and fulfilling ministry among a supportive staff. His world was bigger than he imagined and his dream job did exist.

You're not blind. We will talk more about this in chapter 18, but it is important here to note that having solid relationships with people in other places can expand your field of vision. It's like having "operatives" who can give you good information about a church, denomination, or cultural context. One of the great benefits of developing a variety of relationships is this dividend of being able to see more clearly into the unfamiliar terrain that is common to all ministries.

Some years ago a pastor was considering a senior pastorate in another city. He had received materials from the church describing their demographics and vision for the future. It was a long-standing church of about 150 people. They said they wanted to reach out and meet the twenty-first century head-on. He called and asked what I thought, since I had served there as an interim pastor for several months. Assuring him that they were great people with deep love for one another, I told him they did not seem prepared to pay the price of reaching out beyond their walls. They may have thought they were ready, but I suspected differently.

This brother, who was looking for a church that wanted to break out and become a large, modern congregation, decided to accept their offer. A little over two years later the church dissolved and sold their facility to a growing fellowship that had been renting their building. He received some good insight from me and others but chose to hope for the best. It could have happened but didn't. In the end he realized his misdirected optimism and went on to another fruitful ministry.

12 Mistakes That Stall a Job Search

1. Having a bad attitude
2. Thinking something else will come along
3. Thinking someone else will find you a job
4. Thinking you're more marketable than you are
5. Taking rejection personally
6. Acting desperate
7. Shooting too high (or too low)
8. Looking for a job rather than a good fit
9. Launching a job campaign before you know who you are and what you want to do
10. Asking for "a job" instead of asking for advice, ideas, and referrals
11. Not preparing for interviews
12. Hard-selling (coming on too strong)

You're not naive. Career advisor William Frank shares an insightful list of job-hunting mistakes (see sidebar on page 179).[4] A lot of frustration can be avoided by heeding these pointers.

One mistake that networking can help you with is "shooting too high (or too low)." It's one thing to lose out as number two in a candidate run-off, but approaching ministry positions that are clearly not a good fit only produces feelings of rejection and hopelessness.

One new seminary graduate was applying for the senior pastor position in churches averaging over three hundred in worship attendance. He wasn't getting very much action, so he arranged to come to my office for some placement help. It turns out he was single, under thirty, with no experience in the pulpit or as a minister to adults. The puzzle was solved quickly. He was living in a fantasy world and needed some help coming back to earth. Through a few conversations, he came to realize his need to start by applying for a youth position. He did this, had a blessed ministry, found a wife, had some kids, and is today enjoying a fruitful ministry as a senior pastor and part-time seminary professor. All he needed was a friend who could help him see the possibilities more realistically.

We are not saying God cannot bring you to amazing places regardless of your credentials. But it is wise to seek an abundance of counselors, for through them he keeps us from acting foolishly (Prov. 11:14).

You're not stagnant. "Networking Made Easy" was the title of a newspaper article that asserted that a local networking breakfast sponsored by the chamber of commerce "is the best investment any company can make in growing its business, expanding its client base and connecting with potential purchasers of its product."[5] The world of business recognizes that connecting with key people can keep an enterprise growing. Ministers can benefit by thinking the same way. We sometimes experience a waning of enthusiasm about ministry, getting into a set of habits and approaches that become comfortable but ineffective. Our preaching gets a bit too predictable. Vision fades and the daily grind sets in. Being part of a network of other ministry professionals through personal contact, conferences, and educational venues (such as doctor of ministry programs) can inspire us to renewed commitment to the meaningful work of pastoral ministry.

You're not seen as desperate. Like it or not, a lot of employers, especially church search committees, are cautious about people seeking a job. Katharine Hansen tells it straight when she writes, "People look for jobs, many employers believe, because they are unhappy losers, job-hoppers, or unproductive malcontents who blame poor performance on their employers and believe switching jobs will solve their problems."[6] We're hopeful that none of these apply to you now that you've worked through chapter 6.

In our work with churches we are seeing an increase in this kind of sentiment, and both of us spend a lot of time on the phone with church leaders giving them a "name or two" of potential candidates. We often mention the names of pastors who have established relationships with us and have been keeping in touch. Without such networking you may appear frantic for a job, even though that may not be the case. How to prevent this by building a great lifelong network is our next assignment.

Building a Great Network

By now you are probably saying to yourself, "Yeah, I really want all those benefits of being networked, but how do I do it?" As with anything that is worthwhile, you have to be willing to work hard. Following are the key requirements you will have to fulfill to assure success.

Initiative

There is no way to develop an effective network without being intentional about it. Relationships don't just happen. We have to purpose to invest ourselves in others in order to enjoy the benefits. We have found that not all ministers are naturally outgoing. Many are shy by nature and find interacting with strangers at a conference or joining a ministerial group quite intimidating. If you are going to have a great network, however, you have to find a way past such misgivings and put yourself out there.

It might help to remember that networking is not about asking for a job, but about getting to know others in order to build mutually beneficial resources for life and service. In that sense, it's really just about connecting with others in meaningful ways, which is at the heart of pastoral work. Also, there are a lot of people in your life you know well with whom you are comfortable sharing your thoughts and feelings. In our survey, we asked pastors which resources were most helpful to them when deciding about a career move. Their responses can be seen in figure 13.2. All of these possibilities require initiative but are well within anyone's comfort zone.

Figure 13.2, Q17: When you faced a decision about making a career move, which of the following resources were the most helpful to you?

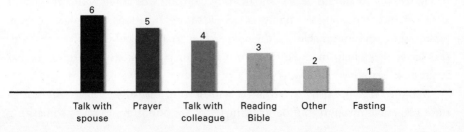

6	5	4	3	2	1
Talk with spouse	Prayer	Talk with colleague	Reading Bible	Other	Fasting

God is sovereign in the calling and sending of his servants, but we have to do our part in the process as well. That includes taking the initiative for your search. Don't think that others will get you a new position or that God will drop it out of the sky. This journey requires your willingness to invest personally and purposely in the details.

A Servant's Heart

Entering into networking relationships gives us an opportunity to serve the needs of others while we ourselves are blessed by their serving us. Taking a genuine interest in others with whom we network is essential. We want to avoid what one Christian businessman finds common in the world of work where everyone is out for him- or herself, "objectifying people, cheapening God's children, perhaps marring the cause of Christ in the process."[7] This type of attitude will only hurt you in the "small world" of Christian ministry. When others hear about your loving and supportive relationships, your stock will rise in the marketplace of pastoral service.

Taking Time

If you're in a hurry to find a position, taking the time to network is a hard pill to swallow. As we mentioned before, networking is a process that needs to be going on over the long haul. In ministry we get so busy with our obligations that purposeful expenditures of time are sometimes overlooked. It's a good idea to put ministerial and denominational meetings, conferences, and ongoing educational opportunities on your to-do list, making them a regular part of your pastoral duties. Through time you will develop a strategic and mutually edifying web of relationships to enhance your present ministry and to provide links for future job searches.

Planning

Successful traveling requires good preparation. The following are some beneficial steps you can take to enhance your networking efforts.

Prepare a networking letter. A networking letter is designed to ask your friends and others for their assistance in your job search by connecting you with people and ministry opportunities. Somewhat like your cover letter (see chapter 12), this concise, one-page document should briefly summarize your personal sense of mission, key strengths, and accomplishments and describe the kind of ministry you're seeking. It should be accompanied by your resume along with a request to review it and send along any names of people or organizations that might provide potential opportunities. Unlike the cover letter to a particular ministry setting, this letter seeks help in expanding your field of possibilities through personal requests to people you know.

Research new contacts received. You will need to investigate the new connections you make through your networking letter. It's important to know something about the new contact and the ministries they represent when you interact with them. The Internet can be a great vehicle for such investigation, as well as your personal friends who alerted you to individuals or organizations in the first place. Be sure to keep good records throughout the entire process.

Develop good open-ended questions. Once you do interact with your growing network, you will want to have crafted a number of helpful questions designed to discover the nature of the person and ministry with which they are associated. For example, you could ask a denominational representative, "What's the biggest challenge your denomination is facing right now?" A pastor of a large congregation could respond to "What, in your opinion, are the most significant must-haves for anyone seeking an associate pastoral position?" The interviewing questions listed in chapter 17 can give you additional ideas as to how these could be framed. Having a few good queries in your pocket will be a great help in many settings and circumstances.

Know what you want to accomplish with each contact. Whether face-to-face (best), through letter (good), or phone (okay), have in mind your goal for that interaction. It may be to get casually acquainted or to share a good meal and learn of one another's ministry. You may want to leave that person with a specific request to consider you as a potential staff member. Then again, the whole purpose may be to gain referrals from your new friend, along with his or her support. Since we are dealing with relationships here, the objectives will be varied and part of a step-by-step process of deepening collegiality.

Have your written materials at hand. When you meet with someone, you will want to make sure you leave them with enough information of the right kind so they can be of help to you once you part ways. Such items as your networking letter, resume, and business card will equip your new acquaintance with the essential stuff. If something is not in writing, it doesn't really exist. So preparing a high-quality networking letter, resume, and business card (optional) is critical to greasing the wheels of your network.

Send a follow-up thank-you letter. In a world of electronic communications, the personal thank-you note, written on real paper and sent by "snail mail" really means a lot to people. Think of the last time you received one—and how it made you feel. Be grateful to those who have taken the time and effort to help you along on your trip. Inform them of your progress, continue to seek their wisdom, and alert them when you find a new position. Such courtesy will serve you and them well in the future.

Awareness

When you started reading this chapter, you most likely were hoping to find a list of places to send your resume to get your foot in the door. Well, that time has finally come. We hope you are convinced that networking is about building and maintaining mutually beneficial relationships. Now you need an awareness of where such connections can be established. Here is our list; it may suggest others to you.

People

Family. Regardless of the circumstances surrounding your desire to find a new ministry, transitions are stressful. The love of family goes a long way in moderating that pressure. And it is not impossible that some close or distant relative could have some good leads for you. It is interesting to speculate why David sent his parents to Moab while King Saul was after his life (1 Sam. 22:3–4). Could it be because David's great-grandmother was Ruth the *Moabitess*? It hardly seems coincidental. Always consider your family as a divine resource.

Friends. You may have good friends scattered about the globe who are involved in or certainly aware of ministry opportunities. They need not be pastors themselves. Most are probably in churches and have their own friends who are involved in still others. These are people who love you and would want to support you with prayer, advice, referrals, and in some instances even financial help.

Ministry colleagues. Probably no one can empathize with your struggles like another pastor. During my decade as a senior pastor in Washington state, a good friend who pastored two hours west of me would visit every month for a couple of days. We'd share our burdens, laugh, cry, and talk ministry. When I moved down to Southern California in 1985, he factored into my job search and remains a dear friend—part of my "A list" when I need some perspective and encouragement.

Mentors. I like this definition of mentoring: "a relational experience in which one person empowers another by sharing God-given resources."[8] If you are blessed, you have one or two people like this in your network. They may include seminary faculty, a seasoned pastor, or parent—the possibilities are many. We serve as mentors to some of our alumni and find it a delight to hear their stories and share in their travels.

Alumni friends. Some seminaries do better than others in helping former students keep in touch with one another. But this is largely a task you need to take on yourself. We find that once graduated, seminarians do a lot of moving around, especially in the early years. It's a challenge to keep track of where they are and what they're doing. Decide that you will keep up with those men and women with whom you have established a solid acquaintance. They will be to you an army of peer mentors and travel companions who will make your journey more enlightened and hopeful. And they will most likely have some great contacts for you to explore.

Denominational leaders. It is not necessary to belong to a particular denomination in order to include their leaders in your network. In my last year of seminary, my wife and I met the regional director of the Evangelical Free Church of Canada in British Columbia. I was not licensed or ordained yet, but we desired to know more about the possibilities in Canada. During what could be called an "informational interview," we shared our calling and desire to pastor a local congregation. Though we didn't receive a call to one of his churches then, two years later he called and asked if we would like to consider a couple of options near Vancouver. Although we were happy to stay put, we saw the value of that long-ago meeting.

Search committee members. In your travels you will meet a lot of great people in search committees even if you don't end up being their candidate. Make it a point to thank them for their time and attention, and then ask them to keep you in mind as they talk to friends and family in other churches. You may not be the right fit for their congregation but just the ticket for one they know about elsewhere. Search committees like getting names from other committees because it saves them time. Who wouldn't want a list of the top five possibilities from another church's search process? So keep in touch with those people who encouraged you along the way, and give them the information they need to be an advocate for you with those in that special fraternity of pastoral search committees.

Places

Ministerial associations. While you may not think you have the time for such things, ministerial meetings, whether local or denominational, can be a great source of support. "People of the cloth" enjoy a level of mutual understanding that is truly refreshing and encouraging. In addition, there are a number of professional organizations related to various specialized areas of ministry. Groups like Leadership Network (www.leadnet.org; created in 1984 to serve senior pastors of large congregations), the Children's Christian Ministry Association (www.ccma-network.com), and a host of other specialized groups offer excellent networking opportunities.

Ministry conferences. Pastors' conferences abound, many related to the types of associations mentioned above. Ministers of all descriptions can benefit from gatherings like the National Pastors Convention, held yearly and sponsored by Zondervan, in partnership with Leadership and InterVarsity Press. Inner-city youth workers can enjoy conferences like those sponsored by Urban Youth Workers Institute, based in Buena Park, California (www.uywi.org).

Pastors interested in the prospect of teaching in college or seminary settings would do well to attend conferences where leaders of such institutions tend to gather. Our seminary has secured a number of professors as a result of continued networking at the Evangelical Theological Society annual conferences.

The Internet. The advent of the Internet has exponentially increased the networking capability of people around the world. Trying to decide where to look can be a bit overwhelming, however. We suggest you include your seminary placement service, along with those of other like-minded schools having an "open" site (nonalumni are allowed to access listings). Many include a list of other Web locations where ministry opportunities are listed, such as ChurchStaffing.com. Though only 10 percent of the pastors in our survey reported finding their current position through the Internet, 19 percent started their search at the computer, and it remains a great place to see what's out there and identify potential ministries.

Professional search firms. In chapter 15 you will find more about utilizing the professional search firm. If you have the desire and resources, they can be of great assistance in your journey. Like travel agents, they know what's available and have methods of helping you with a host of issues related to the pastoral transition process.

Community. It would be a big mistake not to include individuals and organizations located in your immediate community. As mentioned in chapter 12, a good reference from a businessperson or local leader would add significantly to your search documents. You may consider joining the Rotary, the Exchange Club, the Kiwanis, or some other community group dedicated to the betterment of the community at large. One Oregon pastor loved to restore classic hot rods and joined the local car club. He didn't advertise his pastor status, but he became their unofficial chaplain and enjoyed several years of good fun and great fellowship with these men and women.

Travel Warning!

You already know that confidentiality is a big issue at this point in your journey. If you are like the 51 percent of pastors in our survey who wouldn't tell their present ministry they were searching until they were assured of a new position, you will have to emphasize the need for tight lips among your network. But that's hard to manage, since you're asking people to spread the word that you're available. So, once you start down this road, be prepared to get wind of a certain smell—those bridges burning behind you.

But, if your heart is set on a move, that won't matter in the long term. It might make your leaving a bit more complicated, but in the end you will have made your destination—to honor the Lord and his call on your life. If anything is worth the risk, that would be it.

CHAPTER 14

UNEXPECTED DETOURS

Exploring the Ins and Outs of Midlife Career Change

MICHAEL ANTHONY

As for the days of our life, they contain seventy years,
Or if due to strength, eighty years,
Yet their pride is but labor and sorrow;
For soon it is gone and we fly away....
So teach us to number our days,
That we may present to You a heart of wisdom.
Psalm 90:10, 12

One of my areas of academic expertise is management and organizational planning. I am a planner by nature, and I function best when things go according to plan. When it comes to traveling, especially with other people in a Third World country, I prefer not to get hit with too many surprises. With that in mind, you can imagine how I felt when I led a team of twenty college students to Haiti to conduct famine relief in the late 1980s. Times were tense in Haiti, with talks of anarchy and revolt bubbling to the surface. We boarded our plane in Los Angeles at midnight, expecting to have a short layover in Miami and be on the ground in Port au Prince by midafternoon. We would load our equipment onto several trucks waiting for us at the airport and quickly head up into the interior plateau region before darkness fell over the city.

Unbeknownst to us as we flew across the United States that night, the Haitian government would be thrown into turmoil from a coup attempt. Shooting erupted in the capital, and bodies were lying in the streets. Eastern Airlines refused to travel to Port au Prince and canceled all flights for the foreseeable future. When I arrived in Miami with my team, I was pretty anxious about having all my plans fall apart halfway there. Eastern Airlines tried to get us to board a flight that afternoon and return home. I refused. We spent the rest of the day and most of that evening at a hotel trying to come up with plan B. I kept asking myself, "How could God bring us to this point?" We had spent months raising the necessary funds, training as a team, and building significant prayer support. "Why, God? What are you thinking?" I prayed.

I must have made a hundred phone calls to friends, trying to come up with another option. By dawn I had a plan. If we could get Eastern Airlines to agree to reroute our destination to Santo Domingo, the capital city of the Dominican Republic, we could partner with Youth For Christ on a construction project they were conducting in a remote rural area. Understand what was about to happen. I'd never been to the Dominican Republic before. I'd never met the man who said he could provide for our team. I didn't know where we were going to sleep or what kind of project we would be working on. Was I crazy for thinking God had something else he wanted us to do?

The next morning I was able to convince Eastern Airlines to change our tickets at the last minute, and as we boarded the plane, one of the students looked at me with a good deal of anxiety and asked, "Dr. Anthony, is this God's will?" It was a good question! I told him that I didn't know but that I could probably answer that question on the way home in ten days.

The trip was a success, and I have returned to the Dominican Republic with other teams and for training conferences about fifteen times since that experience. It was God's will, but the midcourse adjustment was not without significant risk, soul searching, and reaching out in faith to find God's will.

You may be feeling that same level of stress right now. You're traveling with your family team, trying to figure out what God has in mind for you at this midlife season. Your plans have radically changed, and you aren't sure what direction to take. If this describes your situation, this chapter is for you.

This chapter is designed with two kinds of ministry leaders in mind. First, I want to address those who are starting out in a career or vocational ministry in midlife. You're asking questions, such as, "What is God doing with my life? Can this really be happening to me? I never thought I'd consider going into the ministry at this stage of my life journey."

You may also be traveling with a spouse who is asking her or his own set of questions: "Is this God's will for our lives, and how can you be so sure? I never married a seminary student, and I sure never thought I'd end up as a pastor's spouse. This isn't the kind of direction I thought I'd be going when I said, 'I do,' some years ago."

The second kind of ministry leader this chapter is written for is the pastor who is approaching midlife in ministry and is suddenly coming face-to-face with some significant issues that have the potential of bringing about major life change. Midlife effects all of us in different ways, and much has been written to help guide us through this season. However, as we approach midlife as a pastor, we face unique situations that need to be addressed. Navigating the midlife pastorate may require some course adjustments and retooling. You have aging parents to care for, new grandchildren you want to be near, health considerations, and perhaps a family business that's calling you to reconsider your choice of pastoral ministry. Midlife for you comes with a good many concerns that need to be addressed.

Metaphors of Midlife: Stages, Eras, and Passages

Different authors use varying metaphors to define and describe midlife. The renowned psychoanalyst Erik Erikson divided the human life span into eight stages. The first five deal with birth through adolescence. The last three focus on adulthood: early, middle, and later. Midlife is characterized by those who develop intimate relationships with others and make meaningful contributions to those in their community. Those at midlife who are unable to do this may experience a sense of personal and relational stagnation.[1]

Daniel Levinson wrote a popular book in the late 1970s titled *The Seasons of a Man's Life*. He divides the life span into four eras. The third era is labeled "midlife" and encompasses those between forty and sixty years of age. It is a season marked by deep personal questioning and reflection. People in midlife ask questions about life's meaning and purpose. Are they happy with life at this point, and what, if anything, needs to change before they move into the final era? For 80 percent of the men interviewed in his book, this era was accompanied by moderate or severe crisis.[2]

Perhaps one of the most popular authors to write about midlife is Gail Sheehy, whose bestseller *Passages* was published in 1974.[3] Sheehy based her own theory of midlife development on the contributions of Erikson, Levinson, and Roger Gould. She didn't like using *crisis* to describe midlife, as she found it to be too pejorative. She preferred to use *passage* as a term to describe the various stages of human development. Midlife for men involved separating from parents and embracing one's own life course. Healthy men were also able to invest in activities beyond themselves that brought value to those in the community around them.

Each of these popular theorists identifies a distinct period of time known as midlife. Although he or she may have different ideas about when midlife begins and ends, each researcher sees a distinct set of behaviors characterizing people in their midlife years. Knowing what is normative for men and women in this critical life juncture is essential for ministry leaders. Later in the chapter, I briefly detail these normative character qualities as they relate to your context of ministry calling.

Called to Ministry at Midlife

God seems to revel in selecting for pastoral service those who could have been voted "Least Likely to Enter the Ministry." Time and again throughout history, men and women have been busy minding their own business when suddenly God has shown up and rocked their world with a divine appointment—one that couldn't be ignored or denied. Moses received his appointment while herding sheep; Jonah never expected God to call him either. Jesus couldn't have picked a more unlikely group of followers than the Twelve. Likewise, I doubt Saul expected God to appear to him on the dusty road to Damascus. Speaking of this, Eddie Gibbs writes:

> For too long the church has operated with a long list of requirements that an individual must meet in order to be considered for leadership. This flies in the face of the evidence of how significant leaders have emerged among the people of God over the course of history. Jesus did not start out with such a list; otherwise He would not have chosen any of His original team of disciples. Instead He selected unlikely individuals who were teachable and whose lives He could shape through His presence among them.[4]

If you're sensing God's call and you're between thirty-five and fifty-five years old, you certainly aren't alone on this journey. Surprisingly, many men and women have decided to transition from their previous careers and begin preparing to enter the ministry during their midlife years. For many, life in the corporate world didn't provide the level of deep satisfaction they were expecting.

Biblical Leaders Called after Midlife

Noah was 500 years old when he began his work on the ark. Since he lived to the age of 950, it can be said that he began his ministry in midlife.

Moses was eighty when he began his ministry assignment of leading God's people out of Egypt.

Joshua was at least seventy when Moses commissioned him to lead the nation of Israel.

Caleb was eighty-five years old when he told Joshua, "Give me this hill country" (Josh. 14:12), even though he knew it would take strength beyond his own to finish the task of inhabiting the land.

Sure, they enjoyed the trappings of affluence—the corner office, administrative assistants to order around, and the occasional business trip complete with hotels and restaurants. But ask anyone who has lived that lifestyle for any length of time, and he or she will tell you the thrill wears off quickly. Living out of a suitcase and trying to stay connected to young children from 35,000 feet is no fun at all. For these reasons—and a hundred more—people are reassessing their original vocational choice.

These individuals are known as "second-career clergy" because they have decided to enter the professional ministry later in life after their first career of choice. Many of these midlifers will apply to attend a seminary to receive graduate-level instruction. Half of all theology students planning on becoming pastors in the United States and Canada are thirty-five years old or older, so they won't be alone.[5] Nationwide, 56 percent of senior or sole pastors of congregations came into their ministry after serving in another career for at least five years. Many of them were school teachers or retired military who simply wanted to give God their years of service. When such midlifers receive a call from God, they often seek out graduate theological training.

Midlife seminary students are becoming an increasingly large percentage of the population, as evidence suggests in the sidebar below.[6] Thirty years ago seminary students came to the clergy at an average age of twenty-seven. Today the average age is thirty-five and rising. Seventy-two percent of Protestant pastors started in another career, and most denominations and faiths report an influx of older students.[7]

Changing one's focus and starting a graduate degree, however, will not suddenly make life more meaningful and complete. Leaving the security of a paying career to reenter the halls of academia is unsettling for most returning students. These transition years can be a very difficult change for some. "Different adjustments are required of the midlife adult who becomes unemployed, perhaps for

Midlife Pastors in Training

From 1991 through 2001, students in their forties constituted the fastest-growing age group among Christian theological students.
Currently, 25 percent of male students and nearly half of all female students who are pursuing the M.Div. degree are over forty.
Nearly one-third of students pursuing an M.Div. are women. In the fifty-or-older age group, female students outnumber men.

the first time ever. This may be the most difficult time of life to be unemployed if one has been employed steadily and work is a central part of the individual's identity. . . . Yet some find that unemployment gives them the opportunity to rethink the kind of work they want to do and eventually move in a more satisfying direction."[8] As a result, they come out of seminary with both theological training and a renewed passion for impacting the world in the name of Christ.

If you find yourself on this quest, I suggest you give some serious consideration to your calling (1 Cor. 1:26). Part 1 of this book will become your transition guide. Take the time to be sure your spouse is on the same page and that both of you are committed to your new career direction. If your spouse isn't ready to make the move, then see that as a "wait" sign from God and pray for him to prepare the way for you. If this is God's will, he will need to open some doors and change a few hearts to make your change possible. He is capable of doing that, but it may be on a different timetable from what you expect.

You will also want to partner with someone willing to mentor you in ministry. Meet with your pastor and share your heart about the direction you feel God is calling you to take. Ask for his or her advice and counsel about what the next steps should be. Don't be surprised if he or she offers you a ministry position, probably on a volunteer basis. This will give you an opportunity to see and experience the ministry from an insider's point of view. Experiencing ministry leadership is probably the best way to know if God has placed a call on your life. It will provide you with an opportunity to discover and develop your giftedness and allow you to explore areas where you may want to serve in a leadership role.

Don't be alarmed if the first few experiences don't work out as well as you had hoped. It takes some time to find the right fit. Just because you don't feel comfortable teaching high-energy middle school students doesn't mean you won't make an excellent Bible teacher for older adults. It usually takes a while to find the right place of service. Not all ministries happen in the local church, and that may take some getting used to if all you have ever known about ministry is the local church. God may have something for you on the mission field where your unique primary career is in desperate need — only now you can do it with a direct effect on building his kingdom. Christian camps, schools, and other parachurch ministries are also great alternatives for people entering the ministry during midlife.

Clergy Midlife Concerns

The term *midlife* is often associated with *crisis*. Most of the popular literature would have us believe that at the age of thirty-five we will awaken one morning with a strange desire to leave our career, abandon our family, buy a red sports car, and drive off into the sunset with someone half our age. It's as if we are destined to lose our minds and any semblance of rational thought. And although there may be examples of such events occurring, they are definitely the exception rather than the norm. Reality for most men and women at this season of life is anything but this Hollywood portrayal. Midlife can be particularly troublesome to one's marriage because of the complexities of interpersonal relationships involved.

Most marriages begin with great dreams and hopes of life fulfillment on the part of both the husband and the wife. Somewhere along the way, love sometimes gets lost and isn't even missed. Suddenly the stark loneliness of realizing that you are starving to death for intimacy within the most intimate of relationships becomes reality when you need him (or her) and you have forgotten how to reach out.

Middle age is a difficult time for both men and women. A person between the ages of thirty-five and fifty-five has been portrayed as one trying to walk with children hanging around his neck and parents riding on his back. Midlife is a crisis-ridden time. You wonder if your kids will make it on their own, and you try to figure out how to make life as pleasant and easy for elderly parents as possible. There seems to be no space between the two generations; you are being squeezed in the middle.[9]

This season of adulthood is characterized by a deep sense of contemplative thought concerning life's purpose. By now one's marriage and first career have been experienced, and expectations that haven't been met may lead to disappointment and despair. A desire to try something new before "it's too late" makes some men and women panic as they calculate the time left in their midlife.

The bottom line is that midlife is all about acknowledging change. Our bodies and our appearance begin to change. Children grow up and leave home on their quest to achieve their life's purposes. Communities and neighborhoods change. Parents experience life-threatening illnesses or die, causing us to reflect on our own mortality. Retirement planning now becomes an important event that can no longer be postponed. The typical midlife crisis is nothing more than our effort to take control of things that we have so little control over. If we can adapt to these changes and remain flexible, we can avoid some of the stereotypical responses associated with those who have failed to navigate this portion of the journey.[10]

In the following pages, I briefly discuss the common changes that occur during midlife so that readers might receive some comfort in knowing that what they are experiencing is common to all men and women passing through this stage of life.

Physical Changes

As one author puts it, "When you don't rush the net as you used to in a game of tennis, it may mean that you are terribly out of shape, or it just might indicate that the physical changes of middle life are beginning to show."[11] More is known about the physical changes that will occur during this season of life than the others that are to follow.

For men, the changes may include a receding hairline, graying hair, dry skin, liver spots on the skin, weakened eyesight, reduced endurance, intermittent sleep habits, weight gain, mild forgetfulness, prostate problems, increased snoring, high blood pressure, and an increased risk of stroke and heart disease. Muscle tone and strength decrease. There is also some degree of irreparable cellular degeneration in the brain. There can be some erectile dysfunction. In essence, there is moderate decline in almost all areas of physical functioning.

For women, the changes may include the cessation of the menstrual cycle, thinning hair, vaginal dryness, feelings of anxiety and depression, arthritis, increased risk of stroke and heart disease, emotional mood swings, sleeplessness, and fatigue.

Midlife adults need to learn to pace themselves. Gone are the days when they could burn the candle at both ends, pulling all-nighters to finish up work assignments and not suffering health consequences for doing so. Eventually, they are going to pay the price, and that goes for pastors too. One ministry leader writes, "We church folks were encouraged to burn ourselves out for God—conjuring images of one so weary with well doing he begins to smolder at the collar and eventually spontaneously combusts, to perpetual sainthood."[12] While passion for a life spent in the ministry can be a helpful trait, passion without boundaries can eventually lead to a lifestyle of self-destruction.[13]

Marital Changes

It may seem that after years of marriage you and your spouse can read each other's minds, but that simply isn't literally true. A marriage may begin with mutual interests and a high level of shared intimacy. But as children enter the home and the pressures associated with a minister's job begin to emerge, serious fractures can occur in the marriage relationship. Later, "in the middle years which are marked by personal stock-taking, the faults of one's mate seem to stand out more glaringly. Personal unhappiness finds a scapegoat in the unpleasant qualities of one's husband or wife—and intimacy fades."[14] It's time to pay attention to these subtle changes, because at no other period of the human life span is a male pastor more susceptible to having an affair than during these midlife years. There are many reasons for this, but chief among them is the level of recognition and compensation that pastors receive.

Those who marry clergy should be aware of the paradox of ministry as a vocation. While ministry requires the same arduous process of education and professional validation as other professions, ministers cannot expect to enjoy the same kinds of rewards, status, or authority granted by the culture to other professions. Financial problems are a major strain, leading to divorce in clergy marriages.

Insofar as the standard of living is an index of success, inadequate salaries can also contribute to the nagging sense of inadequacy that sends clergy seeking solace in the arms of someone other than the marriage partner.[15]

Most men and women marry by their midtwenties. Now, fifteen to twenty years later, the couple has children passing through the turbulent adolescent stage where hormones are raging and young teens are testing the limits of their boundaries as they try to live more like independent adults. The problem is that they aren't fully ready to be launched out of the nest yet, and the tension that creates can permeate the entire home. You now have two of the three factors necessary for the perfect storm: parents living in increasing isolation and children in the adolescent stage.

Add the third relational factor, dependence of elderly parents, and you have all the elements for the perfect storm. As our parents grow older, they increasingly depend on us for assistance. As their health declines, we need to step in and provide the loving support they deserve. But that is not to say it will come without a price. When one's parents are no longer able to care for themselves and there are no other means of assistance, it generally means that the children have to bring them into their home. This adds relational pressure as additional family members living in the same house can foster stress and misunderstanding. The pastor may respond by leaving for work earlier and remaining at the office longer. When this happens, the caregiving spouse is under increasing stress, and it is only a matter of time before things erupt at home.

Sexual Changes

Midlife is a time when one's physical changes can impact sexual functioning as well. One study has found that more than half of all men between the ages of forty and seventy have some degree of erectile dysfunction.[16] A host of physical conditions can influence erectile dysfunction, including high blood pressure, diabetes, and depression. Likewise, increased use of prescription medications, cigarettes, alcohol, and even some nonprescription drugs can have a negative effect on normal sexual functioning. Hormonal adjustments, which are commonly associated with the cessation of the menstrual cycle in women, also occur in men.[17]

> The majority of studies on sex and aging confirm that most individuals in late life retain sexual interest and ability. However, as one might suppose, the frequency of the activity declines in the later years.... 95 percent of men between the ages of 46 and 50 had weekly intercourse, compared with only 28 percent of men between the ages of 66 and 71. In many instances, medications, illnesses, partner availability, relationship problems, erection difficulties, or age-related changes in sexual responsiveness are responsible for discontinuation of sexual activity.[18]

Sexual changes are a normal part of midlife, but they certainly need not define who you are. As with other physical changes, they should be embraced if there are no medical solutions; if they present problems in your marriage, they should be discussed openly with your spouse and/or medical provider.

Vocational Changes

The first half of life is spent trying to achieve success. We strive to ascend culture's material ladder of success only to find when we finally get to the top that it is placed on the side of the wrong building. Life's second half is not about material success, but rather about personal meaning and purpose. This second half of the journey requires us to move away from traditional notions of success to significance. Significance is expressed from the inside out and isn't flaunted. It involves a spiritual transformation that doesn't come to us naturally, for it flies in the face of common thinking. It requires abandoning competition, power, and prestige and acting out the daily life of a "holy fool."[19] With this mind-set we are free to consider vocational objectives that transcend thoughts of wealth, affluence, and prosperity.

For those who are already in ministry during their midlife years, some cautioning is in order. You might be tempted to think that because you are a ministry leader, you won't be susceptible to the crisis that is often associated with midlife. A number of studies have been conducted on ministers to determine if they too were vulnerable to the upheavals that are often associated with the midlife crisis. For the most part, clergy are no different from those in their congregations when it comes to weathering midlife storms.

> It would appear from these studies that commitment to ministry is affected by what is happening in one's life in the parish and in one's family. . . . An important implication to ministers: when commitment seems to wane, look for what else is happening in one's life. . . . Commitment will go higher and lower across one's lifetime; do not be surprised when it goes to a low point. Instead, a wise minister, in consultation with other people, will look closely at roots, goals, interests, and competencies as one continues to shape a ministerial career.[20]

As one author lamented, "There is no proverbial fountain of youth — no magic potion to erase the years. Genes, life experiences, and aging are factors affecting our health over which we have little control."[21] The desire to hang on to lost youth can lead people to make seriously inept decisions with lifelong consequences. Such decisions should not be characteristic of the Christian at midlife.

> Midlife to the Christian should be a time of harvest. By now his mind should be richly infused with God's word. His thoughts should be filled

with God's peace that passes understanding. He should meet all of the challenges of midlife whether they be physical, spiritual, or emotional. His life should shine like a beacon on a world where people are so consumed with fear of dying but do not know where to turn except to satisfy the desires of their own instincts and to cling more desperately to the time that is slipping through their fingers.[22]

Midlife as a Season for Growth

In one study of midlife adults, as many as 89 percent associated this period of life with compassion, caring for others, and making purposeful contributions in their community. They wanted to grow closer to their spouse, their children, and their grandchildren. They wanted to help their children financially so they wouldn't have the same pressures they went through raising a young family. They also wanted to be close to their friends and provide assistance where it was needed. In short, they wanted to invest in others.[23]

Midlife is seen as a time of assessing losses and gains. For those who consider only the loss side of the equation, midlife is viewed as a crisis of epic proportions. However, for those who see midlife as a time of reflection and healthy self-examination, it can reap significant positive results.

Midlifers can come through this season of life with a rich sense of meaningful purpose as they consider ways to invest in the lives of others. As ministry leaders entering the pastorate at midlife, they are poised to invest in others with passion and reckless abandon. Life becomes more focused, and life is measured more by inner peace than by material possessions.

The best antidote to midlife is maintaining one's perspective. There is no substitute for experience. Those entering the ministry at midlife have a distinct advantage over their younger colleagues. Sure, life events may remind us that we are mere mortals traveling down an ever-diminishing road. However, with our unique vantage point and keen sense of partnership with God, we can make profound contributions to the kingdom of God.

PART 4

GETTING THERE FROM HERE

CHAPTER 15

USING A TRAVEL AGENT

Dealing with Professional Search Firms

MICHAEL ANTHONY

A plan in the heart of a man is like deep water,
But a man of understanding draws it out.
Proverbs 20:5

An Awkward Dance

I will never forget the time I went to my first dance. This was nothing like square dancing in the gym at school during rainy days. Remember that? When physical education couldn't be held outside because of the rain, teachers at my junior high school would combine the boys' and girls' classes and meet in the gym for square dancing. At least in that setting you got paired up with someone whether you liked it or not and everyone had to dance. Dancing wasn't optional.

The first real dance I ever attended was at the country club my parents belonged to when I was a young teenager. I got a new pair of shoes and dressed in what I thought was an attractive outfit. I did everything I could to make myself look appealing. After all, this wasn't the school gym, and here dancing *was* optional. For some of us who were too shy or hesitant to "strut our stuff," it was more painful than a visit to the dentist. It took me hours to get up the nerve to ask a girl to dance, and in hindsight I realize she only said yes out of pity.

Stepping onto the dance floor, I panicked! I wasn't sure what my role was. I knew in theory I was supposed to lead, but I had no clue how to actually do it. Fast dance, slow dance, it all had the same result—stepping on toes, bumping my partner, feeling insecure, and looking awkward. Somehow I got through it, but I can't say the experience was much fun. Maybe that is why to this day I'm not a big fan of dancing.

Partnering with a search firm to find a new pastoral position may feel like an awkward dance with a partner you barely know. You aren't sure who is supposed to do what. Do I initiate the call, or do they? Am I supposed to secure a contract for services, or do they? Is it my responsibility to pay them for what they do, or is that someone else's job? It can feel awkward if it's your first time dancing with a search firm. Some toes may get stepped on during the process, and maybe some of your insecurities will come to the surface: What if I don't meet their expectations? What if they don't like me? What if no one asks me to dance? It can be a frightening experience for a pastor.

Theology of Engagement

Early in my ministry experience, I asked Brian, a seasoned ministry veteran, how he discovered where God wanted him to serve. "With so many churches and ministry organizations out there, how do you go about finding the one God has for you?" I'll never forget his answer. He said, "I never tell people I want a new ministry job. I simply let God know, and then I wait for the phone to ring. When it does, I assume it is God calling me with a new ministry assignment. I take whatever is offered."

My mentor had an approach to job hunting based on a passive theology of engagement. He took no action on his own (not even to write a resume) and simply waited for God to do all the work. I have come to realize that there is a fine line between being spiritual and being lazy.

Another approach to job hunting that I have witnessed over the years is one in which the pastor crafts a resume and broadcasts it across the planet via the Internet. It is sent to hundreds of Christian ministries in countries he couldn't find on a map. At the same time, he also sends it out to every friend he has ever known. This shotgun approach ensures that every living soul knows that he is looking for a new ministry position. It is the first item of conversation when he calls on the phone, and it dominates every hour of his day. One way or another, he is going to help God get the word out.

This pastor doesn't realize it, but when his friends see him coming, they duck for cover. They don't return his calls, and they avoid any personal contact with him while he is "on the hunt." His theology of engagement is equally faulty because it is based on a view of God as incompetent or inept. Though he wouldn't admit it, he would say God needed his help by providing the muscle and manpower to get the job done right.

Both extremes are based on a faulty theology. Lack of activity and hyperactivity are both signs of a dysfunctional view of how ministry positions are secured. Engaging a new ministry career doesn't have to depend on either extreme. There is a better way that doesn't sacrifice your family or friends during the journey.

Many pastors in the twenty-first century are now employing the use of a search firm. This organization partners with candidates and ministries to help make matches.

One reason some pastors avoid the use of search firms is because they view the role of the search firm much like Yente in *Fiddler on the Roof*. In this humorous portrayal of a marriage matchmaker, Yente is more concerned about her own reputation as the matchmaker in the community than in understanding the needs of the people she is pairing. The result is fear, anxiety, and a belief that God has little or no part in the process.

Nothing is further from the truth. God is deeply concerned about the pairing of your ministry gifts with the needs of the ministry you are called to serve. The role of the search firm is to facilitate that pairing and should be marked by prayerful partnership with the Holy Spirit and sensitivity to both the candidate and ministry organization.

Let's face it: when it came to finding a ministry location in which to serve in the Old Testament, things seemed so much easier. God spoke in a dramatic vision or miraculous intervention, and there was no doubt where God wanted the servant to go. When God spoke to Abraham and Moses, they simply responded, and the match between spiritual leader and congregation was made. Samuel heard God speak, and in no time at all Samuel cracked open the flask and a new king was anointed. There were no interviews, no resumes to circulate, no committees to convene, and no votes taken! The Old Testament example of selecting prophets, kings, and other spiritual leaders was one of divine appointment. God did all the work. How much easier could it be?

In the New Testament, God changed the process. Jesus handpicked his twelve protégés, and these were put in place to continue on in the ministry soon after his departure. Shortly thereafter the apostle Paul came on the scene and began the process of establishing new churches in areas where people had never witnessed Jesus' ministry. These small groups of converts, many of them Gentile, needed direction and leadership. There weren't enough apostles to go around.

We find ministry leaders in the New Testament possessing specific gifts as prerequisites for service. Ministry required a pairing of the giftedness of the ministry leader and the ministry itself. After all, if the church needed an evangelist, it made no sense for God to send them a counselor. The new churches that were founded by James, Paul, Barnabas, or Titus had ministry leaders who were appointed by these early church leaders. Paul's letters provided selection criteria, and the Holy Spirit gave them insight and discernment as they chose elders to carry on in their absence. In time, as the apostles died, these elders assumed a role in the selection of ministry leaders. At first the church acquired a centralized form of governance with appointments being handed down by those in authority (e.g., pope, cardinals, bishops, etc.), but eventually, as a result of the Reformation period, the congregation wanted some say in the matter.

The local body wanted to play more of a role in the selection of their ministry leaders as they became more biblically literate and theologically trained themselves. Relying less on the appointment by leaders who were too far removed from knowing and understanding the unique needs of their particular community, local churches took the matter into their own hands and became engaged in the selection of the ministry leaders by forming search committees to lead the process.

Today we find a wide variety of methods being used for selecting ministry leaders. Some denominations still use a hierarchical structure for appointments, while others opt for a congregational decision. We are not declaring one method right and the other wrong, Rather, we are saying that different methods are being

The Pastor's Guide to Using a Search Consultant

Knowing how the search industry works will make you a better candidate. Many false assumptions need to be corrected. Here is a brief summary of what you need to know:

1. Search firms don't work for you. They work for the ministry that has hired them and agreed to pay their expenses. So don't expect them to return your calls or sit and listen to your traveling story.
2. Search consultants multitask. Dozens of meetings and phone calls and countless details are involved in matching a candidate with a ministry opening.
3. Search consultants are busy people. Following are some of their responsibilities:
   - Marketing themselves to potential ministries
   - Conducting research on ministries and candidates
   - Screening candidates
   - Interviewing candidates
   - Presenting candidates to the ministry
   - Preparing candidates for interviews
   - Debriefing candidates after interviews
   - Presenting compensation packages to candidates
   - Negotiating differences
4. There are two types of search firms: retainer firms and contingency firms.

used today, and one had better be aware of the nuances of each before venturing out on the journey.

The Purpose of a Search Firm

If you have never worked with a search firm before, this might be like breaking a new trail for you. You aren't alone. In our survey we discovered that only 14 percent of our pastors had used a search firm to find a new ministry, while 60 percent said they would consider using one the next time around. These numbers are increasing each year as search firms grow in both professional competency and popularity. To maximize their effectiveness for you as a pastoral candidate, it will be helpful to know what to expect from them as they represent you before the church.

Who Pays the Bill?

You will need to understand from the outset that in the majority of cases search firms are hired by the ministry (e.g., church, school, mission, camp, etc.) to fulfill a specific task. Since the ministry organization pays their bills, it is natural that their allegiance will be to that organization, not to you. They will not, however, leave you out on a limb when the going gets tough. A good search firm will never put you in that position. But knowing who hires them and for what purpose will help you work with them in a mutually beneficial manner.

Rarely is a professional search firm used for recruiting a pastor in a small or medium-sized church. For the most part, professional search consultants are employed when the church is of significant size, generally multithousand. It takes a fairly large ministry to be able to pay the fees that these firms charge. Robert Dingman, a professional search consultant, offers the following guidelines for churches considering using a search firm.[1] Knowing some of these guidelines may be helpful from your perspective as well.

1. Avoid the firm that works on a contingent fee basis. Use a retainer-based firm.
2. Seek a firm that specializes in (or exclusively does) search work with a highly trained staff, not one that offers it as one of many services.
3. In selecting a firm, speak with the person who will conduct the search, not someone else.
4. Hire a firm that assures you of their professional competence from both outside and inside the religious world. Being well connected among Christians is not a fully reliable credential.
5. Talk to other organizations, similar to your own, that the search firm has previously served.

6. Interview several search firms before you choose.
7. Try to determine if the consultant's current workload allows for sufficient attention to your needs.
8. Choose a consultant you feel you can trust and will enjoy working with.
9. Review your internal candidates to be sure you aren't missing someone who is promotable. If you aren't sure, have the consultant evaluate the internal possibilities as well.
10. If your search committee is not overwhelmingly supportive of using a search firm, don't do it. As an outsider, the consultant hopes to work with a group that is not torn by internal politics, particularly on the point of his being a key part of the selection process.

From the candidate's point of view, you may want to consider using a professional search consultant when several things are evident:

1. *You are looking for a position outside the bounds of your denomination.* Rarely will a search firm be employed to fill a pastoral position and limit themselves to candidates within one specific denomination. The pool is much smaller and thus more restrictive. That minimizes the odds of completing a successful search.

2. *You are looking for a position that is national in scope and larger than the average ministry.* The reason for this is simple. Search firms are rarely regional. They usually have contacts all over the country and prefer not to limit themselves to finding a candidate in one geographic location.

3. *You are looking for or are open to considering a ministry that is outside the traditional church position.* That is because most professional search firms represent a very small number of churches. Most Christian colleges, seminaries, camps, mission organizations, publishing companies, and the like use search firms to fill executive leadership openings, as these ministries can afford to pay the fees that professional search firms require.

4. *You are looking for either a senior pastor or executive pastor position.* In almost all cases, the search firm will be employed by the church to find a candidate for one of these two senior-level positions. Rarely does a search firm get involved with any position lower on an organizational chart.

The Search Consultant's Role

As you can see in the sidebar on page 204, the ministry that has employed the services of a professional search firm is willing to pay this firm a sizable sum of money to find a suitable candidate. Expectations are high, and it is imperative that they find the best candidate for the opening. To do that, the firm will go to the ministry board (or search committee of the church) and conduct a full assessment of the culture, context, and ethos of the ministry organization. The following are ten steps on the firm's checklist.

1. *Interview with the governing board and/or search committee.* When a search firm conducts this comprehensive assessment, they are looking for more than where the person's job fits on the organizational chart. They are also looking at the culture of the ministry, the community surrounding the ministry, the institutional personality that is evident, any obstacles (internal and external) in the hiring process, and the unity of the board at the top levels of the organization. Furthermore, they are assessing the demographic changes that have recently taken place (or perhaps may take place in the immediate future) along with the financial health of the ministry. The reputation of the ministry among its constituents is not to be underestimated. These issues, and dozens more, are on the mind of the search consultant.

The professional search consultant needs to have a firm grasp of these issues to honestly represent the ministry before potential candidates. The last thing a professional search consultant wants to do is appear unprofessional or unknowledgeable about the details and specifics of the job or ministry itself.

2. *Development of the ministry profile.* If the ministry organization hasn't already done so, the professional search consultant can help them develop a ministry profile. This document outlines the demographics of the community surrounding the ministry, the historical trends, expectations of the candidate, qualifications of those they are seeking (e.g., education, experience, doctrinal beliefs, etc.), and any other important pieces of information the search committee wants a potential candidate to know *before* applying for the job. Any candidate looking at the ministry will want to contact the search consultant and ask for a copy of the ministry profile *before* making a decision about applying.

Once the documents are in order (e.g., ministry profile, job description, etc.), they are put into a packet and made available to applicants who contact the firm. Once the candidate completes the application materials and returns them, he or she can expect to hear from the professional search consultant in a relatively short period of time.

3. *Preliminary screening of candidates.* If it is obvious to the consultant that there is no match between the ministry and the candidate, the consultant will send a diplomatic rejection letter. (The number of candidates who throw their resume in the hopper much like a quarterback throwing a "Hail Mary" pass in the last seconds of the game is surprising. These candidates never make it to the next step in the process.) However, if there seems to be some potential, even if it may appear remote at this point, the consultant will initiate a phone contact with the candidate to conduct a preliminary interview.

4. *Initial telephone contact.* In this interview the consultant is trying to fill in any gaps that may have come up in the application materials. Any blanks not filled in on the form will raise a yellow flag. Remember, the question was asked

for a reason, and the search firm expects an answer. Dodging a question raises more questions. Beyond making sure the application is complete, the consultant will ask a number of questions to determine the veracity of your answers. The consultant will also need accurate names and dates to initiate a background investigation. He will contact the schools you list on your resume to verify the degrees you hold and any honors associated with them. Their motto at this stage in the process is "Trust but verify."

5. *Primary reference checks.* The consultant will begin contacting the references you listed on the application. He will contact those individuals and ask them a series of questions about your past job performance, personal integrity, and Christian character. He wants to know not only if you fulfilled the responsibilities of your job but also how you treated those you supervised, what your spiritual gift(s) are, and what kind of reputation you have both inside and outside the ministry context. These are called primary level interviews, and the consultant doesn't expect to hear anything negative from these people. After all, why would you list them as references if you knew they wouldn't speak favorably of you? The last question they will ask these individuals is predictable: "Can you give me the names and numbers of three other individuals I could contact regarding this candidate?"

6. *Secondary and tertiary reference checks.* From here the consultant contacts these secondary-level individuals. Now the consultant is digging a little deeper and making contact with people who might not necessarily think you can walk on water. In fact, some of these people may not be on your Christmas card list. Again, questions related to your past ministry performance and character will be the topic of conversation. Since you don't know who these people might be, you have no way of preparing them with the answers you want them to give—and the consultant knows it. Then, again, the consultant will raise that final question and will begin to question third-level references of the candidate.

By now the consultant will be getting a pattern of answers. No longer will he be hearing the carefully scripted answers you provided the individuals you put on your application materials. Now he will be speaking with those with whom you have served on committees, your secretary, past employees you supervised, and perhaps even a few people who have an ax to grind. If he begins to hear the same answers, he will stop here. If the answers are new and worth exploring in more detail, the process will continue until he has overturned every stone.

Skilled professional search consultants know that no one who has served in a significant leadership position does so without making a few enemies along the way. Making tough decisions is part of leadership, and hearing from those who have been on the receiving end of bad news gives insight into the candidate's personality, character, and Christian commitment.

7. *Face-to-face meeting(s).* The next step in the process will be a face-to-face meeting with the search consultant. Don't be surprised if there is more than one of these. At one of them, they will also invite your spouse to attend to determine the level of commitment you both have in ministry. The goal of this step is to eliminate anyone who doesn't fit the ministry profile. Another member of the search firm may attend this meeting. Together they will ask questions about your expectations, motives, doctrinal compatibility, and heartfelt issues.

8. *Background checks.* A thorough background search will also include a criminal background check and credit report. Obviously, if you are at the point of being on the receiving end of this level of inquiry, there is some encouragement in knowing that you are working your way onto the short list of potential candidates.

9. *Introduction to the search committee.* You may be thinking at this point that being screened for the ministry is like applying for a job with the Federal Bureau of Investigation. Well, if you thought getting this far was hard, hang on to your hat, because it's about to get even harder. I won't go into detail here about the steps that follow; that material will be covered in the next chapter. Suffice it to say here that the job of the search consultant has been to prepare you (and the other candidates) for the search committee interview(s). The next few steps depend on the type of church or ministry involved. Some search committees make a recommendation and present the candidate for approval to the church board. In other cases the candidate is presented to the denomination for approval, and many times the candidate is presented to the congregation for approval. At any rate, the final stage of the process is initiated.

10. *Compensation package negotiations.* More detail will be provided in chapter 20 on this step. Here, however, we should mention that the search consultant, rather than the church's search committee or governing board, should be the one to negotiate the benefits package with the candidate. The rationale for this is simple. If the negotiating becomes strained, it undermines the relationships with those whom the new pastor will be working with once he comes to the ministry. Some frank and necessary things can be said and worked out in private between the candidate and the consultant, who in turn can diplomatically negotiate with the ministry. As a buffer, the search consultant provides a helpful and necessary service to both the candidate and the ministry.

The Candidate's Role

Now that you have seen what is involved from the search consultant's point of view, you have a clearer picture of who you are going to the dance with. However, the search consultant is only the mediator between you and your partner. He isn't actually your partner.

The sidebar below lists a number of advantages associated with using a search consultant.[2]

Making a Good Match

This may be your first experience with a search firm and you aren't sure what to expect. How do you even know if the search consultant you are using is a good one? Here is a simple three-question litmus test. (1) Is the consultant knowledgeable about the ministry he is representing? A good consultant has done his homework and has the facts and figures about the ministry at his fingertips. (2) Does the consultant have integrity in his dealings with the church and with you as a candidate? Ask him about his spiritual walk with the Lord, where he attends church, why he is in this career, how many years he has served in this capacity, how many successful searches he has completed, who some of his client churches are, and what kinds of ministries (besides churches) he has provided services for in the past. (3) How conscientious is the consultant? If he is good, he won't simply ask for a copy of your resume. He will take the time to talk to you about your philosophy of ministry, the motives of your heart, your theological distinctives, and issues that are important to you and your family.[3]

Your part in this career transition dance has several parts. First, you will need to be forthright about the answers you are providing and make every effort to be

Advantages of Using a Search Consultant

1. *Presentation.* A search consultant introducing you to a church search committee makes you stand out from the other candidates in the crowded field. You are put forward by a trusted professional rather than through your own self-serving efforts.
2. *Security.* A church that hires a search firm is generally on stronger ground financially and is more committed to your future success.
3. *Confidentiality.* You have guaranteed confidentiality with a search firm.
4. *Preparation.* The search consultant will work with you to make sure that you are prepared for the plethora of interviews and visits you will experience.
5. *Negotiation.* The search consultant will assist you in negotiating your benefits package.
6. *Buffering.* The consultant serves as a useful information channel between you and the church.

yourself at the many meetings and interviews. It is natural that you want to put your best foot forward, but you also have to be honest. Herein lies the tension that candidates face when going through the interview process. "How am I to be honest to those I'm speaking to when I also feel the need to be diplomatic and not shoot myself in the foot along the way?" You may be tempted to say that the board chairman at your last church was anything but honest and professional in his dealings with you, but you can't say that. Instead, you might say something like, "The previous board chairman and I found ourselves in healthy discussions regarding the nature of the church and our ministry's role in accomplishing God's plan." That's a nice way of saying, "We kept butting heads, and I couldn't get him to get on board with my vision for where the church needed to go. I finally gave up and quit!"

Second, you will need to do your homework before attending any meetings or worship services at prospective churches. The next three chapters will provide you with more specific issues you will be facing at this stage of the process. The most important thing you can do, however, is pray and prepare your answers by doing some honest assessment regarding your ministry strengths and weaknesses. Look for diplomatic ways to express both. You don't want to appear arrogant when presenting your strengths, but you don't want to be too self-effacing when presenting your weaknesses.

When you are revealing a negative quality about your character or professional conduct, it is best to frame it in a positive tone. For example, if you aren't very good with administrative assignments, don't say, "One of my weaknesses is that I hate doing things that involve administration." A more positive way to say that would be, "I've discovered I am more productive when I partner with people who can come alongside and use their gifts as well. I have been able to do that with secretaries and staff members who are skilled in doing administrative activities." This allows you to be honest about your weaknesses while at the same time revealing your insights on how to turn a weakness into a strength (e.g., delegating administrative responsibilities).

Third, don't waste anybody's time. Let the recruiter know immediately if you sense the church isn't a good fit with your expectations. Then offer to be a resource to help facilitate the pairing of a candidate with the church if you know of someone else who might make a good fit.

Fourth, don't use the search firm or the church where you are candidating to bargain with your current church for a better benefits package. Knowing that you are interested in leaving and also talking to a search consultant may make your church board scramble to increase your benefits package so as not to lose you. Bargaining with the board, however, is a cheap trick and often backfires.

Finally, be diligent to return any phone calls and/or requests for information that come to you from a search consultant. His job is to keep things on track and moving. If you frustrate him, he may move on to another candidate who is willing to respond at the rate he likes to travel. The old adage "If you snooze, you lose" can be true in this dance.

We have entered into a new era of pairing ministries with pastors. Modern corporate techniques are being integrated with time-honored and biblically based traditions. Nevertheless, there will never be a substitute for a search committee's prayerfully consulting God and asking him to reveal the candidate of his choosing. In the counsel of many, we find safety, so forming a search committee is almost always part of a good beginning. Technology, however, also provides tremendous assistance. Resumes can be posted, communication can be passed along at lightning speed, and information can be shared and processed among many people without them having to gather together in a face-to-face meeting. One's theology of engagement may need to be reviewed as search consultants enter the picture to serve the needs of ministries and ministers alike. No one ever said this journeying experience would be easy, but it's nice to know that there are consultants who are willing to travel down this path with you to provide encouragement and support along the way.

CHAPTER 16

THE LONG WAIT TILL DAWN

Dealing with the Church Search Committee

MICK BOERSMA

Hope deferred makes the heart sick,
But desire fulfilled is a tree of life.
Proverbs 13:12

Looking out the window, I could see cars and buses stalled on the freeway below. We were landing in the middle of a snowstorm, and the scene beneath me was one of winter wonder and commuter chaos. As the last plane was granted clearance to land late that afternoon, we made our way gingerly to the gate. Glad to be safely on the ground, we entered the terminal only to hear that all freeways were closed, all hotels full, and no taxi or bus service would be available until early the next morning.

There we were—all our bags, two young daughters, a building full of strangers, hungry, with the prospect of spending the night in SeaTac airport. The man coming to pick us up was nowhere in sight. And since this was before cell phones, we had no way of knowing when or if he would be arriving to spirit us off to our warm and comfortable home. My wife and I found a corner and started to make it "home." We found some dinner—and then waited. Time stood still. Only fourteen hours before dawn. Would the snow stop? Would we ever get out of here? Why did we fly in December?

"Mr. Boersma, please come to the ticket counter. Your party is waiting." Those were such beautiful words to hear! Others around us offered envious glances. Our friend had managed to get through the icy bedlam, a trip of thirty-five miles that had taken him six hours to navigate. As he gingerly drove through the stalled vehicles on Interstate 5, we were treated to his tale of near misses, rescues, and detours that were part of his journey. We had not been aware of how challenging his act of kindness was, but we were grateful for his loving service to us and happy to be on our way home.

Dealing with a church search committee is challenging and can bring to the surface emotions similar to those faced by my family and me that snowy night. We are at the mercy of others, have little or no control over the circumstances, and feel every tick of the clock as we wait to be "rescued" from our present circumstances. In this chapter we are going to get better acquainted with the church search committee.

Who Are These Search Committee Members?

Search committees are not for those who get weak in the knees when the pressure builds. However effectively they may accomplish their task, for the most part these are good and sincere people who want to do the right thing. It is very costly for a church to make a bad decision, and they are given a charge to keep that from happening. These saints give vast amounts of time and emotional energy, and we should never fail to appreciate their sacrifices. Some of the characteristics of search committee members are listed below.

They are not professionals. Few search committee members have had experience in hiring others. Happily, several resources are available for church search committees, providing step-by-step procedures and resources.[1] Sadly, not all committees avail themselves of such help and therefore may struggle in the process. The sidebar below suggests the ideal makeup of a pastoral search committee.[2]

They are political. Search committee members are people with interests they or others who support them want satisfied. Most committees are made up of a combination of church leaders and laypeople (and church staff on rare occasions) who are chosen by congregational vote. Several sources we checked advised against having couples serving, as this would dilute the representative nature of the group. I recall meeting with a search committee of fifteen members on one

The Ideal Search Committee Includes

- A person with management know-how
- Someone who is theologically astute
- A party with interviewing and assessment skills
- A writer
- Someone with a feel for financial matters
- A person with good logical and analytical abilities
- A number of deeply spiritual people
- Someone who knows the background of the organization and any denominational ties it may have

occasion. Every major special interest was represented in that group. While it was an exhausting few hours, it did give me a sense of where the church was at, what was important to them, and how they felt about the various programmatic elements of their ministry. It is wise to pay close attention to the makeup of this group, as it will give you a better "read" on the ministry you are applying to.

They are powerful. Even though the search committee only recommends candidates to the governing board, they are the ones making the important decisions all along the way. As in those legendary "smoke-filled rooms" where political candidates are chosen, the church search committee determines who is on the ballot. Most carry this power reluctantly and struggle in making such decisions, knowing people's careers are in the balance. That is why it is so important that this group be composed of spiritually mature believers. When this is not the case, members may be swayed by pressures, leading to poor choices.

They are idealists. One of our students, an accomplished businessperson who has served on a church search committee, said, "In business we look for the *best* person for the job. In the church we look for *the* person for the job." Looking for a good match is one thing; waiting for the *perfect* match is quite another. This can affect the search process in two ways. First, the committee may focus only on the church's positive qualities, being in denial of serious flaws that make their opportunity less than appealing to qualified candidates. Second, their pastoral profile may have unrealistic expectations. We have seen hundreds of pastoral profiles over the years, and most have this in common: Jesus himself would probably fail to qualify.

The combination of idealized self-assessments and pastoral expectations, along with a sense that God's perfect choice is out there can make for a challenging time with a search committee. We certainly believe that God's hand is in this process, but it is helpful to understand that committees can often bog down because they are struggling with knowing and doing God's will as they make their important decisions.

They are laypeople. While we assert the priesthood of all believers and rejoice in the equality of all in the body of Christ, we also recognize that believers have differing gifts and roles (Rom. 12:4–8; 1 Cor. 12). Few search committee members truly understand the unique nature and challenges of being in a pastoral position. Because of this, they may not know all of the questions that should be addressed nor appreciate the critical nature of various issues related to pastoral service. This is why it is important to formulate good "pastoral perspective" questions for those interviews as they happen (see the end of chapter 17).

They are meeting strangers. The relationship between pastors and church search committees has been compared to that between people dating. While most people spend a lot of time together before "walking down the aisle," pastors and churches don't have that kind of time to invest. The relationship starts from a dead stop in many cases and thus makes the process long and sometimes confusing. Communication is difficult to establish in any relationship, and misunderstandings are bound to occur between you and the committee. People make assumptions, words mean different things to different people — you get the drift.

This is not an exhaustive list of characteristics by any means, but it is good to have an idea of the types of people who will be interviewing you. While it will take time to get acquainted with those you meet on your journey, your trip will be much more enjoyable if you get to know them and appreciate their life circumstances, challenges, and perspectives.

What Itinerary Are They Following?

Every church does things differently. A New York pastor we know filled the pulpit a few times for a congregation without a pastor. A few weeks later he answered a knock at his door; the congregational elders had come to ask him to be their next pastor. After an hour or so of casual conversation, the deal was done. That was nearly ten years ago, and he is still there.

That doesn't happen very often, of course. More than likely the process will be long and drawn out, requiring tenacity on everyone's part. Search committees do have a basic pattern of operation, however. Many denominations provide handbooks to their churches, spelling out well-reasoned sequences for the pastoral search.[3] From the variety of approaches recommended, we offer a summary of the typical steps taken by a church search committee.

1. *Administer a church self-assessment.* When a pastor leaves a ministry, many churches elect to take the opportunity to reexamine that person's ministry area, or even the entire church. Some employ the services of church consultants, who typically provide resources designed to collect information and tools to begin crafting a profile for the next pastor, help lay a foundation for future ministry, and even help the congregation work through the grief process over the departure of their former pastor.

Many churches do not take time to assess their situation and may run the risk of failing to address critical issues, work out long-simmering conflicts, or address significant differences of philosophy of ministry and expectations. When this happens, the next pastor gets saddled with the consequences. If the church you are applying to has not done some soul searching, it will be wise to help them explore some of these areas throughout the search process, particularly during interviews.

2. *Create church, community, and pastoral position profiles.* The fruit of self-assessment documents is helpful for the aspiring candidate and the committee itself. If this process is done honestly, the resultant information helps everyone

determine the possibility of a good fit. As with any dating service, you need accurate input to find a good match.

You will find varying degrees of completeness in these documents, but basic points should be covered as outlined in the sidebar below. And when it comes to the position profile, be prepared for anything. In the hundreds we have seen, the variety and extent of requirements is astounding. They tend to be overwhelming, but don't be discouraged. One search committee confessed, "We spent the first year aiming too high, looking for the forty- to fifty-year-old superstar with a proven track record at a large church."[4] They adjusted their parameters and found a great match.

3. *Identify potential candidates.* More than 38 percent of the pastors in our research sought help from friends and colleagues in finding their current ministry position. This reflects the tendency of search committees to first seek personal recommendations from key individuals—denominational leaders, seminary placement directors, friends in other ministries, and other pastors. One church put it this way: "At this time we do not want to put any information on a bulletin board that might go out to a number of people; rather, we would like your input on an individual basis that might match a qualified applicant to our situation."

Helpful Profile Information

About the Church
- Location
- Denominational affiliation
- History of the church
- Attendance patterns
- Doctrinal position
- Philosophy of ministry
- Staff
- Facilities
- Finances
- Mission
- Vision (future plans)
- Organizational structure
- Programs

About the Community
- Location
- Demographics
- Educational resources
- Recreational opportunities
- Industry (what people do)

About the Ministry Position
- Gifts and abilities
- Education
- Experience
- Ministry style
- Personal character
- Job responsibilities
- Supervisory relationships
- Vacation, salary (maybe)

We receive many such requests, and it underscores the importance for you to build and maintain good networks throughout your ministry life (see chapter 13). While this is often the first step, search committees will also list their position on various seminary websites. One committee chair I talked to bemoaned the fact that one of his members listed their position on a major secular job board. They received more than five hundred resumes, many from people who were not even Christians. Still, ministerial placement sites are a good way to identify potential ministries for you and to secure possible candidates for the search committee.

4. *Process incoming resumes.* Once again we enter the "smoke-filled room." What goes on here is anyone's guess. Committees use all kinds of methods for determining which candidates to follow up on and which to round file. As we mentioned in chapter 12, a poorly constructed resume can land you in the recycle bin right off. So can applying for a position for which you obviously do not meet basic qualifications as listed in their position profile. And flooding the mail with resumes has never been a wise move.

Many search committees, once they identify potential candidates, send them a lengthy questionnaire. These are usually quite comprehensive and can take the job seeker many hours to complete. The committee figures that if you are serious about this position, you will spend the time and effort. Also, if your answers aren't what they are looking for, you can be more easily eliminated. Here's a tip: Be yourself. Answer the questions honestly — you want them to love you for who you are, not for what you think they want you to be.

Committees may also construct a sort of "must have" grid, passing up anyone who does not measure up to those critical expectations. Many others use what has been referred to as the "Delphi technique." This is where each member ranks candidates surviving the initial cut. Through a process of discussion and successive revotes, a clear "winner" emerges. This consensus approach can be very helpful and often results in unanimous recommendations from the search committee to the governing board. Committees are usually secretive about how they determine God's will in this step, but most take the responsibility very seriously and want to do the right thing.

5. *Focus on top contenders.* When the list has been narrowed to candidates with good potential, a number of actions will be taken by most committees. Some will send the candidate additional clarifying questions. Phone interviews are not uncommon at this stage either. Being well prepared for such encounters is important (see chapter 17). We are not the greatest fans of phone interviews, because so much of communication is nonverbal. But at this point it can give both parties a better sense of one another.

Checking references often begins at this point. Some committees find that doing this *after* the initial phone interview with a potential candidate helps them tailor the right questions for the reference. In one case when I was serving as a reference, I had a great conversation with a chairman who sought further commentary on some difficulties one of their candidates had at a former church. My perspective helped clarify some reservations he had and enabled the search committee to fairly assess his potential.

Finally, this is often the time when a committee will send out a "search party" to visit the candidate on his or her turf. There are good reasons for doing this: (1) they can see the whole person interacting with real people; (2) they can see the type of people the candidate attracts; (3) they can show the candidate that they are seriously interested (this helps if the candidate is reluctant to consider a move); and (4) they will be drawn together as they travel together.[5] A great challenge here is maintaining confidentiality. In large ministries this is not as difficult as in smaller congregations. Search committees have to try carefully to blend in. Not all are successful.

6. *Conduct face-to-face interviews.* We will focus on interviews in the next chapter. Here is where the candidate gets to meet people on *their* turf. It is your chance to look around and get a feel for the people and the ministry. This interview does not guarantee you will be their primary candidate, but it does comprise a great "date" where you can actually have some meaningful and probative conversations.

Should things go well in this interview, you will be advised that you are either one of their top candidates or you are "the one." If not, you will be thanked and assured that you have their prayers. Several pastors reach this point, only to be told "no thanks." It may be heartbreaking for you and discouraging for the committee, as you have both put a lot of effort and emotion into the process.

If you are a serious contender, the committee will most likely ask your permission to do background checks on your credit and criminal history. Verification of your identity and educational claims may also be made. This is becoming much more common, and you should consider it a reasonable request.

7. *Set up official candidacy.* Once the committee has decided on their candidate of choice, they will recommend this person to the governing board. We have heard of some churches trotting out two or three different people on successive weekends and holding a sort of "beauty contest." This is a disastrous way to pick a new pastor because it can blur the focus on priorities and can create dissension. Happily, it rarely happens, and we would counsel you never to agree to such an arrangement.

In most all cases, if you are being brought to a church to candidate, the committee and board have determined you are their new pastor. In some sense, the official candidacy is a formality. But it is a rigorous and critical time for you and them. Perhaps you have heard the term "hell week" in conjunction with early season physical training for sports teams. Many churches will arrange for their candidate to spend a week performing whatever ministry the position requires (preaching, teaching, etc.), meeting with boards and committees, and generally getting acquainted with the flock. In addition, time will be given for house hunting and checking out the greater community. We will spend some time on these and other important tasks in chapters 18 and 21.

8. *Take the vote.* Of course, in the case of many staff positions, a vote by the congregation is not conducted. Senior staff and elders make that decision. But in most churches the fellowship gathers to affirm the candidate. Constitution bylaws often specify the percentage necessary to call a pastor. We would look for something higher than the 75 to 80 percent stipulated in most of these documents. And we would suggest you not lay out a "fleece" percentage. If you vow to say yes if the vote is 95 percent and it comes out 94.5 percent, you have just put yourself in an unnecessary moral dilemma.

This is usually the time when a concrete financial package is offered. Though certain aspects may have already been discussed, the real negotiating happens now. This is a delicate and important topic, so we have dedicated chapter 20 to that discussion.

9. *Prepare for moving day.* Many committees are also given the task of helping the new pastor settle into his or her new surroundings. They will keep in communication as you close out your present ministry or job situation. They may be the ones to arrange for moving vans and initial housing needs. A thoughtful congregation will care for these and other considerations. In our final chapter, we will talk about the end of this incredible journey and how to make your first days with your new flock a blessed and growing experience.

What Can I Expect on This Trip with the Search Committee?

Remember, this is a journey with strangers. A colleague of ours who leads trips to Israel once said, "In traveling internationally, expect the unexpected and be ready to change the itinerary at a moment's notice — flexibility is everything." Trips are more enjoyable if you are prepared for the unexpected. Here are some things you can look forward to — in no particular order.

Frustration. To the candidate, search committees operate at a snail's pace. It is easy to forget they have lives, jobs, and families. Other factors that can drag out the process include the tenure of the former pastor, the reason he or she left, the size of the church, its denomination, the time of year, and even constitutional restrictions. While knowing these factors are possible, it is still hard to be the one waiting at the mailbox.

Delayed communication is often a source of pain. One pastor's wife put it this way: "We have often waited months between phases of a committee's search before hearing any response from them. We totally understand that search committees are not doing this full-time, that they have jobs and families; but please appoint a correspondence secretary and keep those on your list up to date."[6]

There will be many reasons for frustration, perhaps the most significant being that you have little control over the process. Leaders naturally struggle with this, but as we will see at the end of this chapter, there are some things we have the ability to manage.

Rejection. One pastor who responded to our survey had this to say about his rejection experience:

> All of the churches we were considering are closed doors. This week has been discouraging, to say the least, as they one by one moved off of our list. I'm very affirmed that I received serious attention, made it so far along down the road, got interviews, etc. Those who considered me saw great potential from my materials. However, it ended up this way: [Church One]—Concerned about life experience (age). [Church Two]—Made it to top three and was told that there were no negatives against me, but decided to go with someone who is a senior pastor now, fifty years old, and an empty nester. [Church Three]—After we flew up there and the committee deliberated for almost two months, the ten-member committee could not come to consensus about me and decided that their indecision was a sign they needed to release us, not wanting to string us along.

Unlike this brother, candidates are usually not told the reasons for not being selected. Many committees use form letters.

Exhilaration. It is always exciting to visit a new place, see the possibilities, and meet great people. The candidating process is filled with such opportunities. As you interact with other ministries, you will see different philosophies and models that will expand your universe and make you more aware of the amazing diversity in God's work. It may be hard to keep your emotions in check if you are not selected as the new pastor, but the risk is well worth it as you experience the exciting potential in different locations.

You may also come to know the encouraging sense of validation. Many pastors have discovered during the search process that they are blessed to be where they are and experience a resolve to continue there with a renewed sense of vision. I enjoyed three more years of service after being passed over for a new position. And God used those years to prepare me for the fulfilling work here at the seminary.

Growth. There is no getting around it—the search process is a trial. James tells us that life experienced in the grace of God leads to personal spiritual growth (James 1:2–4). We see God work through seemingly impossible circumstances. Our relationships with family and friends become sweeter as we struggle together and prayerfully seek his will. We will establish new Christian friendships that will enrich our lives. And as is true with most growth, we like the results but would rather not have to go through the process. We close this chapter with a handful of suggestions for your making the most of the search committee process.

How Can I Make This Journey a Blessing to All?

Attitude is everything here. As we have said before, we should seek to serve, to be a shepherd to these dear people who have committed themselves to the arduous task of serving on a search committee. It is not about *getting* the job, but about *doing* the job. Here are a few ways you can serve the church search committee and bring honor to the Lord Jesus Christ.

1. *Be honest.* Don't shape your profile materials to fit the job opening. Be yourself and provide good information to the committee. Misrepresenting yourself is not only wrong, but it will make it necessary to continue the charade long after the call has been given. There is nothing wrong with putting one's best foot forward—just make sure it's your foot.

2. *Be gracious.* It is in your best interest not to take shortcomings exhibited by the search committee as personal affronts. Give these folks room to mess up. You'll mess up too. Far better to establish a relationship based on grace than to make the exchange one of conflict and resentment.

3. *Be prompt.* Even if the committee is slow in getting back to you, respond to requests with due diligence. Remember, you are showing them by your actions the kind of work ethic and approach to responsibility that will characterize your ministry. Who knows, they may learn a thing or two from your courteous and thorough responses.

4. *Be prayerful.* The pastors we surveyed indicated that prayer was the second most important influence on their search process, just after talking with their spouse.

Pray for the search committee, your present ministry, your family, and your friends. Seek God's wisdom and comfort as you make your way through the challenging steps of the search process.

Conclusion

In working with church search committees, the only thing you can control is how you respond. When we were stranded at the airport that snowy winter night, there were a lot of things I could not do. But I could find some seats, purchase carryout food, and assure my young daughters that we were okay and that this would be an exciting adventure. Yes, I was perturbed at first, tired and wanting to be home. But I remembered something my dad taught me as a child. When we took trips, he would live by the maxim: Half the fun of a trip is how you get there. The destination is important, of course. The dawn is a welcome sight. Yet the uncertainty and challenge of the night makes it so.

CHAPTER 17

ARE WE ALMOST THERE?

Preparing for the Interviewing Process

MICHAEL ANTHONY

He who answers before listening—
that is his folly and his shame....
The heart of the discerning acquires knowledge;
the ears of the wise seek it out.
Proverbs 18:13, 15 NIV

The airport was packed with expectant travelers. People swarmed over the defenseless airline agents at the counter, asking endless questions about the long delays. "Where's the plane?" "How soon before it arrives?" "Will we be able to make our connecting flights?" The agents held their tempers in check and managed to board as many passengers as possible once the plane arrived. Our flight made a stop in La Pas, Bolivia—for refueling, we were told, even though the itinerary wasn't all that long—on our way from Lima, Peru, to Santa Cruz, Bolivia. What was even stranger was that after we had all deplaned, the flight took off empty, leaving us wondering, *What's going on?* No one at the ticker counter had an explanation, so we sat for hours waiting for a plane to be dispatched to pick us up. Because of the extreme altitude, people were succumbing to high-altitude sickness. Tempers flared, and angry passengers were threatening physical violence if they didn't get a flight out immediately. I kept asking myself questions, such as, How much longer can this take? How much farther do we have to go? and, Am I almost there? The delay seemed endless.

Perhaps you have asked those questions during your career transition journey. At times your journey may seem endless. Phone calls, interviews, resumes, faxes, committee meetings, more phone calls, correspondence, references, Web browsing, networking, more phone calls, and endless hours of waiting. In exhaustion you ask, "God, am I almost there?" But before you round the bend and head for the finish line, you will find one last challenging hurdle before the job offer comes your way: interviewing at your prospective church.

Why So Many Questions?

With the endless supply of questions coming your way, many of which are repetitive, you might be tempted to say, "Why so many questions?" Well, the answer is really pretty simple. Your answers reveal to people who don't know you a little about yourself—your motives, passion, philosophy of ministry, spiritual relationship with God, and life priorities. People need answers before they feel confident to cast a vote. The endless array of questions also gives you an opportunity to hear what is important to those asking them. If you keep hearing the same questions being asked about your philosophy of worship style, you can be sure that this is an important topic at the church where you are candidating. It reveals something of their heart concern as well. Maybe they have been burned before and want to make sure it doesn't happen again. If you have ears to hear, you can pick up a great deal about the needs and concerns of those to whom you may one day be called to shepherd.

In addition to hearing the questions themselves, be sensitive to the tone used when the questions are being asked. Is the person asking a question just because it is his or her turn as they go around the room, or is there something behind this particular question? The tone or manner in which the question is framed may reveal something about the atmosphere of the meeting, the attitude of the person asking, or whether the individual asking has an ax to grind. Remember, Jesus faced many questions over the course of his earthly career, and his level of sensitivity to the person asking the question revealed a great deal about the opposition facing him at times.

Preparing for Formal Interviews

You will be interviewed multiple times in the process of securing a new ministry. If you have been contacted by a search firm, you will have a different path than the candidate who simply sends his or her resume to the chairperson of the search firm and then waits for the phone to ring. If the church you are pursuing is using a search firm, you will want to make sure you read chapter 15. Assuming the church you have sent your resume to hasn't chosen to hire such a firm, you will have a fairly predictable path for your interview process.

The Initial Interview

Generally speaking, the search committee will meet to review the resumes they have received from members of the congregation and other interested parties. Once they have looked through this plethora of materials, they will select several resumes that they want to examine more closely. At some point along the way, one of the members of the committee will call you for an initial interview.

This interview is designed to clarify any questions that may have come up during the committee's preliminary reading of your materials. Perhaps you failed to include an important date or omitted the name of a previous supervisor. At any rate, they are still at the rough screening stage and are calling for further information.

In some cases, this preliminary interview is to get an initial read on who you are as a ministry leader. The committee wants to hear what you sound like, clarify your passions for ministry, and hear you state your career objectives in your own words. They want to hear your heart speak in ways that the printed page cannot. Perhaps the person conducting this initial interview has a mutual friend who went to school with you and will use this connection to open a dialogue. Maybe the interviewer once lived in the city you're currently residing in and saw that as a point of contact between the two of you, and that's why he or she was selected by the committee to make the call.

This initial interview is designed for screening purposes. The person conducting the interview wants to hear a little bit about your journey thus far in ministry. He or she will ask questions like the following:

- What are your strengths and weaknesses?
- What are your spiritual gifts?
- How long have you been at your present ministry?
- Why are you seeking a change at this time?
- How does your spouse feel about making a move?
- What are your doctrinal or theological distinctives?

If you are really wise and attentive, you will hear something in the questions being asked that will reveal the concerns and biases of the person conducting the interview. The questions may also reveal something of the condition of the church or the leadership in question.

For example, if you have the same question asked repeatedly (although in different words), it might reveal what's going on at the church during this current season. What do you think is happening at a church when you have the following questions posed during your initial interview? "Tell me about your views on women in leadership." "Do you feel women should be allowed to teach any class at church or just serve in the nursery?" "What kind of ministry does your wife have at your current church?" "Would you ever allow a woman to speak from the pulpit?" "Do you have any problems reporting to a female church moderator?" Questions like these may reveal the current stress points at the church. If you hear repeated questions along the same theme, you may want to ask a few of your own.

This initial conversation may appear low-key and "off the record," but don't think for a minute that it's not important. Remember, if you don't impress this first contact, you will probably never get a second one. You need to win this key leader over to your side so that when the conversation is over, you leave him or her wanting to run into the next search committee meeting shouting, "I've found our new pastor!" Just being warm and friendly isn't enough. Remember, you aren't trying to become their next best friend, you're trying to become their pastor. Speak as a pastor and spiritual leader.

Never, under any circumstances, should you say anything negative about anyone at your current ministry location. Don't criticize what is going on in your life at the moment. It may be tempting to tell the person you are leaving because you can't stand the double-minded board chairman, but what you may not realize is that the board chairman is the interviewee's second cousin. Not only have you failed the interview, but you may also have expedited a transition out of your current position.

When asked, "Why are you leaving your current position?" simply state that you sense a call from God to transition into a new season of ministry where you can maximize your area(s) of giftedness. Nothing more needs to be said about the conditions where you are currently serving.

Once this initial interview is concluded, you will either receive a "Thank you for applying" letter that says, in essence, "Thank you but no thank you," or you will receive an invitation to move to the next level of interviews.

The Committee Interview

Once you have been selected by the committee to move to the next phase of the process, you will be invited to come for a formal interview. This interview will usually be with the church's search committee. In very large churches, a sub-committee may meet with you first, but for our purposes in this book, we will assume you have made it through that step and you are coming face-to-face with the search committee.

Between your previous interview with the individual member of the search committee and now, you should have done your homework. You should have done some serious research into the church, its community demographics, the denomination it belongs to, its past leadership, and its current conditions. If you are fortunate, you will have been able to track down a few colleagues who know members of the congregation. You don't need to go so far as to hire a private investigator to gather your information, but that level of thoroughness is what we have in mind.

The reason why you need to do your homework is simple. It will provide you with two things. First, it will give you an understanding of the needs of the church and help you know whether your gift mix is a match for their needs. Such knowledge gives you a distinct advantage during this phase of questioning. Second, it tells those who are doing the interview that you care enough to track down information on the church and are prepared for this stage of the journey. Having come to this stage prepared communicates a great deal to the committee. It tells them you are serious about this job opportunity and that you know you have what it takes to do the job.

Walking into the search committee meeting unprepared and with a cavalier attitude won't win you any points with the members of the committee. Remember, they have invested months of their lives in late-night meetings trying to research the best candidates for their church. They have spent the necessary time doing their homework, and they expect you to come equally prepared, having done yours. They have earned the right to be at the meeting. The big question on their minds is whether you have earned your right to attend. They will soon find out!

There is no way to ascertain at this point precisely what questions you will be asked at the formal interview, but there are some fairly predictable ones. The first question you field once the pleasantries and introductions are over is almost always the same. Knowing what it is and coming prepared to answer it right out of the block will give you a decisive advantage, so come prepared by writing out your answer like a script. Actually, this first question isn't a question at all. It's a directive: "Tell us about yourself."

You may think this suggests a simple answer that you could respond to in your sleep. But there is far more to this question than meets the eye (or ear, as the case may be). Think about what they're asking. They have already examined your resume, done a credit check on you, made sure your academic degree is legitimate, watched a video of your preaching, and conducted background reference checks by calling every supervisor you have ever worked for. They already know you better than you can imagine. So why do they start with such a predictable beginning? Because it reveals your priorities and your ability to focus a volume of information into a concise summary.

This is not the time to start with "I was born at a very early age" and continue through your life at annual intervals. Even at a minute per year, you will kill your interview before you graduate from kindergarten. All the interviewer wants is a sip from the faucet, not a torrent from the fire hydrant. The lesson to be learned here can be summed up in a few basic rules taken from the field of journalism. When telling an important story, such as that of your life,

- put the important stuff up front,
- use action verbs, and
- employ one idea per sentence.

Don't overestimate the attention span of those attending this meeting. Remember, they have probably already worked a full day at the office, and you are competing with all the other important details of their day. When it comes to verbal autobiographies, less is always better. Write out your response in advance and practice delivering it in front of a mirror. You should not only sound engaging, but you should look engaging as well. Maintain good eye contact with those on the search committee as you respond. You should be able to state your response to this directive while snowboarding down a mountain.[1]

Remember that this is not a simple question to see if you know who you are and where you have come from. It is a test to see if you can prioritize years of professional ministry experience and summarize why you believe your ministry gifts and talents are the best fit for their church's leadership needs. Do you mention your family? How have childhood experiences impacted who you have become? How have you responded to setbacks? Was your academic preparation purposeful or random? Are you a planner, or do you rely on fate (or luck) to guide your path? These are the kinds of issues that are on the table — not where you were born and where you went to school.

Don't begin with something tedious like "I was born in South Africa to missionary parents who sent me away to school in Kenya every year. It was lonely, and I wish I had grown up in the United States." Instead, respond with something like this: "I was born in South Africa and spent my childhood years traveling through a variety of countries. While at times it was quite a challenge, it also allowed me to develop an appreciation for communicating in cross-cultural settings and helped me to gain confidence in my leadership abilities at an early age."

See the difference? They already know from your resume where you were born and who your parents are. That's not what they want to hear. So communicate what you learned from your childhood experience and how it helped mold you into the kind of ministry leader that will benefit their church. Share examples from your spiritual journey that reveal your character and your core values (which should align with the church's if possible), and indicate where your path of ministry preparation gives clear evidence of why you should be given the job.

Common Interview Questions

Mick and I have gathered a list of questions that you might expect to find in an interview with the search committee. This list is by no means complete, but it will give you some idea of their concerns. Take the time to work out your answers, and come prepared with a confident knowledge of how you will respond once they are posed.

There is no way of knowing the exact questions you will face during the interview process. Some fit into broad categories, such as theology, philosophy of ministry, leadership/management style, and so on, whereas others will be very specific. In any case, you will probably encounter many of the questions cited below.

1. How do you view the process whereby we received the Scripture? That is, how much involvement and latitude was given by men under the inspiration of the Holy Spirit to show their humanity?
2. Do you see the possibility of errors being contained in the text as it was originally given from God?
3. What do you believe about the person and work of the Holy Spirit in the church today?
4. What are your beliefs regarding the nature of spiritual gifts?
5. What is your vision for ministry, and how does it relate to the Great Commission?
6. How does the humility of Christ affect the character of your ministry and leadership?
7. Whose ideas have had the greatest impact on you?
8. Name two recent books you have read and discuss their impact on your thinking.
9. How would you characterize your relationship with Christ?
10. Discuss how you develop your personal devotional life.
11. How do you show your family (if married) that they are a major priority to you?
12. Do you have a system to manage your time, and do you feel you are effective at it?
13. What is your style of dealing with interpersonal conflict?
14. What are your personal interests or hobbies?
15. What has been your experience with both traditional and contemporary forms of music and worship, and which do you prefer?
16. How would you characterize your style of leadership?
17. If you have an idea for something you would like to start as a ministry of the church, how would you work with church leadership to make it happen? How would you work with your staff?
18. What spiritual gifts and abilities has God granted you?
19. What major events or experiences of your past have affected you most profoundly?
20. What is your understanding about how God makes his will known as to whether you should accept this new position if it is offered?
21. Why did you feel it was time to seek this opportunity for ministry or to leave your previous one?

22. What are some of the goals that you have, both personally and professionally, that could be consistent with ministry at this church?
23. How do you address the topic of financial giving in the pulpit?
24. How will you deal with conflict between yourself and members of the church board? Church congregation? Church staff?
25. How will you foster a positive reputation of our church in the community?
26. Describe your convictions about the family and what the church should be doing to impact the community through family ministry.
27. How does your spouse view her or his role as the spouse of a minister?
28. How will moving to a new church and/or community impact your spouse and/or family?
29. What is your preference regarding worship style?
30. What do you understand the relationship between social concerns and evangelism to be?
31. What kinds of mission experiences have you had? How have they shaped your worldview?
32. Why are you considering leaving your present ministry position?
33. What is your preferred approach to church governance and why?
34. What is your view regarding the place of the church and political issues?
35. Who are you currently mentoring in ministry? Describe your priorities in this regard.
36. What are your personal strengths and weaknesses in ministry?
37. Would you describe yourself more as a leader or manager?
38. What was your favorite class in seminary? Least favorite?
39. Would you describe yourself as a self-starter?
40. What programs have you developed in past ministries? Were they successful?
41. Discuss any theological issues you are currently wrestling with.
42. What past experiences have helped shape your personal core values?
43. How many people have you led to Christ through personal evangelism?
44. What experiences have you had conducting church discipline?
45. Discuss your personal philosophy regarding debt.
46. Describe any accountability relationships you have right now.
47. Are there any relationship failures from your past that need to be resolved?
48. Provide an example from your past where you had a vision, developed a ministry program based on that vision, and saw it to fulfillment.
49. Have you had any experience serving at a church during a building campaign?
50. If you came to this church, would you have any outside ministry obligations, such as speaking at camps, chaplaincy, writing projects, teaching at a seminary, etc.?

If you have answered these questions (and no doubt many more) well, your next step along this ministry journey is the congregational interview. It makes the search committee interview seem pretty tame and predictable. After all, the search committee has had the advantage of scouring your resume in advance, hearing firsthand from your friends and former colleagues how well you have served in ministry. The members of the congregation, however, do not have that advantage. Many may come with misconceptions about what they have heard about you, and a few who prefer another candidate may come to the meeting with a personal agenda that isn't very well hidden.

The Congregational Interview

Not all churches conduct an all-church congregational interview. It is usually part of the selection process at some point in churches that have a congregational form of governance. However, even those churches that are elder ruled or where the pastor is selected by a denominational leader (e.g., bishop, superintendent, etc.) may still conduct a congregational interview for the purpose of allowing the members of the church to ask questions and get to know you better.

It would be misleading for us to say that these meetings are enjoyable. They rarely are fun, because there is no way to prepare for the questions you will be asked. Some questions make sense, such as, "Tell us why you would consider leaving your current ministry to come to our church," or "If you were to come here, what changes would you make in the first year?" But there may also be those in attendance who come prepared to make you look foolish or unprepared in hopes of making the candidate of their choice look better (even if he or she isn't even being considered by the search committee). Sometimes a person brings a question to a congregational interview because he wants to show the congregation how informed he is about current conditions in the church. It might be a loaded question presented to embarrass the previous pastor or a member of the church board. It is hard to predict or to prepare for such questions, and the skill of a diplomat is needed to answer them without falling into a trap.

As you respond to the questions that are presented, ask yourself if there is an underlying issue that may transcend the question itself. Who is doing the asking? What is the tone of the person posing the question? Is he or she sitting alone or in the midst of a large group? Is this the congregation's E. F. Hutton asking a trick question or the lone voice of a caring individual? Ask God for a discerning spirit as you hear the questions and pray also for a wise response.

Recall that Jesus had his share of troublemakers who followed him around asking questions too. Many of these questions were intended to trip him up or to defend the questioner's own personal or religious agenda. Go into such meetings with the assurance that if God wants you to be the chosen shepherd of the church, no man or woman dare stand in opposition of his selection. God is more than capable of fighting his own battles. Be polite, and don't be afraid to say that you prefer to focus on the future rather than the past.

Season your speech with references from Scripture, but don't answer each question with a litany of Bible verses. This isn't a game of Bible trivia, and people won't be impressed as much by the amount of Scripture you can quote as by hearing you apply a passage relevant to the specific needs of this congregation. Can you speak with a balance between truth and grace? Are you loving? Does your tone communicate a legalistic attitude? Can you be vulnerable with your answers? Can you give examples that allow others to laugh at your humanity? Do your responses reveal your core values? These are the kinds of things the people really want to discover about you.

Remember also that your appearance is being judged as much as the competency of your answers. People expect their pastor to look the part, so come to this meeting as you would on Sunday morning. Come to the meeting with your heart prepared, your thoughts collected, and wearing what you feel is appropriate given your audience.

Dealing with the Oops Factor

It is not uncommon to leave an interview wishing you could take back something you said. If you find this happens, here is what you can do to correct the problem:

1. Don't panic if you find you didn't respond well to a question you were asked.
2. When you have finished your current response, go back to the individual and say, "I'm sorry, I think I may have misunderstood your question. Would you mind if I rephrase it to see if I understand just what you mean?"
3. Proceed to rephrase the question. Ask if your understanding is correct.
4. Take this opportunity to clarify your response and correct anything you said earlier.
5. Let your questioner know that you would be happy to continue the dialogue after the interview.

When You Misspeak

It's pretty tough responding to questions without much knowledge of what is going to be asked. Why do you think presidents do it so seldom? Sometimes you say something, and as the words come out of your mouth, you wish you could take them back. But you can't. Your answer is out there as a permanent record.

Inevitably you will get asked a question that makes you feel uncomfortable or that you don't quite understand. You do your best to answer it, but it keeps coming back to your mind as the interview goes on. It happens to everyone. How do you handle that when it happens?

Don't leave the interview with regrets. Authors Ronni Eisenberg and Kate Kelly suggest in their helpful book *Organize Your Job Search*, that you deal with the "What I should have said" factor by saying, "Excuse me, I'm not certain I fully understood the question you asked earlier about.... I should have explained...." The fact that you had the presence of mind to clarify your thoughts and revisit an issue will get you points, and the best part is that you won't leave the interview feeling regretful that you just "blew the interview" in front of all those people.[2]

After the Interview

You have now run the gauntlet of formal interviews. You have met with the search committee and fielded their questions (interrogation?), and you have made it through the congregational interview as well. Where do you go from here?

Now you enter one of the most challenging times along the career journey: you wait for the phone to ring.

During this season of waiting, the search committee is meeting to discuss your interviews with them and before the congregation. More than likely, they are also bringing in additional candidates from their short list (usually no more than three people) and are running them through the same series of formal interviews.

You are not powerless, however, and don't have to sit back and remain aloof. After a few days have passed, call the chairperson of the search committee to express your appreciation for the time that the committee invested in making your recent visit a pleasant experience for you and your spouse. Taking the time to call demonstrates that interpersonal relations are important to you. Some candidates simply prefer to send a note to say thanks, but a phone call is far more beneficial for several reasons:

1. It allows you to get a general feel for how your visit was received by the search committee and/or the congregation.
2. You can ask if there are any questions that need further clarification from the interview(s). Ask if he or she felt your responses were clearly understood by everyone involved.

3. You can follow up on any details or items of information that you wanted to provide while you were there or that were requested of you in one of your meetings.

4. You can clarify or correct any information you provided as a response in one of your meetings.

5. If you sense a good rapport with the chairperson of the search committee, you can ask what the timetable is for making a decision.

None of the things on this list are available to you if you simply drop a note in the mail saying thanks for the interview(s). This follow-up call allows you to do so much more. In some cases, it might make the difference between getting the position or not, because the search committee may be operating off of misinformation based on your response to a question. Your clarification may make the difference in them considering your application.

How to Fail Your Interview

In a helpful book entitled *The Insider's Guide to Finding a Job*, Wendy Enelow and Shelly Goldman provide some helpful insights on what *not* to say during your interview(s).[3] The following is a list of common mistakes that will not only sink your interview, but may also facilitate your departure to the airport.

1. *Not preparing enough.* Fundamentally, the biggest mistake people make is that they do not prepare adequately for the interview(s). A few hours just isn't enough. Plan, prepare, and discover everything you can about the job in advance. It's not only important, it's essential!

2. *Not knowing your greatest selling points.* You should come prepared with a brief sound bite that answers the question, Why should we hire you for this position? If you can't answer that question in a clean and well-crafted statement within three minutes, you are in trouble!

3. *Not asking the right questions.* At some point the committee will ask you what questions you have about the job. This is where you need to come prepared with some questions that reveal your grasp of the situation and your ability to solve the issues they are facing. Talk like a member of the team, not as someone from the outside looking in. They are looking for a team player, so the sooner you talk like one, the better you will look to them.

4. *Not asking for the job.* Don't be afraid to let the person/committee know that you are interested in filling the position (if you are) and to enquire about the next step in the interviewing process. Playing "hard to get" is generally not viewed in a positive light by those in charge of hiring a candidate.

5. *Asking about the salary.* The interview isn't the time to request specifics about the salary or compensation package. There will be time enough to discuss

those matters if they decide to hire you. Asking questions about the salary at this stage in the process makes it look as if you are overly focused on financial issues. Instead, ask questions about how performance will be evaluated, and close the interview with a summary of how you will meet those performance expectations.

Sure, mistakes are made by both parties during the interview stage. Perhaps some meetings aren't programmed as well as they could have been. Maybe your responses seemed a bit fragmented or you misunderstood a question or two. That doesn't have to spell the end of the process. It simply means that you might have to do a little bit of work making up for getting off to a bumpy start. Besides, having gone through the interview stage is helpful for both you and the ministry. You each learn some lessons, and you're both better off for the experience. Don't lose heart if you aren't selected. Use it as a learning experience, and you'll be that much better off when the next one comes along.

Going through the formal interview stage of the journey can be a daunting task. It is one of the scariest parts of the entire job search. But if you plan well in advance by doing your homework and preparing responses to expected questions (see the list on pages 230 – 31), you can do much to alleviate the stress and fear associated with this stage of the pastoral appointment. Formal interviews are designed to reveal information that is not apparent on your resume or application. Much like the engagement period for a young couple in love, it takes the relationship beyond the dating stage to a more serious (and sometimes intimidating) stage of development. It is necessary and helpful for all parties involved, but no one ever said this part of the journey would be easy or fun.

CHAPTER 18

SCOUTING THE LAND OF MILK AND HONEY

Visiting the Church and Community

MICK BOERSMA

They gave Moses this account: "We went into the land to which you sent us, and it does flow with milk and honey!"
Numbers 13:27 NIV

After a relatively short period of exchanging documents and enjoying a few phone conversations with members of the search committee, my wife and I found ourselves driving through the majestic forests of western Washington on our way to candidate at Country Bible Church. Raised in the country myself, I had an image of a small, white-frame building, complete with bell tower and hitching post. The parsonage would be from the set of *Little House on the Prairie*, except it would have electricity and plumbing.

Imagine our surprise when we arrived in the community and found a 3,500-square-foot home and the most picturesque worship center in town, a facility that drew engaged couples by the dozen to request a wedding in its glass-ended sanctuary. We were on scene in our new community, ready to plunge into five adventure-filled days of candidacy for the senior pastor position. Here was a place we had never seen before, a culture significantly different from our own, and a group of people willing to take the risk of sharing the future with us. Five crucial days, and our lives would never be the same.

At this point in your journey, you have been selected as the candidate for a particular ministry position. Paperwork has been exchanged, initial interviews have been done, and all that remains is for the search committee (with the approval of the official church board) to present you to the congregation as their official candidate. In this chapter we will consider candidacy week. A great time of discovery and sharing, it could be compared to the exploration undertaken by those twelve Israelite leaders into the Promised Land. Their future depended on collecting accurate information and, of course, the power of the living God who promised it to them in the first place.

As you find yourself an official candidate preparing to "spy out the land," it is crucial to approach the adventure well prepared. We offer a checklist of considerations that, if heeded, will help ensure a successful candidacy experience and prepare you for a rich season of ministry.

Candidating Week Essentials
Never Travel Alone

Under no circumstances should you ever agree to candidate at a church without your spouse—and even your children. Your loved ones need to experience this adventure with you. They need to sense the atmosphere, meet the people, and take in the landscape. Sharing this trip together is the only way to hope for a good decision once the vote is taken and the offer presented.

I have also found that a spouse and children catch a lot of things we miss. They have radar that identifies anomalies to which we are insensitive. They are interested in certain features of the community that may not interest us. They see possibilities that we don't even consider. Perhaps that's one reason Moses sent twelve men instead of just one into the Promised Land. In the end, only two saw the real picture. And had the people listened to Joshua and Caleb, they could have avoided forty years in the wilderness!

Be Prepared

By this time you will have provided a resume and other materials requested by the search committee and experienced a number of interviews. Yet the official candidacy week will involve more interviews and interactions with all kinds of people and ministries. Being ready for all this is a must.

1. *Pray.* The great majority of pastors in our survey found prayer to be a most important discipline during the time of transition, second only to sharing with their spouses. Enlist the prayers of friends, family, and colleagues who are aware of your situation. Regular communion with the Father will bring wisdom and peace of mind, very much needed in these heady days of investigation (Phil. 4:6–7; James 1:5).

2. *Get rest.* The typical candidate schedule in most churches is quite rigorous. While some associate positions will require a few days, most senior pastor openings will call for an eight-day schedule, including two Sundays. You will be asked to preach both Sundays and meet with a host of committees and ministries during a fast-paced and exhausting schedule. Regardless of the position being filled, you will have meetings with the official board, church staff, volunteer leaders, and congregation members. Unless a parsonage is provided, you will likely have a guided tour through the community and a visit with a Realtor.

Many itineraries I have seen don't leave much opportunity for rest and relaxation, so it is important that you get what rest you can *before* this week of frantic activity begins. While preparing for a candidacy week can itself be exhausting, you will want to pace yourself and make sure you arrive there in good physical, mental, and spiritual shape. If they offer to fly you and your family out for the week, take the offer. Let the host church be as gracious as they want to be. Offering to drive the thousand miles might seem magnanimous of you, but it will leave you tired once you get there.

3. *Have your research in hand.* We didn't have the Internet in 1970 when my wife and I candidated at our first church, so we didn't know much about our future home when we arrived. Today you have the opportunity to uncover all kinds of information about the church and community through their websites. In addition, you should have received important details from the church through the materials they sent you during the early days of the process (see the sidebar on page 217 for a list of items to look for). Take time to prepare a set of questions this information prompts, and look for opportune times to bring them to the table.

Be Flexible

Candidating week is quite a phenomenon. It's sort of like "speed dating," a modern concept where people sit down together for five minutes, share all they can about themselves, then switch to other partners when the bell rings. At the end of the night, daters decide who they would like to talk to a second time. A lot is riding on just a few minutes of hurried conversation.

Having just a few days to interact face-to-face with your future fellowship gives rise to the need for flexibility on everyone's part. Myriad interests capture the hearts of God's people, and they all want to know what you think about them. Everyone will want a small piece of you, and orchestrating a schedule that will allow for maximum exposure will be a challenge for you and your hosts. Be available to everyone and give them all the time and attention your energy will allow. You can always catch up on sleep when you get home. The five days we spent with the people at Country Bible Church were fun and furious. We saw more of the town and its people than we ever imagined we could. Upon our return to California, we took two weeks off before loading the moving van and heading north on Interstate 5.

Be Observant

The focus here is on the *passive* aspects of your investigation of the church and community. You need to be watching, listening, and getting a feel for this opportunity as you spend time interacting with the people and their environment. While it may not be practical in some cases, staying with a church family during candidating week can offer a more intimate glimpse into the hearts and minds of your new acquaintances.

My wife and I had no children when we candidated, and we were able to stay with two different families during those five days. The first night was with the treasurer, a longtime member, fine man, and purveyor of conservative fiscal practice (a glimpse of things to come). The following evenings were at the home of a young deacon, his wife, and four children. This couple had a habit of staying up until 2:00 every morning, but we managed to beg our leave and hit the sheets by at least midnight. Being with these dear folks gave us a sense that they were the kind of people we could grow to love very deeply. Our prediction was true.

Any congregation is composed of various groups representing a number of interests, passions, and perspectives. W. Bud Phillips, a professor and expert in church ministry, has identified eight major subsystems that are present within most congregations.[1] Keep the sidebar below handy as you seek to identify and better understand the various groups within the church.

In addition, note how the people in the church respond to your preaching and teaching and how they interact with one another. Is the worship joyful and sincere? Do people bring their Bibles to Sunday services? Do the facilities reflect an appreciation for excellence and good stewardship? One of our surveyed pas-

Eight Subsystems of a Local Church

Worship and Celebration: those who work hard at creative and meaningful worship

Education and Nurture: those committed to teaching and education ministry

Communal: those who greet and seek to assimilate and welcome others

Reparative: those who develop support communities for people needing the church's love

Maintenance and Sustenance: those concerned about financial and facility matters

Transient and/or Transitional: those not staying long in the community but wanting to make a contribution

Evangelism: those who focus on bringing the gospel to others outside the church

Outreach: those who see the importance of supporting the wounded, poor, and disadvantaged in the local community

tors noted that as he candidated at various churches he and his wife would ask themselves, "Would we attend this church if we weren't part of the staff?" That is a valuable question to ponder as you look and listen.

Be Inquisitive

In this section we speak of the *active* part of your investigation: questions to ask and things to do. We will look first at questions concerning the church and then at the community at large.

Concerning the church. As mentioned above, you have already received a lot of information from the church through personal interviews with its leadership and perspectives from other colleagues and pastors who know something about your new setting. From those prior contacts, you will want to create a list of

---

Be Inquisitive about ...

- The most significant historical events in this ministry
- What drew people to this congregation in the first place
- The more difficult times experienced by this ministry
- The top two or three areas needing attention right now
- Long-term vision for church and various ministries
- What people would change if resources were not an issue
- The best programs the church has going now
- How the church is involved in the community and desires to be involved
- What former pastors did particularly well
- Areas in which former pastors struggled
- Length of time former pastors served at the church
- The circumstances under which the last pastor left
- The most frequent sources of conflict within the church family
- How decisions are made (the formal and informal power structures)
- Ways the church has helped its pastors grow and become more effective
- Roles typically taken by spouse and children of the pastor
- Expectations regarding schedule and priorities of the pastor
- How compensation issues are handled
- Financial health and giving patterns of the church
- Things people would change or add to the facilities

clarifying questions designed to get closer to the heart of particular issues that concern you.

Also, be prepared to ask the various church committees that will interview you (see chapter 17) some questions of your own. They will appreciate your interest and initiative, even if they aren't expecting you to be so curious. I have had many conversations with pastors who wished they would have asked more questions during the candidating process. One in our survey offered this advice: "The little things that bug you at the start may end up being the reason why you leave a few years later." Don't assume anything, explore everything.

When you are on location, visit a few pastors from other churches in the area. Spend some time getting their read on the community and the reputation of your future church. There will be no time more suitable for them to give you an honest appraisal, and it will go a long way in identifying potential ministry friends and establishing good relationships with these congregations and their pastors.

Concerning the community. By this time in the process, you have spent a lot of energy looking at the church in question. On-site candidating, however, gives you your first real opportunity to scope out the local community. I have discovered that a lot of pastors don't spend enough time and effort getting to know their surroundings. They neglect this part of the search process at their own peril. After all, your people *are* this community. To be familiar with the town is to be knowledgeable of the church within it. Here are ten key features you will want to examine as you scout out your promised land.

1. *Culture.* Foreign missionaries spend a lot of time on this one, but pastors moving about the country often don't. This is a big oversight, as culture shock is very real and calls for careful analysis and preparation. One pastor noted that "cultural mismatches give the biggest trouble," and many others cited this as a major challenge during the transition process.

A resource I routinely share with my students and alumni pastors is a schematic of the United States mainland created by Joel Garreau in a book he authored several years ago. In the *Nine Nations of North America*, he identifies and describes the several "nations" that exist within the continent (see the sidebar on page 243).[2] The significant differences among the nations are noted as well as helpful contrasts and qualities that make each nation unique. If you know people who live in the area you are considering, be sure to get their firsthand assessments of it.

To help you with a little of your own sleuthing, here is a list of culture questions you will find handy as you interact with the new neighborhood.

1. Who are the prominent people in this community (in politics, athletics, religion, the arts, etc.)?
2. Who are this community's heroes and heroines?

3. What is the ethnic makeup of this community? Are other languages frequently spoken?
4. What are the most important community observances and celebrations?
5. How do the various churches and religious groups get along in this community? What is their reputation among the nonchurched?
6. Is divorce common and accepted? Is cohabitation socially acceptable?
7. What is the attitude toward gambling and use of alcohol in this community?
8. Do people value personal visitation in this community? Is it acceptable to drop in on folks or are appointments necessary?
9. What foods are most popular here, and how are they usually prepared?
10. What things are taboo in this community?
11. What is the usual dress code for work and casual times?
12. Are people in this community "on time" for things, or is the culture more event oriented?
13. How do people greet one another and say good-bye? Do they shake hands? Is hugging okay?
14. What are the favorite leisure and recreational activities of adults? Of youth?
15. What sports (and professional teams) are popular?
16. How will your financial position and living conditions compare with those of the majority of people living in this community?

To get the best answers to these and other questions, take a lesson from the Australians and plan a "walkabout." Hit Main Street, the mall, and any other venues where you will rub elbows with the public. People love to talk about their community. During a faculty retreat in one of our local mountain communities,

The Nine Nations of North America and Their Capitals

1. The Empty Quarter — Denver
2. Ecotopia — San Francisco
3. The Breadbasket — Kansas City
4. Mexamerica — Los Angeles
5. Quebec — Quebec City
6. New England — Boston
7. The Foundry — Detroit
8. Dixie — Atlanta
9. The Islands — Miami

I plopped down in a Realtor's office and simply asked him what kind of people bought homes in the area. He didn't stop for fifteen minutes. I probably got to know more about that village than some of its inhabitants, and I enjoyed the conversation immensely.

2. *Education.* There are three circumstances that typically make education a big issue for a pastor when candidating: you have school-aged children, your spouse is a schoolteacher and desires employment in the district, or you would like to pursue advanced studies requiring campus-based instruction. In addition to those three items, the condition of the schools will affect your future, since this local feature impacts most of the families in your ministry.

One relatively easy way to get a head start on this investigation is through the United States Department of Education.[3] Visiting their website leads you to a number of vehicles that will provide a wide array of information on both public and private schools. State departments of education are also a good place to look. In addition, most real estate websites provide profiles on public schools because this information usually affects home prices in the area.

But the best place to assess the educational climate in your new community is at ground level, face-to-face with the people who matter—teachers, students, and their parents. If you aren't sure what to ask, the list of strategies that follows will enable you to get to the important issues.[4] Have it with you when visiting the school and talking to the locals.

Special Circumstances

1. For those who prefer Christian education, it is important to discover what options are available. Get references and recommendations from those who have children attending different Christian schools. Find out why they chose the one they did. If the nearest Christian school is a distance away, find out if there is a carpool or bus for transportation.

2. For those who homeschool, it's a good idea to find out if others in the church homeschool their children and talk to them about homeschool groups in the area. Certain public schools and local colleges provide support through training, facilities, and materials.

3. Those moving to foreign mission locations must wrestle with decisions about where and how their children will receive an adequate education. Mission agencies usually provide help and counsel in this challenging area of planning.

1. Talk to parents in the church about the local schools—particularly those with children your kids' age or with those who have already been through the system. Knowing where the good schools are can help determine where you look for housing.

2. Some districts have different programs at different schools and allow children to attend the school best suited to their needs (e.g., vocational studies, education, agriculture, music or the arts, etc.). Some schools have a program that earns them a reputation (e.g., award-winning music groups or science programs). Learn what programs are available both within the district and in nearby areas and how transfers are done.

3. Ask about the school's score on national and state testing. Where does it rank in comparison to other schools in the state and in the area? Are the children testing out below or above the state and national averages at each grade level? How well are they meeting the goals for the national "No Child Left Behind" initiative? How well are the children from this school doing at passing the exit exam for graduation from high school (required in many states)? How many of the students go on to college?

4. If moving to a major metropolitan area, you will want to know how many of the students are non-English-speaking and how the system handles that challenge. It is important to know that your child won't be held back by others or become bored and disinterested in school, but will be given challenging opportunities.

5. It is helpful to know the sort of teachers the school has. How many years have they been teaching on the average? Is there any sort of mentor program in place for new teachers? Are there any master teachers on site?

6. Along with the student-to-teacher ratio, it is good to know what sort of classified help is available in the classroom. How many aides? For students with special needs, this becomes particularly important, as it is often the aide who helps the children as much or more than the teacher.

7. What sort of programs do they have for children with special needs? Is tutoring available if children fall behind?

8. In regard to curriculum, it is a good idea to look through the textbooks that are used, as well as explore the school's method of teaching reading, writing, and math. The amount of homework is a concern to some parents as well.

9. Find out what approach the school takes on issues of special concern to Christians (e.g., sexuality, marriage and family, creation, and religion-related issues like meditation). Some schools allow for release-time Bible classes during the school day, which are taught by pastors.

10. In regard to facilities and equipment, access to computers is becoming more a part of education. Does the school have a computer lab? Are there

computers in the classrooms? Does the school participate in any online learn-ing programs?

11. Extracurricular activities are a plus, especially in the lives of teens. Find out what sports, music, art, and drama programs and clubs are available.

12. What sort of behavioral standards are upheld? How is discipline administered?

13. How does the school communicate with parents? Under what circumstances would you expect to hear from the teacher?

14. What venues are available at the school to parents who want to be actively involved in their children's education (e.g., parent-teacher organization, class-room assistant, room mother, field trip chaperone)?

3. *Economy.* You will want to find out what the people in your new con-gregation do for a living. While the search committee may have provided some information, you now have the opportunity to hear how people feel about their occupations. Take time to visit their places of work, see what concerns they deal with on a daily basis, and become familiar with the vast array of things people do to make a living. Of course, you will only have time for a snapshot, but it will help you to see the community for what it really is.

General information about the economies of various areas of the country can be obtained through the United States Census Bureau.[5] Statistics can be secured from any state and a large number of business sectors within each. And don't forget to ask the local businesspeople how things are going. My experience is that they will be honest with you and offer their opinion on what the govern-ment can do to improve things. That brings us to the next key feature of your new community.

4. *Politics.* In today's world, politics is not just about how one views the role of the federal government in the fifty states. It encompasses a wide array of vital social and ethical issues that affect everyone's life. States are colored red or blue, depending on how their people vote. In some places, being a Christian means pressure to vote for a certain candidate or belong to a particular political party. What do people in the community expect the role of religion to be in the market-place of public political debate? How should religious leaders lead?

There are legal limits to what churches and pastors can do in the political arena. But every church and town has its own way of dealing with this, and it is wise for the pastoral candidate to draw perspective from the congregation and its leaders. You can find out how the area voted in national elections from the Federal Election Commission.[6] Such insight can help you determine the kinds of issues being debated by your community and the presence or lack of consensus among its inhabitants.

5. *Population.* Visit the United States Census Bureau website to gain access to a great deal of useful information.[7] You can discover how the population in various states is aging, where people are moving to, whether an area is growing or declining, and how ethnic patterns are changing. Information like this can help you see what kinds of issues may be a part of your future ministry.

6. *Housing.* During your candidating week, you will be given time to look for housing—unless the church provides it, of course. You can do your homework beforehand by accessing some of the many Realtor websites. They will cover neighborhoods, values, appreciation, schools, and safety. Take your time. Don't sign anything until you have peace about it. If you are married, include your spouse in every decision. It might be a good idea to rent for a few months and give yourself time to check out what the community has to offer. We lived in the church-owned home for eight years. When we finally built our own house, we were aware that certain parts of the area received more wind than others and that some acreages were inexpensive but would not perk (accommodate a septic system). Once again, do your homework!

7. *Recreation.* If you like downhill skiing, most of Nebraska will be a chal- lenge for you. Surfers need special grace to pastor in Arizona. Every place has its unique offerings when it comes to recreation. And it is important that you address this issue when candidating. Reinvigorating your zeal, enthusiasm, and energy is necessary for you and your family to thrive in ministry. Your examination of the new community should include getting a sense of what kinds of recreational activities are available and whether you will be able to afford them. Family mem- bers may have to be willing to develop new recreation interests.

8. *Spiritual climate.* In visits with alumni here and overseas, some of our graduates have told us of the spiritual darkness enveloping their communities. Witchcraft is common in some places. Other towns are havens for New Age groups and cults of various kinds. Still other parts of this world are post-Chris- tian, living in a darkened state of pseudo-religiosity in which most people believe in God but live as though he does not really exist.

On the other hand, some ministers find themselves on the crest of great spiritual awakening. We know of pastors whose churches are bursting with new converts in communities abuzz with spiritual energy. I believe God calls his people to both kinds of places, and while we shouldn't judge his will based on the current spiritual climate, it is a good idea to know what kind of condition your community is experiencing. It will help you know how to pray and prepare for the journey ahead. Ask congregants what they see around them. Begin during this candidating week to uncover the spiritual history of your community. Such insight will sharpen you and your church as you together develop a vision for the future.

9. *Atmospheric climate.* Several of our survey participants noted what a challenge different weather patterns were for them and their families. Candidating in July in Iowa won't prepare you for Iowa in January. Climate is an important item to cover in your investigation. You can find good information about any area through the United States Department of Commerce's National Climatic Data Center.[8] This site gives weather patterns covering decades and a realistic picture of climatic features of most areas of the country.

Climate is a significant feature of any area. Begin during your candidating week to better understand it and its implications on your future ministry there. You will find people eager to offer their opinions, and you will begin to form warm and lasting relationships in the process.

10. *Community services.* There are places in this world where such a term has no meaning. You are on your own for virtually everything. Most of us will never live in such places, but wherever we go, we will find varying degrees of community services available to us, and it's helpful to know what's out there. We speak of things like police and fire protection, medical care, and social services. What about parks, street maintenance, and city government? Are retail outlets readily available? Can I get my vehicles repaired nearby?

Again, you don't base God's call on how robust the community services are, but they will be a part of your reality when you come to minister. You and your family may have to ask if you are prepared to do without some conveniences. Will you be able to graciously receive a lesser quality or speed of service than you have experienced before? No one likes the new guy on the block who constantly complains about how great things were back in "Perfect Town, USA." Chances are they will wish he'd go back there!

Conclusion

Enjoy the trip. Look over the land. Uncover all you can. Accept the realities. Understand that getting the whole picture will take time and never will be fully realized. If you sense God's leading to accept the offer, love the people he is giving you and plan to stay a long time.

Have faith. One pastor put it this way: "If you want to discover distant lands, don't be afraid to lose sight of the shore." Nineteenth-century Quaker and poet John Greenleaf Whittier offered this observation: "For of all sad words of tongue or pen, the saddest are these: 'It might have been!'" When your investigation has revealed as much as a candidating process will allow, and God makes it clear he wants you to take the land, go for it. The Israelites suffered much because of the faithlessness of ten men. May you keep company with Joshua and Caleb, men of faith and character who saw the challenges of the land but trusted in their Lord's ability to make it theirs.

CHAPTER 19

OBEYING THE TOUR GUIDE

Discerning God's Call

MICHAEL ANTHONY

Let me hear Your lovingkindness in the morning;
For I trust in You;
Teach me the way in which I should walk;
For to You I lift up my soul.
Psalm 143:8

The tour guide had just stopped the vehicle. I was staring into the eyes of an adult male African lion sitting under a bush just forty feet away. There was nothing between his teeth and me — no zoo barricades, strong steel bars, or towering walls. The tour guide noticed this huge beast as we were driving along. It appeared to him that the lion had recently eaten a meal and was *probably* not in the mood to do anything but rest. I was hoping he knew what he was talking about when I released the door handle from my grip. I stepped out of the Jeep to capture the moment on film.

The tour guide instructed me on what to do and what not to do. He kept his rifle at the ready in case the lion decided to lunge and charge. We both knew there was little to no chance of getting back into the Jeep in time. I had to rely on the training and knowledge of my tour guide or I would become the lion's next meal. I have never paid more attention to a tour guide in all my life.

Pastors across North America are listening to another kind of tour guide — one who not only holds the knowledge of personal safety and peace, but that of professional fulfillment and career satisfaction as well. Disregarding this tour guide has its own set of consequences. Some have failed to heed his instructions and have suffered irreparable damage. I'm talking, of course, about our heavenly Father, the eternal tour guide of our faith and ministry.

Hearing an earthly tour guide when he is standing a few feet away from you is one thing; hearing God speak is quite another. Their voices just don't sound quite the same. I have known of people who have said they heard God speak to them in an audible voice, but God does not often operate that way. So how are we to discern his direction?

Voice Recognition

Hearing the voice and recognizing its origin can be two very different things for some. I remember a time when I answered the phone and began talking to the person on the other end only to discover a few minutes into the call that the person I was speaking to wasn't who I thought he was. It was pretty embarrassing to say the least. "Sorry, Bill. I thought you were Tom." Try that the next time your spouse calls you at your office and see how well it goes over. She'll be thinking, *How could he not recognize my voice after all these years?* Perhaps God thinks the same thing when we don't recognize his voice.

When a call comes from a church to become their new minister, you will be faced with an important decision regarding whether God is speaking to you or you are hearing the voice of a well-meaning search committee member. You had better get it right, because there is a lot at stake in the decision that rests on your shoulders.

What can you do to determine God's will once that call comes in? A few suggestions follow.

1. *Clear your mind of the current distractions and do some assessment.* Get away from the turmoil and pressures associated with your current ministry setting. Ask yourself, "Am I doing what really fulfills my original calling? Am I using my God-given spiritual gift(s) to their fullest capability? Do I have a peace deep in my spirit that I'm doing what God has asked me to do?" If the answer to these three questions is a resounding "yes," then stay put and rest in the knowledge that you are where God wants you to be—even in the midst of turmoil and pressures. If the answer to these questions is uncertain or a resounding no, it may be time to start asking God for a fresh direction.

2. *Spend a season of time in the Word of God searching for guidance.* God often speaks through a passage of Scripture. Allow the Holy Spirit to apply his Word to your current ministry context. Remember the words of King David, "Your word is a lamp to my feet and a light to my path" (Ps. 119:105).

3. *Spend a significant time in prayer asking God for guidance.* Ultimately, your life is in God's hands, and you are simply asking for marching orders so you can faithfully serve him. Consider supplementing this time of prayer with a season of fasting. Giving you his direction is God's responsibility. If you hear something, take action. But if you hear nothing, stay put.

4. *Talk it over with your spouse and get her or his input.* God calls a husband and wife as a team rather than just one individual. Both of you are created in the image of God and possess the same Holy Spirit. "When a wife says it's time to leave, she may not be driven by selfishness or fear but by clear-headed conviction. If your wife is in touch with God, herself, and you, listen carefully. God has a habit of putting opposites together to provide a better field of vision."[1]

5. *Seek wise counsel from those who have your best interests at heart.* Ask those who have served as mentors to you and ask other spiritually minded men and women who know you well and understand your current ministry experience what they feel is God's will for you concerning his call.

Circumstantial Confirmation: Does God Still Give Signs?

This is the part of the chapter where I'm going to get controversial, so I may as well add a disclaimer here. Asking God for a fleece is clearly biblical, as we saw in chapter 1. Many Bible teachers, however, see this as an act of spiritual immaturity, and I can understand their position. After all, we have several advantages today that the Old Testament saints didn't have. For example, we have the full scope of God's Scriptures, we have the Holy Spirit living inside of us to lead and guide us, and finally, we have far more hindsight. Let's face it, signs can be pretty difficult to interpret too. As Garry Friesen puts it, "The only time that circumstances can be 'read' is when a divine interpretation is placed upon them by supernatural revelation. Apart from such revelation, circumstances may be taken to mean almost anything."[2]

Is God obligated to answer our request for a sign? Absolutely not! But does he? In many instances I'd have to say that he does. Perhaps it is because he recognizes our own weaknesses and lack of faith, but I have heard many stories from pastors who asked God for a fleece and he provided direction through it. Some would say it's a coincidence, but I try to keep an open mind. Since I have heard a great many of these stories, I would like to offer some suggestions:

1. *Don't ask God for a sign to do something that he has already clearly told you to do in his Word* (e.g., witness to those around you, serve him in your community, use your gifts to minister to others, give a portion of your income to the needs of those less fortunate, etc.). He has already told you to do it, so get on with it.

2. *Make the fleece fit the request.* Don't tell God that you will only go to seminary if he strikes down your codependent parent with lightening so you will feel a sense of release. That's a little extreme, don't you think?

3. *Relate the sign to the request.* A deacon at my church once told me about the sign he used to determine whether he should marry his girlfriend. He told God, "If she opens the door wearing that cute pink poodle skirt, the white sweater, and a blue hair ribbon, I'll know she is the one." That's what she wore when she opened

the door, so he proposed to her. Don't make life-impacting decisions based on hair ribbons and poodle skirts. If you are trying to determine God's call on your life to go to a particular school, for instance, apply to the school first and let the admissions officer speak for God and use the sign of an acceptance or rejection letter to guide you.

4. *Do what is in your heart.* Psalm 37:4 says, "Delight yourself in the LORD; and He will give you the desires of your heart." When I am counseling someone who has to choose between two perfectly acceptable options and he doesn't know which one to pick, I tell him to select the one he wants most, then to firmly set a date in his mind when he will make his decision public. Then I tell him to wait a few days and see if he has a peace about the decision he is about to announce. If so, he should announce it as planned and move forward. If he doesn't have a peace about the direction that he has set his heart on, then he should change it to the other option and give it some time too. Philippians 4:6–7 says, "Do not be anxious about anything, but in everything, by prayer and petition, with thanksgiving, present your requests to God. And the peace of God, which transcends all understanding, will guard [the *Amplified Bible* translates that word as 'arbitrate'] your hearts and your minds in Christ Jesus" (NIV). He will allow his Holy Spirit to arbitrate, or judge, the merits of a decision by giving you his peace. If you have a peace about it, decision made.

5. *Do what is expedient.* Don't waste a lot of time trying to make a decision if it needs to be made in a timely manner. For example, if you have to decide whether to accept a church's invitation, give them a reasonable amount of time (generally two weeks is sufficient) and then begin following steps 1 through 4 above. If you still don't have a clear answer from God after two weeks, you don't have God's peace and the answer is most likely "no."

Here is another example. Perhaps you are waiting to hear if God has called you to attend seminary. You apply to two schools and await his answer. You receive an answer on January 15 congratulating you on your acceptance at one school, but your spot will only be held until February 15, after which time it will be given to another applicant. By February 15 you have only heard from the one school. Do you wait until you hear from the second school or send in your deposit? The answer according to this principle is send in your deposit before you lose your spot. By waiting to hear from the second school, you may lose out on attending both of them. What happens if you get an acceptance letter from the second seminary a week later? Throw it away and forget about it. God is sovereign, and if he had wanted you to attend the second school, he would have provided the invitation by the deadline.

6. *Keep your word and don't look back.* Once you determine what your "sign" will be, set your mind to act on it if and when it is confirmed. Don't be like Gideon who kept adding to his fleece as he went along. God's patience may run out.

The Dilemma of Two Open Doors

You may find yourself in a position where two churches issue you a call at the same time. Right now you might like to have that problem, but such a dilemma can be nerve-racking as you try to figure out which one is God's will. Here is what I suggest: Follow the steps cited above first. Then if you still don't know which one to take, examine the motives of your heart and make sure they are pure. Now pick the one you think is the best fit for your giftedness, and start packing your bags. In the event that you have two equally compelling options, God may be saying, "I can use you equally as well in either setting. I trust you; you decide."

The dilemma of two open doors can be mind-boggling and can start you down a path of asking for signs and miraculous activities that would rival Israel's exodus from Egypt. Don't succumb to immature requests for signs and wonders over every little decision you make. That's why God gave us his Word, his Holy Spirit, prayer, and the wise counsel of others. Our service is of the utmost importance to God, and he will take the responsibility of informing us of his direction when the time is right.

Confusing the Message

Some people have clearly not been very effective in hearing God's voice or discerning his message. For any number of reasons, the voices that impact our decision-making ability get confused and distorted. When that happens, sometimes it helps to pull away from the noise surrounding us and give God a clear channel into our souls. For some, it will involve more than a weekend of solitude and become a more prolonged season of concerted study.

It may even involve "testing the waters" to see if there is any verification to what you are hearing. As Edmund Clowney, a retired seminary president, writes, "Uncertainty about a call to ministry may indicate with certainty a call to theological training. Even when God does not call a man to pastoral work, he often leads through seminary study to other ministries of teaching and to informed leadership in the church."[3] If you are transitioning between church ministries and you have never had a season of seminary training, it might be a good opportunity for you to receive some as you are waiting to hear his voice. If you are on the verge of being forced to resign, it may offer you a face-saving way to depart by enrolling in seminary to pursue additional theological training or an advanced degree. Perhaps there you will hear God's voice regarding his plans for your future.

Sometimes there are too many voices coming at us simultaneously and they prevent us from hearing God speak. If those who spoke to us on God's behalf had pure motives, we could depend on them for guidance. However, most people, including ourselves, seldom operate with pure motives. I remember dating a young woman during my young adult years. We had only gone out a few times when she told me God had informed her that I was to become her husband. It freaked me out! I told her that to the best of my knowledge, God could speak to me too, and until he gave me the same message, it wasn't going to happen. Talk about mixed motives!

Perhaps your wife's parents want you to attend seminary in the city where they live. Do they want you to be near them because it's a great school or because they want to be near their new grandbaby? Do they speak for God? It's not always easy sorting out confusing voices.

Pastors need to have a special conviction in their hearts that they are fulfilling God's destiny with their lives. God's call is a response to greatness, to fulfill what we were created for. Our reason for being comes face-to-face with God's opportunity, causing powerful and exciting things to happen. Pastor John Jackson of Carson Valley Christian Center puts it this way: "Genuine calling is a powerful antidote to the emptiness of boredom or discouragement, to the meaninglessness of superficial, scattered activities, and to the drive to prove ourselves. Calling is not about the size of a church or about the scope of a ministry — it's about following the heart of God. This is the crucial point that many miss."[4]

The process of forming a clear vision begins with hearing from God. God's call in our lives is shaped by three crucial elements: (1) our grasp of the heart of God, which determines our motivation; (2) our grip on the needs of people around us, which shapes the direction of our service; and (3) the gifts God has given us, which determine the effectiveness of our service.[5]

The call of God is designed to communicate his plans for your life. Understand right from the beginning of this journey that you are his child serving according to his purposes. Since he is the only one who can provide clear and unequivocal direction to you, it is his responsibility to make things happen in such a manner that you will know what his direction for your life is. It isn't a game to God, and it shouldn't be one for you either. He will make his call known to you in his time and using his sovereign methods. As the Lord tells us through the prophet Isaiah, his ways are higher than our ways (Isa. 55:8).

CHAPTER 20

CAN I AFFORD THIS TRIP?

Negotiating the Compensation Package

MICHAEL ANTHONY

The elders who direct the affairs of the church well are worthy of double honor, especially those whose work is preaching and teaching. For the Scripture says, "Do not muzzle the ox while it is treading out the grain," and "The worker deserves his wages."
1 Timothy 5:17 – 18 NIV

A few years ago I was in the interior plateau region of central Haiti with a team of college students on a short-term mission trip. I was walking through the local market when I looked back and discovered that one of my students was missing. I backtracked and discovered her in a heated debate with a local street vendor. She had picked up a small tin cup and was trying to negotiate a price for it. Unfortunately, the student had given the woman a ten-dollar bill for a twenty-five-cent cup. With so much cash in hand, the woman who was selling the cup had decided to increase the price substantially in the hopes that the student would get frustrated and walk away. Her plan almost worked.

The student was nearly in tears because the woman refused to give her any change when I walked into the scene. I got pretty animated, slapping my hands together and arguing with heated passion. To the uninformed, I may have appeared rude. But to the locals, I was negotiating like one of them. I retrieved the correct change for the student, and we walked away. My student learned some important lessons that day about the art of negotiating in a foreign culture: negotiate the price before you show your money, bring a friend who knows the culture, and don't be afraid to express your passion.

Few ministers know the art of negotiating their salaries when they enter into this final phase of the job search. They find it distasteful and shy away from anything that seems like self-promotion. They get timid and meek, almost asking to get taken advantage of by those on the committee who know what they are doing. By acting this way, they find themselves at a distinct disadvantage because, like my student, they are not accustomed to the art of "closing the deal."

Effective negotiation leads to a fair and reasonable compensation package for both the pastor and the church. "But," as one expert writes, "because nothing comes easy, negotiating compensation is tough. Indeed, most people fall apart on salary negotiations. Because there is such stress, anxiety, and discomfort with the confrontation and risk-taking negotiating entails, most employees get the short end of the bargain."[1]

Myths about Salary Negotiations

This stage in the career journey is accompanied by a host of myths and misconceptions. Dispelling some of these myths will help you see salary negotiation from a more accurate perspective. Following are five common myths surrounding negotiating compensation packages with the local church.[2]

Myth #1: "People in the church won't like me if I stand up for a higher salary." People appreciate honesty and would rather have a pastor who can address real-life issues fairly and directly rather than hide behind pretense.

Myth #2: "I'm not a lawyer; I'm a proclaimer of the gospel." Each person has negotiating skills that are learned in childhood.

Myth #3: "The church is poor and can't afford to do better." Some churches are already doing all they can financially. However, many are not, and they need to be challenged to step out in faith. The interim pastor may need to speak on stewardship prior to your arrival.

Myth #4: "The church's giving to missions will have to go down if they increase my salary." A healthy program of missions support starts with a healthy local church base. This is accomplished by properly funding its pastoral leaders who are fundamental to its stability and growth.

Myth #5: "Part-time pastors aren't real pastors." The early church started out with lay leaders. Eventually they became so involved with their responsibilities that they needed to receive financial support so they could give themselves wholeheartedly to the work of the local church. In time this led the way to a professional clergy. Some churches don't need a full-time pastor, but for those who do, the pastor needs to be funded appropriately if he or she is to give the ministry highest priority.

Doing Your Own Negotiating

Many pastors would prefer to let someone else do the talking for them when it comes to salary negotiations. If it's so tough to do, why not just let someone else do it for them? The reason is simple: no one can speak as passionately and convincingly about his or her role as the pastor.

Sure, it would be nice to have a search consultant do all the heavy lifting in terms of securing your compensation package for you (see chapter 15), but most ministers will have to do it themselves. This chapter is designed to give you the skills necessary to negotiate successfully. Following are suggestions to guide you in the negotiating process.

Suggestion 1. Never negotiate a compensation package during your first meeting. If you bring up the topic, it will come across as your central focus. If they address it first, they will come across as desperate. Neither is a good position from which to negotiate.

You will want to have a conversation in which compensation is addressed before you get back on the plane, but it should be one of the last meetings you have with the search committee or governing board. In many cases, they may need to secure a vote from the church prior to making an offer, but sometimes the committee likes to have this conversation prior to the candidate's departure so they know what needs to be done to secure his or her acceptance.

Suggestion 2. Come into the meeting with this committee with confidence and composure. Present yourself as professional and secure in your giftedness and capabilities. Avoid saying, "I can work for whatever you want to offer me." That isn't spiritual; it's foolish. Ultimately, you want a compensation package that is fair and reasonable for both parties.

Start the meeting with prayer and recognize that both you and the church want to serve Christ's kingdom as stewards of his resources. Be courteous and polite even if the first offer on the table is well below what you feel the position is worth or what you can afford to live on. They may simply be low-balling you to see your response. As much as you would like to think they are negotiating with everyone's best interests in mind, remember that they are there to represent the church, and their responsibility is to avoid "giving away the farm." Remember too that many of these committee members do this for a living in their secular environments, and this is the only presentation format they know. It isn't biblical, but it's their only frame of reference.

Suggestion 3. Don't take the first offer presented unless you are absolutely certain that it contains everything you and your family need. "The No. 1 mistake made during salary negotiations is giving up too quickly. You must remember that the salary you accept will affect your earning capabilities for several years to come."[3] If you have a firm grasp on your needs and the package offered seems fair and reasonable, say, "Thank you for your offer. I would like to take some time to pray about it and discuss it with my wife." Wait until you get home to shout, "Hallelujah! Thank you, Jesus!"

Suggestion 4. Do your homework in advance and determine what you need to live on as a family. Come into the meeting with a good working knowledge of your own family budget. Bring notes if you need them, but put them in a file folder that can be opened for reference purposes but not left out in the open for curious eyes to read.

If you have done some research in advance, you should have a pretty good idea of the salary range that is reasonable for the position. You can gather this information by asking denominational leaders in that community, other pastors of comparable churches, seminary classmates in the area, search consultants who specialize in servicing the needs of churches, or any local seminary professors.[4] Another helpful source for the Consumer Price Index (CPI) and average salaries of selected white-collar occupations can be obtained from your State Department of Labor or the U.S. Department of Labor, Bureau of Labor Statistics.[5] Much of this data is also available online. Another helpful source is the Effective Buying Index (EBI) found in the *Sales and Marketing Management* magazine available at your local library or bookstore.

Negotiating Dos and Don'ts

Do

1. Investigate the salary range of the ministry based on comparable data.
2. Know the lowest amount you are willing to accept.
3. Remember that the person with whom you are negotiating may be the person with whom you also work once you accept the job.
4. Be realistic.
5. Understand the perspective of the church.
6. Postpone discussing compensation until after all of the interviews and meetings are finished.
7. Get *everything* in writing.

Don't

1. Lie about the amount you are currently making.
2. Volunteer your salary history.
3. Discuss salary during your first meeting.
4. Negotiate in bad faith — be honest and fair.
5. Accept an offer without concerted prayer and discussion with your spouse.
6. Be afraid to ask for a full range of benefits.
7. Accept a position if you don't have peace about it.

Suggestion 5. Never provide a salary history with your application materials, and do not include it on your resume either. *Never* respond to the question, "How much did you make at your former ministry?" or "How much are you currently making?"

"Employers use salary history for a variety of reasons. They want to see if your current salary is beyond the salary range for the position you are seeking, if you have made steady progress on salary in previous positions, and to gain the edge in salary negotiations—since they will have all your information and you will have very little of theirs."[6]

Never lie about your answer; instead, tactfully deflect the question. Politely say that your previous salary figures are private and not a basis for determining your salary in this position since there are different factors involved. That should satisfy anyone with an ounce of propriety. If it doesn't, remain firm and tell them you don't divulge such information. Then say politely with a smile, "Next question?"

Suggestion 6. Don't be overly emotional or offend anyone on the other side of the table. Statements such as, "You might let your family live in a house like that, but I'd never do that to anyone I love," expresses too much personal emotion and will be viewed as an attack. A better way to respond is to say, "The parsonage is lovely in the summer, but the lack of insulation makes maintaining heat problematic in the winter months." Once you put someone on the defensive, they have a difficult time hearing what you are saying and become more reluctant to give in to your requests.[7] Remember, once the negotiations are finalized, you must work with these individuals, and you certainly don't want to start your ministry with hard feelings over compensation negotiations.

Negotiating Styles

Negotiating one's compensation package is one of the most challenging conversations you will have as you enter your new ministry position. Rarely do seminaries equip students with the skills necessary to conduct the kind of bargaining needed at this stage of the transition process. Some pastors, especially those whose journey has been particularly long and painful, are tempted to take any offer that gets laid on the table, whether it is realistic or not. If you are feeling that way now, take a minute and gather your thoughts. Determine not to say, "Oh, whatever you feel is fine. My family and I will live on whatever you feel led to give us."

Our job is to give you the knowledge necessary to walk away from the table feeling confident that you and your family will have what you need to enjoy a reasonable lifestyle in the community where you are conducting your ministry. If you receive less than you feel you are worth due to poor negotiations, every paycheck you receive will remind you of your undervalued position. As such, you will grow embittered and probably face stress and tension at home. It is not in the best interest of either you or your church to be put in such a position.

Harvard University conducted a study and identified two contrasting styles of negotiating a compensation package. The first approach, *positional bargaining*, is the most common style used in the corporate world (it's pretty common in churches too). In this style the sides announce their positions as "This is how much I want to receive" and "This is how little we want to pay you." From there they proceed to negotiate toward some middle ground between these two starting points. The second style, *principled bargaining*, is characterized by both parties sharing a common commitment to fairness, justice, and honor. They focus on determining "what is fair" in light of these principles. It is a far better style of negotiation because neither side emphasizes "What is the most I can get out of this?"[8] It allows both parties to walk away from the negotiations feeling as if each entity has been dealt with fairly and in a manner of mutual respect.

Contents of Compensation

There is much more to a compensation package than salary, and if you don't understand that from the beginning, you will be deeply disappointed with the end result of your discussions. Negotiations need to start with a reality check for both parties involved. That reality check is made by taking an accurate look at the job description to be sure that it is up to date and that it accurately reflects the current position (not what was developed eight years ago prior to the last minister who held the job). The reality check also needs to include an honest look at your resume to determine the level of education, experience, and expertise that you bring to the church. Both the church's job description and your resume are critical documents at this stage.

In addition to salary, a number of other important elements need to be considered in the development of a comprehensive compensation package. Each element will be explored in this section.

Salary. Trying to determine what is a fair and reasonable salary sometimes requires the wisdom of Solomon because so many variables are involved. What is considered fair and reasonable to one pastor in a small rural town in Nebraska would never begin to cover the expenses for another pastor serving a megachurch in Miami. The cost of living is just too different to make any reasonable comparisons. Calculating what is "fair and reasonable" will have to take place in the context of the local community itself, because comparisons even within a particular state or country aren't very accurate. It is even more difficult in multiple staff churches (see the sidebar on page 261).[9]

For decades one traditional measure used to set the senior pastor's salary has been to compare it with that of a schoolteacher in the region. Such a comparison is unrealistic, however, and nowhere near accurate for a number of reasons. First, most pastors have a graduate degree, but few schoolteachers are required to have much more than a bachelor's degree. It is usually a school administrator that has a graduate degree.

Second, the salary of a schoolteacher is based on nine months of employment. Teachers generally have two weeks off over Christmas, a week for spring break, several long holiday weekends, and eight to ten weeks during the summer. A senior pastor doesn't get that much time off.

Third, teachers don't have the kind of responsibility and accountability that senior pastors have. Most senior pastors have to report to a governing board, supervise a staff, and account for the stability of the church's finances and attendance. They are also on call 24/7. Teachers do not have to meet the same level of accountability and time commitment. Therefore, some prefer to use the salary of an attorney, community college professor, or business leader in the community as a more accurate standard of comparison.

Multiple Staff Salaries

When your church has more than one staff member, it is important that you establish a scale that considers the equitability of the salaries. It isn't necessary that everyone get the same benefits, but there should be some incremental progression. See the following for examples.

Senior minister. This salary is to be established on an annual basis, and it becomes the base salary for other pastoral staff members.

Senior associate minister. This is an executive pastor or someone who has significant leadership and supervisory responsibilities. He or she would receive approximately 75 to 85 percent of the base salary.

Associate minister. This would include such ministers as the children's pastor, youth pastor, and missions pastor. This individual may have a seminary degree and provide leadership over a particular ministry department. He or she would receive approximately 70 to 80 percent of the base salary.

Entry-level minister. These are individuals who are just starting out in ministry and have not attended seminary or Bible college. They have responsibilities beyond a volunteer but don't have significant duties. They require a high level of supervision and would receive approximately 65 to 75 percent of the base salary.

One clergy compensation expert puts it this way:

> When making a presentation to a church board, compare the clergy position to that of a company CEO. Clergy perform the duties of counselors, teachers, leaders, administrators, employers, ambassadors to the community and students, plus they often have family responsibilities. After walking board members through a typical work week, I ask, "Do any of you want to apply for this position?" In this way, board members come to see the job as more than sermons and service.[10]

Keep in mind that the average lay board member doesn't know how to compare salaries of clergy with those of other members of the community. They rarely know what the person sitting next to them on the pew receives each year, and they aren't about to share their own financial details with others on the committee either. In short, they are just as clueless as the next person. But they are the ones in charge, so you will have to be patient.

Probably the most "fair and reasonable" way to put a dollar value on the senior pastor's position is to compare salary figures with those in the community who have similar education, experience, and work responsibilities. You may also consider doing a survey of other pastors in the area to see how similar churches compare with yours. If you associate with a particular denomination, they probably already have this information available. It's just a matter of accessing the information for your use.

Social Security. Most ordained pastors are considered "common law employees" by the Internal Revenue Service (IRS) for the purpose of federal income tax, but they are considered self-employed by the Social Security Administration. This distinction can lead to numerous disagreements regarding who has jurisdiction when it comes to matters of taxation and Social Security withholdings. Even many CPAs are confused when it comes to deciphering tax laws in relation to the minister.

Ministers who have not opted out of paying the Social Security and Medicare tax will need to have FICA withholdings taken out of their pay. This can be done either by the church or individually. If it is done by the church, you want to be sure that it is included in your compensation package as a benefit and not deducted out of your net take-home pay.

If your church doesn't withhold your monthly or quarterly payment to the Social Security Administration, you will be responsible for making both portions of the payment. This amounts to 7.65 percent of base salary plus housing allowance, or where a parsonage is provided, 7.65 percent of base salary plus the greater of 30 percent of the base salary or the fair rental value of the parsonage.[11] If this isn't included in your compensation package and you have not opted out of Social Security, you will be required to make quarterly payments to cover this expense. In essence, plan on a little more than 15 percent of your salary going to cover Social Security and Medicare tax.

Parsonage. You may be offered the church's parsonage to live in if the church owns one. It is becoming increasingly rare for pastors to choose to live in a parsonage unless it is their first ministry out of seminary. In most cases pastors prefer to purchase their own homes so they can accumulate home equity while they are serving in their ministry position. For many pastors, accruing home equity is the only form of retirement savings or investment they can afford. Living in the church's parsonage has a number of advantages and disadvantages, and you would do well to consider those if this benefit is offered to you. At the very least, make sure you walk through the parsonage to consider its "livability" if it is a required piece of the compensation package.

If you are expected to live in the parsonage, you will want to know what kinds of guidelines are expected of you and of the congregation members. For example, I know one pastor who was expected to conduct Sunday school classes in the parsonage basement on Sunday mornings. That meant anybody who wanted to enter the pastor's house on Sunday morning to get a tour of the "facility" was allowed to do so as they worked their way down to the basement.

Will the living room also be a classroom for the church? Will the kitchen be used as a "kitchen annex" on Sunday mornings as people come through looking for refreshments? Some women in the church make it their business to tour the parsonage each Sunday morning during "open house" and take inventory and make mental notes of damage and personalized decorations. The horror stories about such invasiveness could fill a book.

Housing allowance. The church board does not actually provide a housing allowance. It is granted to you by the Internal Revenue Service if you are a licensed member of the clergy (you need not be ordained to enjoy this benefit). However,

Compensation Checklist

1. Salary
2. Social Security/Medicare tax
3. Parsonage/housing allowance
4. Pension/retirement
5. Health benefits
6. Vacation
7. Holidays
8. Continuing education
9. Sabbatical
10. Automobile reimbursement
11. Moving expenses
12. Relocation

you will want to be sure that you are licensed, and if you are not, now—during your negotiations—is the time to become licensed. All that is involved in the licensing process is for the governing board of the church to vote to license you during a business meeting and to record that vote in the minutes. It costs the church nothing to license you. I suggest you go to the local Christian bookstore and purchase a license certificate for twenty-five cents and have the church board sign it on the evening of their vote. It will be your responsibility to keep that certificate in your files in case you are ever audited by the IRS.

The housing allowance provides you with significant tax benefits. For example, with a housing allowance benefit, you are allowed to deduct the amount that you have paid for your mortgage payment (principal and interest), your property taxes, association dues, cleaning supplies, furnishings, utilities (e.g., gas, electric, water, trash, sewer), home maintenance, home owner's insurance, and refinance fees. Check with a local tax advisor before taking these deductions to be sure they are still in effect. These benefits may change from year to year in the future.

Pension/retirement. As an independent contractor, you may not receive any retirement benefits from your church or denomination. If that is the case, you certainly want to be sure that this topic is discussed when you sit down to negotiate your compensation package. You can be pretty certain that most, if not all, of the members of the negotiating committee have either a pension or retirement plan where they work. It stands to reason that they should make some provision for you as well.

In a secular work environment, many employees are given a pension. In many cases this takes the form of shares of stock in the company. This may be good while the company is growing, but we have seen several large firms in the past few years file bankruptcy, and the result has been devastating for their employees. The employees at Enron were not even allowed to sell their stocks while the company was in the process of filing for bankruptcy, although company policy did not preclude their executives from being able to do so. Such discrepancies in the pension system have led many company employees to opt for a 401(k) system instead.

Named for the clause of the federal tax guidelines for which it was established by Congress, the 401(k) allows company employees to be able to deduct a portion of their before tax income and have it set aside in a portfolio that accrues interest each year. This principal, together with compounding interest, grows depending on what kind of securities the fund is invested in (e.g., stocks, bonds, savings, etc.). Many companies also contribute a portion to provide a benefit for their employees. For example, many companies will match 5 percent of the amount that the employee sets aside each month. Choosing not to participate is tantamount to throwing away free money.

The 401(k) is only available for employees in private companies. However, Congress established a similar program, known as the 403(b) for employees of public schools and/or nonprofit or tax-exempt organizations. A similar plan, known as the Public 475(b) exists for employees of state and/or local government (see chapter 9 for more details about retirement accounts).

I have known some Christian ministries to provide significant incentives to employees to encourage them in their retirement savings. To do so is to communicate sincere understanding and concern for their employees. For example, if a pastor sets aside 5 percent of his or her income, the church might match it with 10 percent of their own. Some larger Christian ministries have been known to provide a match up to 100 percent of the employee's contributions during the last few years of his or her employment in an effort to assist the employee in adequately preparing for retirement.

For this reason you absolutely must ask the negotiating committee what retirement benefits are offered by the church. If nothing is provided, think long and hard before agreeing to accept their offer unless you feel you can take on the burden of your own retirement planning by yourself. It can be done, and many pastors are doing it. Just go into it with your eyes wide open regarding what it will cost you.

Whatever you do, don't neglect to set aside some portion of your monthly income for your retirement. You might think it more spiritual to "trust in the Lord" when you get to that stage in your life, but think about what you will be doing to your spouse if you have nothing saved and you pass away the day after you retire. With no retirement savings, Social Security, or Medicare provisions, life will be bleak. Who will pay for housing, food, and medical expenses during the many years that may lie ahead? That's no way to demonstrate your love for someone who has shared in the sacrifices of your ministry.

Health benefits. No one needs to tell you that medical costs are increasing faster than the rate of inflation. If you have children, you know all too well how quickly an outing can turn into a costly affair. Last month my thirteen-year-old son went skiing, and within ten minutes of his going down the slope, I got a call asking me to come and pick him up and take him to the hospital. He had broken his wrist in five places! I thanked God that he wasn't hurt worse. A few weeks later I got the bill from the hospital, and I thanked God again that I had health insurance.

Medical and dental insurance is a very critical health benefit that needs to be included in your compensation negotiations. You should obtain full coverage for your entire family. You may need to pay a reasonable deductible for the coverage, but it will be well worth it if or when it is ever needed.

Vacation. Some provision should be made for you and your family to get away for seasons of personal refreshment and recreation. There is nothing healthy about not taking a vacation. I once sat on a governing board and heard the president boast about not taking a personal vacation in years. He later resigned after suffering emotional and physical burnout. You can't exempt yourself from the laws of nature. You reap what you sow, and if you neglect to take care of yourself physically, you, and often your family, will eventually pay a price for it.

As a rule of thumb, a pastor should receive a week of vacation for each year he or she has been employed up to what the church board feels is reasonable. Many churches will provide a month during the summer while the pastor's children are off school and another week in January after the hectic Christmas season has passed.

Many churches may require you to be employed as their pastor for at least a year before receiving a vacation benefit. If this is the case, you may want to try to time your departure so that you can enjoy some vacation with your family between the end of your current ministry and the start of your next one. That is not always possible, but it is something to consider.

Holidays. It isn't always possible to take time off during the traditional holidays, such as Thanksgiving, Christmas, and Easter, except, of course, in multiple staff situations where staff members rotate so that they can take turns visiting out-of-state relatives. These are prime seasons for you to perform your pastoral duties. You should, however, be allowed to take the equivalent time off afterward or during a different month. If you can't get a week off to compensate for these holidays, try and negotiate a month of Mondays in addition to your regular days off you so can enjoy some personal renewal.

Continuing education. Most professions expect their workers to stay abreast of changes in their field. Lawyers, police officers, flight attendants, teachers, and those in the medical community are all required to complete a certain number of continuing education hours each year. Failure to do so could mean the loss of credentials, certification, liability insurance coverage, or even employment. Ministers should have the same level of expectation in terms of their ongoing education.

Continuing education is a benefit that most lay leaders understand. However, many pastors fail to secure these benefits because they neglect to ask for it during the negotiation process. This compensation benefit includes costs associated with attending conferences and training seminars (e.g., travel, registration, hotels, meals, etc.), purchasing books and journal subscriptions, paying school tuition, and similar kinds of expenses.

Sabbatical. The Old Testament principle of resting in the seventh year is referred to as a sabbath. It is a time when the land is left alone to rest and be renewed. In the same way, many professionals enjoy a sabbatical rest from their work responsibilities after six years of continuous employment. This benefit is associated most with institutions of higher education. Colleges and universities grant their faculty a sabbatical after six years of teaching for the purpose of pursuing activities they might not otherwise be allowed to engage in due to their teaching responsibilities. These activities generally include such activities as writing a book, conducting extensive research, or speaking internationally.

Only 39 percent of our surveyed pastors were employed at a church where a sabbatical policy was in effect. For those churches that had a sabbatical policy, the amount of time that a pastor was allowed to be gone ranged from two weeks to twelve months with pay. The average was 4.3 months, or approximately one third of a year.

A sabbatical is not to be confused with a vacation. A vacation is a time set aside to rest and be personally renewed and to enjoy time away from work to be with one's family. A sabbatical is quite different. The purpose of a professional sabbatical is for spiritual and professional renewal. This can take several forms but usually includes reading, attending extended conferences, writing, participating in a spiritual retreat and/or short-term mission trip. Planning is best left up to the minister, depending on his or her personal and spiritual needs. Sometimes a sabbatical is started just prior to or right after a family vacation, but it is generally not a good idea to link the two activities due to potential misunderstandings that could result.

The church board should set aside additional funds to cover pulpit supply during the senior minister's sabbatical leave. These funds should amount to a few hundred dollars per Sunday, depending on how many times per weekend the visiting minister is required to speak. This is also a good time to let associate pastors at the church take on the responsibility of preaching. They can exercise their preaching gift without having too much pressure placed on them to "hit the ball out of the park" every time they get up to speak.

One last caveat associated with a sabbatical benefit is that most Christian institutions that offer a sabbatical require a signed contract stipulating a certain number of years of service after returning from the sabbatical. If the minister leaves his or her employment with the church within two years, the minister will have to pay back some of the costs associated with the sabbatical. That prevents a pastor from using his or her sabbatical to secure another position and then terminating his or her employment immediately afterward.

Automobile reimbursement. Some churches leave it up to the minister to deduct automobile expenses at the end of the year on his or her federal and/or state tax return. However, since many ministers do not itemize deductions, they are not eligible to receive reimbursement. For this reason, some churches prefer to reimburse their minister for the expenses associated with ministerial travel. This may include the cost of renting or leasing a car and reimbursement for fuel expenses, minor maintenance costs, and so on. For pastors who have to do a lot of visitation over many miles of country travel, it's best to negotiate expenses associated with leasing a car and buying fuel (since a new car will have low maintenance costs and will be more dependable over large distances).

Moving expenses. Moving across country is a costly venture. Packing, moving, transfer, storage, and unpacking costs add up fast. A church that expects their new minister to shoulder all these costs will have a difficult time recruiting a new pastor unless he or she is desperate to leave a current position. In most cases, the new church covers all reasonable costs associated with moving. Once again, since these costs are pretty high, it is not unusual for the church to stipulate that the new minister must stay at the church for a specific length of time for the debt to be forgiven (usually two to three years). If the minister leaves before that date, he or she must pay back a prorated amount of the moving expenses.

Relocation. Many costs are associated with making a move. Whether it is across town or across the country, some costs can be reduced while others will remain fixed. One of the largest expenses, besides the moving van itself, is the cost associated with selling a home. Generally, Realtor commissions for selling a home are approximately 6 percent of the sales price. In addition, buying a home is expensive too. A down payment, broker fees, escrow fees, title search fees, and the like add up to a significant amount of money. Some churches offer to share in these expenses, but once again the details need to be spelled out clearly and in writing before the job offer is accepted.

The Offer Is in the Mail

Churches are notorious for moving slowly. That is the nature of an organization that relies on volunteers to get things done. You are at the mercy of everyone else's schedule. However, that doesn't mean you sit idly by, waiting for their offer to arrive.

It is customary for the church to secure a congregational vote before making you a formal offer (the search committee or governing board should have negotiated an informal offer before you left). The church may need a week or two to inform the congregation, schedule a vote, and then tabulate the results. Under such circumstances you will probably be told that a formal offer is "forthcoming." Welcome to purgatory!

It is possible that the church simply needs to do due diligence, get the vote, and send you the final offer. In most cases a week or perhaps two at the maximum is acceptable. But what happens if the church stretches out the process for three to four weeks (or longer)? What's taking so long? It may be that the church is bringing in another candidate so the congregation can have options. We would all like to believe that a church is bargaining in good faith, but such ploys have been known to happen. There is nothing wrong with a church bringing in several candidates as long as they communicate up front with each candidate that this is their intention. It is when they don't tell you and present a verbal offer to lead you on while quickly bringing in another candidate that things get unethical.

Is there anything you can do to avoid this from happening? Perhaps not. However, you can motivate the church to keep things moving at a reasonably quick pace by letting them know that you will be candidating and considering offers from other churches until you receive a written offer from them.

If the potential church tells the candidate that they want to hire him or her but the written offer will not be coming for a few days, the candidate should let them know that he or she is fine with the wait but will be interviewing at other churches. If the search committee realizes the candidate is active in a job search and that other churches may be interested, it may increase the church's level of interest in that candidate and, in turn, expedite the delivery of a written offer.[12]

Trust but Verify

It may sound hard-hearted to bring this up, but it needs to be said. Too often misunderstandings about something discussed during the negotiation stage have resulted in disappointments, bitterness, anger, and frustration. No pastor should ever agree to accept a job offer until all of the terms and conditions (including benefits) are spelled out in writing. Every item included in the benefits package should be detailed in the final job offer document. This document may take the form of a formal contract, a letter from the search committee or governing board, or perhaps an email from someone with the legal authority to act on the church's behalf.

It is not uncommon for some final negotiations to take place after the agreements have been spelled out in a meeting. Perhaps once the minister returns home, the committee modifies a particular benefit and the committee chair phones the candidate. When that happens, you should request that the item be included in a follow-up document. If you feel uncomfortable asking for that, you should take the initiative of sending an email to the chairperson stating your understanding of the changes in the offer since your last meeting. This is referred to as a "memorandum of understanding" and is common practice in secular jobs. This way you have it in writing, and it creates a necessary paper trail. You may never need to go back to the document, but it is nice to have it if you need it.

I have been treated more fairly by secular employers than I have been by Christian ministries. Somehow the latter seem to think they can cut corners because "we are all one in the faith." The way to prevent getting taken advantage of is to be sure that the details of a compensation package are spelled out in writing *prior* to acceptance. Once you accept their offer, it is far more difficult to go back and reopen the negotiations after you have discovered you forgot to discuss some important detail.

Negotiating one's compensation package, especially as a pastor, is a challenging and difficult assignment, but it need not be stressful or contentious. "On the contrary, true and principled negotiation can go a long way to building trust and a healthy relationship between pastor and congregation. The pastor can feel empowered by being heard ... and the church can feel that the needs of the overall program and the need to have a responsible budgeting process are met."[13]

Pastors who walk into a meeting to negotiate their compensation package having done their homework will be at a tremendous advantage. They will appear more professional and confident in their leadership. Such a posture will garner the respect of those on the committee and help ensure that the needs of both parties are being addressed. The final outcome will be fair and reasonable, and both sides will walk away feeling as if their interests have been heard and understood. In the end, the final offer will be comprehensive and satisfying to both the congregation and the minister. Such a win-win arrangement allows the congregation to move forward with a pastor who is focused on the future and not distracted by matters of compensation.

CHAPTER 21

ARRIVING AT YOUR DESTINATION

Getting Settled in Your New Community

MICK BOERSMA

Be shepherds of God's flock that is under your care, serving as
overseers—not because you must, but because you are willing, as God
wants you to be; not greedy for money, but eager to serve; not lording it
over those entrusted to you, but being examples to the flock.
1 Peter 5:2–3 NIV

It took me well over ten years, but I finally succeeded. I located a copy of the classic travel movie *If It's Tuesday, This Must Be Belgium* (MGM/United Artists, 1969). Take a busload of strangers on an eighteen-day tour through nine European countries, and you have the makings of a real adventure! If you have ever been on a group tour, you can imagine how the plot unfolds. Luggage gets lost, people get lost, personalities clash, and everyone commits crimes against culture on a daily basis. Yes, it's a movie I love to watch once a year just to remind me of the spills and thrills of traveling life with others.

As your moving van rolls into the new community and you anticipate the beginning of a new phase of ministry, you join a lot of other people in this country who are faced with the challenge of beginning a new chapter in life. According to the U.S. Census Bureau, between 1995 and 2000, over 22 million families relocated within the United States.[1] They all shared the excitement, anticipation, and anxiety that moving brings. Starting well in a new job and community is something everyone desires. In this chapter we will discover what it takes to do just that. After all you have gone through to get here, it is important to carefully consider your entry strategy. Good starts make for long and effective ministries.

Before We Depart: A Word to New Seminary Graduates

Perhaps you are fresh out of seminary and headed for your first ministry position. Like many young pastors-to-be, I went from college straight into seminary.

As my wife and I entered our first pastorate, we were full of zeal and vision for the future. We were in for some surprises, many due to the differences between the world of academia and the local church.

While second-career clergy are often more savvy to these distinctions, we had a lot to learn. See what we discovered, on page 273.

A little knowledge will save you some discouragement and even give you some wisdom in dealing with the changes you will be facing early in your career. And those of you entering ministry after a career in the secular marketplace will find other dissimilarities in addition to these. Expect some adjustments of this nature, and you will be more likely to engage them with a positive attitude.

Readjusting the Rearview Mirror

The term "bury the hatchet" is a phrase borrowed from Native American history. It refers to an Iroquois ceremony in which war axes or other weapons were literally buried in the ground as a symbol of a newly made peace.[2] In previous chapters we addressed the need to deal honestly with emotions and personal baggage as you make your transition. This is especially true as you begin your new pastorate. Precedent to any hope for a healthy future is your willingness to deal decisively with two key issues.

1. *Bitterness, disappointment, and hurts from the past.* When asked what advice he would pass on to others in ministry, one pastor who had experienced his share of trouble responded, "Forgive the past pain and allow God to 'expand your borders' and to exhibit grace." Of course, this is Christlike behavior. But it isn't done without the power of the Holy Spirit through a willing heart. If you have been in ministry any length of time, you have been beaten up a bit. Sheep sometimes bite the shepherd. Carrying resentment and bitterness over these incidents will only hurt you and your new flock.

2. *Assumptions that "it" will happen again here.* "It" could be a conflict in a certain area, a personal failure, particular problems with the board or staff—the list goes on. You can live life one of two ways: either assume the best or assume the worst. I have found life in ministry much more fulfilling when I approach relationships with a positive attitude. Yes, sometimes the "it" does happen. For the most part, however, people need someone to give them a chance to rise above their weaknesses and call them up to greater things. Shepherds do this for their sheep.

If we look too much in the rearview mirror of our life and ministry, we will probably have a spiritual wreck. And if we become absorbed in our past hurt and pain, we are in danger of that pain defining us rather than seeing our identity in Christ. Adoniram Judson, the famous missionary who suffered severely for Christ, said while imprisoned, "The future is just as bright as the promises of God."

SEMINARY	LOCAL CHURCH
Learner/Follower	**Teacher/Leader**
➤ Ask questions	➤ Expected to have answers
➤ Submit to authority	➤ Exert authority
➤ Perform single acts of ministry	➤ Oversee many acts of ministry
➤ Participate	➤ Administrate
Focus on Academics	**Non-Academic**
➤ Scholarship and research	➤ Much less time for study and research
➤ Understanding theology	➤ Theology made practical and simple
➤ Exposure to issues and ideas	➤ New ideas threatening to others
➤ Respect for degrees	➤ May or may not respect degrees
Non-Relational	**Focus on Relational**
➤ Involvement with others optional	➤ Building relationship mandatory
➤ Lecture format	➤ Good communication—listen and speak
➤ Work alone on papers or projects	➤ Work together—cooperate, motivate, counsel
➤ Few or no conflicts	➤ Handling conflict against self and mediating conflict between others
➤ More informational than experiential	➤ Tough problems with negative outcomes
➤ (Few practical skill courses or labs)	➤ Applying what you know—exercising power and authority
Structured	**Unstructured**
➤ Required courses	➤ Self-directed
➤ Assignments	➤ Conflicting expectations Setting own limits, boundaries, goals Fluctuating schedule
➤ Grades	➤ Results intangible—hard to guess
➤ Accountability	➤ Self-discipline in spiritual growth Living with criticism and failure Must seek own support network
Common Social Experience	**Unique Social Experience**
➤ Community of called and committed	➤ Mixed levels of commitment
➤ One of many	➤ Example to all
➤ Temporary—to complete course work	➤ Permanent?—tenure unknown
➤ Everyone a newcomer	➤ Pastor is newcomer
➤ Being single—okay	➤ Being single—often a detriment
➤ Honesty about sin/struggles expected	➤ Honesty about sin/struggles not as acceptable—with discretion
Idealism	**Realism**
➤ Theories of what "should be"	➤ Actualities of what "is"
➤ Gathering ideas and examples	➤ Adapting ideas to own situation
➤ Learning "how to" skills	➤ Trying various approaches
➤ Setting expectations and goals	➤ Adjusting expectations and goals
➤ Creativity encouraged	➤ Tradition and ritual established
➤ Feeling adequate to the task	➤ Discovering inadequacies

Avoiding Costly Mistakes in the Transition

Making a new ministry transition allows you to make a new start. This is a time of setting new precedents. Just as your resume created a first impression, so will your first days in office. You have heard about the so-called honeymoon period new pastors enjoy. It is supposed to last for a few months and provide some mercy while you get your bearings. Well, I like what consultant and researcher Roy Oswald once said about this pastoral honeymoon period: "There is no such thing as a honeymoon period. What might feel like a honeymoon for clergy is really a period of 'suspended judgment.'... Make no mistake—people are watching you very carefully and making judgments all the time."[3]

Our desire is to help you win a favorable judgment in these early days of your new position. We can mess things up in a variety of ways, but some mistakes are more costly than others. In fact, some are so serious they can get you thinking about your next transition even before you have finished unpacking your boxes. Here they are—along with ways to avoid them.

1. *Leaving your family behind.* Of course, you brought them with you—physically. But the tendency will be for you to jump into your new role and get to work. And why not? You have responsibilities spelled out for you and lots of needy people to serve. But what about your spouse and kids? Are their lives as prescribed as yours? Has your spouse found a place to serve, using his or her gifts to God's glory? Have the kids begun to fit into the new church, community, and schools?

Don't make the mistake of neglecting your family's needs as you get busy with ministry work. There is plenty to do. For one thing, you will want to assist in getting the family situated in your new living quarters. Following are some practical ways to do this.[4]

1. Make a positive good-bye to the old home and community—a final party, visits to special places for the last time, a memory walk through the rooms of your empty house.
2. Plan a welcoming ritual for your new home—do a walk-through with your kids before the furniture arrives or plant a tree to commemorate a new beginning.
3. Have everyone's survival necessities where you can easily find them upon arrival—a special blanket, toy, teddy bear, coffeepot, medical supplies.
4. Reestablish family routines quickly (e.g., mealtime and bedtime rituals); keep the rules the same, showing this is the same family but just a different location.
5. Prioritize the unpacking process. Start with the kids' rooms, then yours, then bathrooms, kitchen, family room, etc. Wait on hanging pictures and final arrangements of furniture.

6. Allow the kids some say in setting up their bedrooms. This makes the space theirs and helps them begin to feel at home.

7. Help your children feel comfortable in their new rooms. They may find it hard to sleep; help by talking about how the old and new rooms are different and what's nice about the new one.

8. Get familiar with the neighborhood. Take a walk and introduce yourself to the neighbors; show the kids where their boundaries are; locate fire, police, and other nearby services.

9. Help your pets settle in too. Don't let them roam immediately; help them adjust by limiting their world, then slowly let them explore.

10. Remember to make new friends, but keep the old. Begin the process of meeting people through various activities. Plan phone calls with friends left behind.

As for helping your spouse find a place of ministry in your new setting, especially wives, placement specialist Robert Dingman suggests that four key factors may come into play and should not be ignored.

1. *Competition.* If your wife is an outstanding women's Bible teacher but a teacher is already in place, she may not want to let her giftedness be made public for a while.

2. *Compensation.* If your wife's gifts include musical or organizational skills for which others are paid, arguments could arise over whether she should receive pay.

3. *Moving into the big leagues.* If your new ministry is run with a much higher degree of professionalism than your wife has been accustomed to, she may feel inadequate.

4. *The authority syndrome.* When it is the pastor's wife who's involved, things can get sticky regarding who carries the authority.[5]

Giving your spouse and children their fair share of your time, energy, and emotional support will go a long way in setting you up for a good ministry.

2. *Assuming you will "click" with people easily.* If your last ministry was effective, you enjoyed a depth of relational effectiveness with your people. That did not come easily or cheaply. It won't in your new ministry either. New beginnings are naturally associated with optimism and excitement, but after the celebrations are over, you must begin to settle into the tough business of getting to know your people. Building trusting and effective relationships will take a lot of time and effort, and they will be forged through good times and bad. Not everyone will be as responsive as you would like. Certain personalities will be difficult to embrace.

Take it slow and give yourself time to know your people over the long haul. Don't set unrealistic expectations about winning everyone over with your winsome personality.

3. *Stuffing your emotions.* Moving is a stressful time. In our midthirties my wife and I relocated to Southern California, where we had lived during our college years. I figured the adjustments would be relatively easy. Wrong! It took us a long time to feel at home here. Friendships didn't come quickly, and there were times when I wondered if we had made the right decision. We experienced tears, loneliness, and lingering sadness over the final days in our former pastorate.

We processed these feelings together as a family, taking time to listen to one another and work through the emotions. Nothing was considered out of bounds—everything was put on the table. Even though our daughters were only nine years old, they responded to this openness and made the adjustments in a timely and positive manner. But it wasn't easy. Had we ignored our emotions, I believe these last twenty years would not have proven to be as exhilarating and fulfilling as they have been.

4. *Changing things too fast.* Making changes upon beginning a new job is tempting. People expect it. It shows that you have initiative and vision. But churches aren't corporations, and moving too fast can cost you dearly. Some people would propose that you have about a six-month window to make changes before the concrete begins to harden. The expression "Strike while the iron is hot" comes to mind. We say proceed at your own risk.

Granted, there may be a number of changes your people expect you to make as you begin your pastorate. But changing the service times or going to a contemporary worship service are not among them—at least not now. During the first six to nine months, devote yourself to loving the people and being a historian. You didn't get the whole story during the candidacy process—not by a long shot. Listen and learn from a lot of people before considering any significant changes to the ministry. You don't want to inadvertently harm people by moving ahead too soon.

5. *Entertaining criticisms of the former pastor and others.* Every transition within an organization involves opinions about the person who was just fired or has retired or moved along voluntarily. It's the stuff corporate politics are made of. Sadly, the church is often no different. Some people will want to "share" with you all the blunders the last pastor made or the weaknesses he or she exhibited. Others will want to warn you about those "troublemakers" in the congregation who always vote against progress.

6. *Ignoring unresolved conflicts within the congregation.* While this is not a book on conflict resolution, you may appreciate a three-step process I have found helpful in effecting the ministry of reconciliation. First, enable the individuals involved to express their position(s) on the issue. Often this never happens

because people don't listen to one another. They may need to write out their feelings to start and then share with the other(s) in your presence their honest opinion. When all parties have been able to express themselves—and listen to (hear)—the others' positions, you are ready for step two.

Second, determine what each person in the situation needs from the other. Conflict often results from unmet needs, and once both parties have heard one another out, you should be able to identify a few key needs that are going unmet. The final step involves helping each person identify one need he or she could meet for the other. Baby steps are in order here, and one successful act of sacrifice will lead to others. I'm not a trained counselor, but I have seen a lot of people learn to love one another this way; and through the power of the Holy Spirit a lot of hatchets get buried.

7. *Ministering out of town too much.* For many pastors, the allure of travel and the thrill of being a popular conference speaker is captivating. We all know of nationally renowned pastors whose speaking engagements carry them all over the country. That may be fine in their circumstances, but in the early days of your new position, you are wise to stay home and work hard for your new flock. Start-up tasks are time-consuming, and your people deserve your wholehearted attention during these early days. Once you have earned their respect and trust, they won't mind having you take up some outside commitments.

8. *Trying to become someone else.* From the start of this book, we have encouraged you to be yourself—to be honest and forthright with the search committee. Living up to the expectations of those whom you have just met can be very challenging. At times, attempting to do so may cause you to act or speak in a manner inconsistent with your true nature as you are tempted to become what others want you to be. Don't cave in. Just be yourself.

9. *Putting vision over people.* Vision goes hand in hand with fresh starts. The congregation is looking for new direction, a call to faith, exciting possibilities. You may be tempted to strike out on the adventure and drag people along who aren't ready. It's not that they don't want to come along, but they first need to know that you care about *them*. They need to know that they are more important than your dreams.

10. *Working at a sprinter's pace.* The first days in a new pastorate are busy ones. Everyone will want a little piece of you. They will want to get to know you and share their ministries and ideas. And settling into the community at large with all its pressing demands will be time consuming. One pastor in our survey mentioned that he overworked his first months in a new position for fear he would be fired again as he had been in his former church.

Conversations with hundreds of pastors over the years have revealed that it takes a good two to three years to really get settled into a new ministry. Getting to know people and their culture takes time. Effective pastors pace themselves to avoid burnout. They tell us that making time for self is the only way to establish the foundations for a long-term ministry. Being too busy will only wear you out early and even impair your ability to thrive long-term.[6]

Making a Fresh Start in Your New Pastorate

The common mistakes discussed above can cost you dearly in the early stages of your new pastorate. Here we share disciplines that you can practice to strengthen yourself spiritually so that you are able to engender fruitful and meaningful service for Christ. There are many more possibilities than we list here, but these are crucial to successful ministry.

Write a Letter

It is always proper to RSVP. Though you have already accepted the call at this point, before you arrive there is another way you can encourage your new flock. Write them a brief letter (one page) addressed to the recognized lay leader or senior pastor. In a note enclosed with the letter, request that your letter be published for the congregation at large through its newsletter or weekly worship folder. After an appropriate salutation, make sure you include the following elements.

- Thanks and appreciation for their hospitality, graciousness, and support in calling you to serve with them
- Anticipation and excitement about the future together
- Confidence that the journey ahead will be one of positive expectations and effective shared ministry
- Desire for God's blessing as both you and they adjust to these exciting days of new relationships and vision

Signs You Are Too Busy

- Thinking you are indispensable
- Refusing to delegate anything to anyone
- Never spending time with family or spouse
- Spending time with family and spouse but regretting every minute of it
- Saying, "I'm always behind"
- Feeling guilty when you take time for yourself
- Working harder, not smarter
- Having feelings of guilt when you tell a parishioner "no"

Wrap your comments in genuine warmth and love for your new flock. Let your spouse share in the task. These words will mean the world to your new fellowship and encourage them as they prepare to receive you. Then sign off using the title with which you would like to be addressed (e.g., Pastor Bob, Reverend Smith, etc.).

Pray

We should always be communing with our heavenly Father. And while there are times we may slack off in this privilege, the first days of a new ministry should not be among them. Satan likes to strike at the start of things. He did it in Genesis 3, and we all suffer for it. Even Jesus was not spared as he began his early ministry (Matt. 4; Mark 1; Luke 4). You won't be exempt either.

One of the pastors in our survey shared the following story to reinforce this point. He started as senior pastor at his new church in late fall. The choir and orchestra were preparing the Christmas musical, which would be the highlight of the Advent season in their small city. Three nights before the first performance, he received a call from the police department. They had his worship leader under arrest for a serious crime. A feeling of doom overwhelmed him. Even though the news hit the paper the next day, God graciously provided another music director and the church's reputation was not irreparably harmed.

Satan would love to discourage you early in the trip. Bringing your heart to the throne of God daily, both personally and as a fellowship, will go a long way in setting the stage for a ministry that is well armed for the spiritual battle ahead.

Read Your Bible

Your personal spiritual growth can take a hit in the start-up of a new ministry. Because maintaining a solid devotional time in the Word can get squeezed out of your schedule, you need to resolve your first day on the job to protect this time. Bible reading and prayer provide the wisdom and power of God for your life and ministry. In my pastorate, part of my daily routine was to arrive at the office by 8:00 a.m., a half hour before official office hours. I had never read through the Bible cover-to-cover before. Now I attempted it. It wasn't long before I found myself in 1 Kings, where I came upon a passage that would provide guidance for my years in this wonderful congregation.

> "Now, O LORD my God, you have made your servant king in place of my father David. But I am only a little child and do not know how to carry out my duties. Your servant is here among the people you have chosen, a great people, too numerous to count or number. So give your servant a discerning heart to govern your people and to distinguish between right and wrong. For who is able to govern this great people of yours?" (1 Kings 3:7–9 NIV)

I was no King Solomon. Our congregation numbered 150 — there would be no grand governing, but I did feel like a little child who needed a discerning heart. Soaking in the Scriptures gave me God's perspective on living and serving with his great people. Carving out that thirty minutes a day was one of the best decisions I ever made.

Attend to the Basics

While you are tugged in many directions as people share their ideas about where you should start focusing your energies, make sure you give priority to some key areas of your ministry, such as preaching, visitation, and organization. Giving these a solid start will enable you to branch out later.

While it may be tempting to open with a "state of the union" series, I would encourage you to start by giving messages that help people in their daily lives. This gives you a chance to share your own journey, to help them get to know you through personal illustrations, and to open up opportunities for further interaction as they respond to the Spirit. Leave the vision stuff alone for a while — you all have probably had enough of that during your candidacy. Stay away from controversial doctrines too. Give yourself and your people time to adjust.

You will also need to be with your people right from the start. Set up a schedule that allows you plenty of time out of the office to be with your new friends. It will help acquaint you, sharpen your preaching as you apply the Word more knowledgably to the real needs and circumstances they face, and lead to meaningful counseling opportunities.

People certainly want to know how you will spend your time, so give them a sense of how you plan to organize your workweek by establishing office hours. Most pastors are given flexibility in this area, and it is important that you figure out early on what will work well for you. Publicize these hours in the worship folder for a month or so. Be willing to adjust as you get to know the rhythm of your new community and church.

Begin Building Trusting Relationships

Leading a congregation that doesn't trust you is impossible. Securing that confidence is an order of first importance and involves investing time and energy in relationships with the three main groups in your church — the paid staff, lay leadership, and congregation.

1. *Paid staff.* Whether senior pastor or associate, you have a chance right now to initiate a positive working environment with your colleagues. Dr. Kevin Lawson, one of our faculty friends, did extensive research into what makes for a thriving church staff environment. Reflecting concepts we have already shared throughout this book, he gives the following advice to associate staff: "If you take

seriously the model of servant-leadership portrayed in Jesus' life and teaching with his disciples (Mark 10:42–45), then your first concern as an associate staff member is to strive to understand what your supervisor needs and values from you, and then to serve him by meeting those needs to the best of your ability."[7] These needs include cooperation, loyalty, honesty, competence, initiative, trustworthiness, and open communication.[8]

Lawson's findings provided useful information for senior pastors too. Happy associates reported that their supervisors did a number of beneficial things for them that helped them do well in their ministries.[9]

1. Help develop a sense of partnership in ministry
2. Lead the ministry team through vision
3. Build trust together
4. Are available and approachable
5. Provide support and encouragement in ministry
6. Care for the person as well as the ministry
7. Demonstrate loyalty
8. Keep communication open
9. Give constructive feedback
10. Are a model and mentor in ministry
11. Encourage personal and professional development
12. Pray for and with them

Everything listed here is about forging good relationships. Start now by having regular staff meetings and times of prayer. Plan a staff retreat early in your tenure. Spend some time in outdoor ventures or other mutually enjoyable pastimes. You won't become buddies with everyone, but you will begin the process of getting to know one another and building loyalty and trust.

2. *Lay leaders.* Pastors in our survey indicated that when conflict was a major reason for their leaving a ministry, it was almost always with staff or lay leaders (90 percent). Knowing your governing board is a first step in promoting harmony. As with your staff, there are many venues through which this can be accomplished. Every year our board and staff joined together for three days in a beautiful mountain cabin near Mount Rainier. We cooked together, played in the snow together, and huddled around the massive fireplace to share, confess, envision, and pray. Those were sweet times. And we needed them, for we were sorely tested many times with very difficult issues.

3. *Congregation.* Take the lead in reaching out to your new congregation. Invite people to your home for an open house. Let them know you are interested in visiting their homes as well. Despite cultural differences that may come into play here, you will be surprised how most people welcome the idea. Our

people were very hospitable and proud of their ability to raise great gardens and cook gourmet meals. So during one of my first Sundays as their new pastor, I announced in the pulpit that my wife and I would love to verify their legendary claims. We ended up being invited to dinner in almost every home within the first six months of our pastorate. My fifteen-pound weight gain proved their boasting justified. We were off to a great start!

Continue Exploring Your Community

During your candidacy week (see chapter 18), you started the process of discovery. Now is the time to get out and meet the people who form the community in which you serve. While this should be fun for you, it is also hard work. It's really part of your job too. As a faithful shepherd, you need to know the sheep. Understanding their world gives you such knowledge. So follow up on those interesting sights you first saw when candidating, and purposefully plan more missions of discovery as the early days of your ministry unfold.

Stay Friends with Your Past

As you venture boldly into your future and enjoy all the wonder of a new place, don't forget those you have left behind. Write or call them every so often. Tell them how much you appreciate all they did for you over the years. Draw wisdom and grace from their minds and hearts as you pass through various trials and enjoy hard-fought victories. As a reminder of how appropriate this is, we leave you with the words of Paul, written to his beloved congregation in Philippi:

> Grace and peace to you and from God our Father and the Lord Jesus Christ. I thank my God every time I remember you. In all my payers for all of you, I always pray with joy because of your partnership in the gospel from the first day until now, being confident of this, that he who began a good work in you will carry it on to completion until the day of Christ Jesus. (Philippians 1:2–6 NIV)

We both pray that you will enjoy a rich and long ministry in your new place of service. As you shepherd God's people, may you remain faithful to your call and obedient to your Lord Jesus, and may you continue to grow in love for his church. Bon voyage!

ADVICE FROM FELLOW TRAVELERS

In our survey of pastors, we asked fifty questions about their transition experience. Several of these questions were open-ended, which allowed the pastors to respond with thoughts and feelings about their particular experiences. Since the context of your move may vary a great deal from those who have gone before you, we thought it might be helpful for you to hear how others have survived their transitions. A number of these pastors had made several career transitions, while for a few it was their first. Some moved from one coast to another, while a few simply moved across town. Most moved from one church to another, but some decided to transition into parachurch ministries.

By far, the most difficult question we asked related to their personal reflections associated with being fired or forced to resign. For many the pain was still real, and they could recount stories with vivid clarity even though it had been years since they made their move. Encouragingly, quite a number expressed the words of Joseph when he said, "They meant it for evil, but God meant if for good," and as such, they could praise God for the difficult journey because of how it brought them closer to the Lord, their spouses, and other family members. They wanted to share their painful stories to show others how to navigate troubled times and possibly avoid mishaps.

The following material is divided into two sections. The first deals with the pastors' answers to the questions, "What is your best piece of advice regarding the process of making a pastoral transition?" and "What advice would you give to a pastor about making a move to another church?" The second section deal with responses to the question, "If you have ever been fired or forced to resign from a church ministry, what effect did it have on you personally?" We hope you will find encouragement and comfort in knowing that many have traveled this trail before you and desire for you to navigate difficult days with the strength that is yours in Christ. These pastors want to remind you of the words spoken by the author of Hebrews, "We are surrounded by such a great cloud of witnesses" (12:1 NIV). May you find encouragement and hope in those who are your fellow travelers.

What advice would you offer to a pastor who is in the midst of a career transition?

Forgive the past pain and allow God to "expand your borders." Exhibit grace.
—Hospital chaplain

For the sake of all the churches and believers involved, please only transition if it is something the Lord desires and not simply your desire for a ministry situation that you find more attractive.

—Unknown

Do lots of historical fact finding—know why others left before you.

—Senior associate pastor

There is not enough room on this survey. I thought I was through the grief and anger, but I realize by filling this out that I still wonder why God didn't bless me in ministry.

—Self-employed

Never burn your bridges. God blesses perseverance.

—Senior pastor

Be sure to take ample time to process as a family, to grieve the loss together, and to stay emotionally connected as a family. Guard your heart as the wellspring of your life. Follow the leading of the Spirit, and discern his guidance from the Word. Walk with integrity and submission to his lordship.

—Parachurch leader

Know that wherever you go, there will always be issues. There is no perfect church. If there is, don't go there; you'll make it imperfect.

—Youth pastor

It set us back financially in a way that took years to recover, but family and ministry have flourished. In all, a great thing.

—Associate pastor

Find out why the last pastor left. Also, check to see if they have an unusually high turnover rate of pastors. Don't tell anyone you are looking! I am gratified that even though the transitions have been fairly traumatic, my wife and children have a positive view of ministry.

—Pastor in seminary

Have a community of trusted friends and colleagues who can be a "discerning community" for you as you pursue other options. Be willing to let them ask you tough questions.

—Associate pastor

Don't be stupid. Be shrewd. Get it in writing. Go where you fit. Ask others for help.

—Associate pastor

Be patient. Investigate everything. It does take a toll on children.

—Associate pastor

Know a detailed list of the expectations the church has and discuss it prior to taking the church. Be honest and up-front with your current church about your intentions to leave. Give them as much time as possible before you leave (so they can make the necessary adjustments for being without a pastor).

—Senior pastor

Make sure their vision statement and yours coincide. Ask questions. Do background checks on the church! I found out I was the twelfth pastor asked to leave in a six-year history.

—Youth pastor

Be aware of the emotional cycle of leaving a church; it is similar to a grief process. Be aware of the emotional side of the process for the whole family. Transition lasts longer than just getting to a new position, but be open to God bringing help and healing and reconnection from unexpected places.

—Unknown

Know the real reasons why you are leaving your present church for a "new" one. Have you overstayed your welcome, or are you leaving before your time? Lovingly listen to your family (wife and kids). If it's good for a church and not for them, you lose.

—Associate pastor

Make sure it is what you are looking for. The little things that bug you at the start may end up being the reason why you leave a few years later.

—In transition

Interview them more than they interview you.

—Youth pastor

Make sure God is calling you out of and into your ministry positions. Make sure your spouse feels the same calling. Prepare your kids well. Seek God, seek God, seek God!

—Senior pastor

Have thick skin.

—Associate pastor

Be sure you are well aware of what you are getting into. Ask a lot of questions and then ask some more.

—Senior pastor

Be sure to include support staff in your circle of friends. Be sure they know what is going on. You may be the "boss," but without them you are toast!

—Support staff

Put together a team of trusted people, and use them as a sounding board for the first year. They can keep you from a lot of pitfalls.

—Senior pastor

Ask all the questions you have and the questions your family has, because as much as it is a vocational decision, it is also a family welfare decision. "Will my family benefit and thrive here?"

—Associate pastor

Take a break between ministries.

—Pastor of family ministry

Be a leader and get organizational training in addition to Bible/seminary.

—Senior pastor

Forgive those who have hurt you. Trust God and see him working in all of this. Be able to move beyond anger and fear and how evil people can be.

—Senior pastor

Only dance with one girl at a time (i.e., never candidate at two churches at the same time).

—Senior pastor

It takes time to establish credibility, and credibility is the most important leadership factor. People aren't going to trust you until they feel they know you. You've been given enough to prove that you do what you say you will do. No one is guaranteed to stay with you either. They walk away for the most surprising reasons. That being said, it is important to clarify your core values before you go, and stick to them.

—Senior pastor

Show yourself some grace. Transitions create some internal turmoil that is not necessarily an indicator of a spiritual problem.

—Bible and theology professor

Take the time to absorb the "DNA" of the ministry. Not just what they do but why they do it. Seek out someone who has been at the church for four to five years and ask them what they think about how things are going.

—Teaching pastor

Don't be afraid of mainline denominations. It saved me. Had I not become a Lutheran, I would have tossed out personal experience with that of the community I left.

—Editor

If you have ever been fired or forced to resign from a church ministry, what effect did it have on you personally?

The pain made me second-guess decisions I had to make in future ministry. It left me shell-shocked, and I wondered if ministry was really my calling. I'm glad I didn't quit. Now that I have some perspective on it, it was a blessing from God to be led away from an unhealthy ministry.

—Associate pastor

It demolished some of my views of the city church and the state it was in. My spouse lost respect or confidence in me as a husband and provider. While our children are young, she no longer has the faith for me to enter another vocational ministry position.

—Out of ministry, in education

It was very difficult and made me question where I stood and if I had failed. Even though I have since been comforted by many others who knew the church I was at was extremely lacking in being progressive, it was still a struggle.

—Youth pastor

It was initially demoralizing. I felt I had failed God, the church, myself, and my family. With time, I understood it was God's way of removing me from an unhealthy situation.

—Associate pastor

It shook my confidence and left me doubting my ability and my interpersonal skills. I don't think I am recovered yet, and perhaps that is for the best!

—Associate pastor

The lack of integrity regarding how the senior pastor handled the termination was devastating.

—Left ministry, federal employee

The sense of betrayal I experienced was almost beyond words. It was shocking to see what the elder board was willing to do to justify their actions. Even non-Christians handle people better than that. In hindsight, it was a gift from God that I was forced to resign before the church went through a split.

—Family pastor

It was frustrating that I was not supported by the leadership of the church. In essence, I was painted into a corner. In the end, I experienced freedom from a challenging situation.

—Left ministry

I questioned my call to ministry, and it was extremely frustrating.

—Family pastor

It was the hardest experience I ever went through. Real tough emotionally. Yes, God used it to mold me, but it was damaging also to the psyche and strained some relationships.

—Senior pastor

It was exhausting and stressful from all the pressures and considerations involved. I experienced trauma and grief from the abuse as well as threats. Being foreclosed on a ministry I loved and had a vision for was real hard.

—Senior pastor

I'm still unemployed after sixteen months. I'm angry, more withdrawn, and uncertain.

—Associate pastor

It was very difficult and depressing. I'm just glad it wasn't a moral failure, only a theological disagreement. The hardest part is not knowing if they will give me a positive reference or not.

—Associate pastor

It made me closer to God's leading. I learned the importance of not being out of favor with men but, more importantly, not being out of favor with God. With this maxim, God has a way of leading you to the highest path, and he has angels to protect you, guide you, and provide for you along the way.

—Jail chaplain

It caused me to question my calling, left me struggling with bitterness toward the senior pastor and church board ... yet it was an amazing opportunity for me to get into a healthy ministry situation.

—Associate pastor

It really shook my confidence and made me doubt my calling. It also helped me grow and learn to trust in Christ more.

—Associate pastor

It was devastating. It's caused me disillusionment and made me question my calling. As a result, I am very insecure where I am now.

—Left ministry, probation officer

It was a mix of emotions: complete and utter devastation, depression, anger, hatred, bitterness toward God, rebellion toward the "system" and life, and wondering if all these years were wasted.

—Parachurch leader

It made me bitter for a while, and now I am less trusting of church leaders.

—Christian education director

It made me feel as if church was a business too. I felt used and discarded.

—Associate pastor

It shocked me for a while, but God moved me on to a megachurch where I received more opportunities, exposure, and the chance to pursue a doctoral degree.

—Pastor of small groups

It was devastating. A real Tobiah and Sanballat type of situation. It hurts to be betrayed by those you trusted!

—Senior associate pastor

NOTES

Acknowledgments

1. John C. Laure, "Forced Exits: A Too-Common Ministry Hazard," *Christianity Today* 42, no. 2 (March–April 1996): 72.
2. According to LifeWay Christian Resources of the Southern Baptist Convention, as reported by Wounded Heart Ministries at www.bibleteacher.org/wounded/WH_Art2.htm. Accessed December 14, 2006.
3. Some statistics in this book may not add up to 100 percent because of rounding off the numbers.

Chapter 1: Traveling by the Book

1. Jackson W. Carroll, *God's Potters: Pastoral Leadership and the Shaping of Congregations* (Grand Rapids: Eerdmans, 2006), 165.
2. Kevin Lawson, *How to Thrive in Associate Staff Ministry* (Bethesda, Md.: Alban Institute, 2000), 219.
3. Gordon MacDonald, "God's Calling Plan," *Leadership* 24, no. 4 (Fall 2003): 36.
4. James M. George, "A Theology of God's Call to the Ministry" (unpublished Th.M. thesis, Talbot School of Theology, 1986), 15.
5. Charles M. Horne, *Salvation* (Chicago: Moody, 1971), 114.
6. Darius Salter, *What Really Matters in Ministry* (Grand Rapids: Baker, 1990), 31.
7. Thomas Oden, *Becoming a Minister*, Classical Pastoral Care Series, vol. 1 (Grand Rapids: Baker, 1987), 41.
8. Charles Jefferson, *The Minister as Shepherd* (Fincastle, Va.: Scripture Truth, 1970), 35.
9. Bob Moeller, "Grating Expectations," *Leadership* 27, no. 1 (Winter 1996): 31.
10. For a helpful discussion of the biblical basis of leadership and management in Christian ministries, see chapters 1 and 2 in Michael Anthony and James Estep Jr., *Management Essentials for Christian Ministries* (Nashville: Broadman & Holman, 2005).
11. Barna Research Group, *Unchurched*, "Barna by Topic," www.Barna.org. Accessed December 18, 2006.
12. R. Laird Harris, ed., *Theological Word Book of the Old Testament*, vol. 2 (Chicago: Moody, 1980), entry 1802, 731.
13. Ibid., entry 2109, 830.
14. Phillip Keller, *A Shepherd Looks at Psalm 23* (Grand Rapids: Zondervan, 1970), 35.

Chapter 2: I Have a Dream

1. Nicholas Lore, *The Pathfinder: How to Choose or Change Your Career for a Lifetime of Satisfaction and Success* (New York: Simon & Schuster, 1998), 11–14.

2. Bill Hybels, *Courageous Leadership* (Grand Rapids: Zondervan, 2002), 29–30.

3. George Barna, *Without a Vision the People Perish* (Glendale, Calif.: Barna Research Group, 1991), 28.

4. Gordon Coulter, "Building Mission and Vision," in *Management Essentials for Christian Ministries*, ed. Michael J. Anthony and James Estep Jr. (Nashville: Broadman & Holman, 2005), 64.

5. Barna, *Without a Vision*, 38–39.

6. Ibid., 40–41.

7. Susan Sully, *The Late Bloomer's Guide to Success at Any Age* (New York: HarperCollins, 2000), 36–38.

8. Julie Jansen, *I Don't Know What I Want, but I Know It's Not This* (New York: Penguin, 2003), 28–30. Used by permission of Penguin, a division of Penguin Group (USA) Inc.

Chapter 3: Anatomy of a Carry-on Bag

1. Jackson W. Carroll, "Leadership in a Time of Change," *Circuit Rider* (July–August 2002): citing a research project for *Pulpit & Pew* at Duke Divinity School.

2. John R. Cionca, *Before You Move: A Guide to Making Transitions in Ministry* (Grand Rapids: Kregel, 2004), 35.

3. George Barna, "Awareness of Spiritual Gifts Is Changing," *The Barna Update*, February 5, 2001. Barna Research also offers "The Christian Leader Profile" at www.barna.org. This is an instrument designed to help ministers evaluate their call, character, competencies, and leadership aptitudes.

4. Ibid.

5. The Myers-Briggs Foundation at myersbriggs.org provides testing and professional assessment services.

6. ChangingMinds.org is one of several sites that administers and provides professional interpretation of this instrument, considered one of the most documented and validated measures of normal adult personality available today.

7. The Psychological Publications, Inc., website description can be seen at www.tjta.com. This site provides information on complete training programs and the purchase of all materials associated with the T-JTA.

8. Church Planter Assessment Training. These categories are taken largely from the findings of Dr. Charles Ridley of Indiana University as recorded in Charles R. Ridley and Robert E. Logan with Helena Gerstenberg, *Training for Selection Interviewing: Facilitator's Manual* (Carol Stream, Ill.: ChurchSmart, 1998).

9. R. W. Dingman Co., Inc., www.dingman.com. This professional search firm specializes in finding leadership for corporations and provides services to church and parachurch organizations as well. Accessed November 21, 2006.

Chapter 4: How to Get There from Here

1. Rodney L. Lowman, *The Clinical Practice of Career Assessment: Interests, Abilities, and Personalities* (Washington, D.C.: American Psychological Association, 1991), 8–9.

2. Richard Bolles, "The Pastor's Parachute," *Leadership* 11, no. 3 (Summer 1990): 20.

3. Susan Sully, *The Late Bloomer's Guide to Success at Any Age* (New York: HarperCollins, 2000), 221–22.

4. An excellent discussion of this is found in Christopher Bargeron, "Movin' on Up," in *The Insider's Guide to Finding a Job*, ed. Wendy S. Enelow and Shelly Goldman (Indianapolis: JIST Works, 2004), 45.

5. Paul Hershey and Ken Blanchard, *Management of Organizations: Utilizing Human Resources* (Garden City, N.J.: Prentice Hall, 1969), 382. For a detailed discussion of the use of this criteria in the context of church ministry, see Michelle Anthony, "Developing a Strategic Plan," in *Management Essentials for Christian Ministries*, ed. Michael J. Anthony and James Estep Jr. (Nashville: Broadman & Holman, 2005), 95.

6. Cynthia Ingols and Mary Shapiro, *Take Charge of Your Career* (New York: Barnes & Noble, 2004), 16.

7. Charles W. Broach, "Balancing Your Life Objectives with Your Career Goals," in Enelow and Goldman, *The Insider's Guide to Finding a Job*, 50–51.

Chapter 5: Caution! Turbulent Weather Ahead

1. John N. Vaughan, "The Future: One Hundred Years Later," *The Church Report* (2006): 1, www.thechurchreport.com.

2. Eddie Gibbs, "Leadership Matrix," *Your Church* (January–February 2006): 8.

3. Henry T. Blackaby and Richard Blackaby, "Vision Problems," *Your Church* (March–April 2006): 12.

Chapter 6: Paradise Lost

1. Barry Schwartz, *The Paradox of Choice* (New York: HarperCollins, 2005), 182.

2. Dean R. Hoge and Jacqueline E. Wenger, *Pastors in Transition: Why Clergy Leave Local Church Ministry* (Grand Rapids: Eerdmans, 2005), 49.

3. John. E. Peterson, "The Call of God and Clergy Transitions" (unpublished dissertation, Bethel Theological Seminary, 1993), abstract summary.

4. Kevin Lawson, *How to Thrive in Associate Staff Ministry* (Bethesda, Md.: Alban Institute, 2000), 219.

5. George Barna, "Giving to Churches Rose Substantially in 2003," *The Barna Update* (April 13, 2004), www.barna.org.

6. Hoge and Wenger, *Pastors in Transition*, 49.

7. John C. LaRue Jr., "The Pastor's Family and Money," *Your Church* (November–December 1997): 80.

8. Andy Husmann, "Signs of the Times" (paper presented to the Michigan Baptist General Conference at their annual conference, Tustin, Mich., May 12, 1989).

9. William Bud Phillips, *Pastoral Transitions: From Endings to New Beginnings* (Washington, D.C.: Alban Institute, 1988), 3–4.

10. *When You Seek a Place for Ministry*, 2nd ed. (Ministerial Leadership Office of Mennonite Church Canada and Congregational and Ministerial Leadership of Mennonite Church USA, 2005), www.mennonitechurch.ca.

Chapter 7: Mapping Your Course

1. William Shakespeare, *As You Like It*, act 2, scene 7.
2. *The EFL/ESL Career Exit Strategy Guidebook*, www.Benzhi.com, 2005, 1. This website assists those in the English as a Foreign Language and English as a Second Language teaching profession and has a helpful exit strategy guidebook online.
3. James Antal, *Considering a New Call* (Bethesda, Md.: Alban Institute, 2000), xiii.
4. Ibid., 29–30.
5. Dennis Baker, *A Manual for Pastoral Search Committees of the Conservative Baptist Association of Southern California* (doctoral dissertation, Talbot School of Theology, 1992), 31.
6. Roy M. Oswald, *Running through the Thistles: Terminating Ministerial Relationships with a Parish* (Washington, D.C.: Alban Institute, 1978), 4–5.
7. Jackson W. Carroll and Barbara G. Wheeler, *A Study of Doctor of Ministry Programs* (Hartford, Conn.: Hartford Institute for Religion Research, 1987), 230–31, http://hirr.hartsem.edu/bookshelf/out_of_print_dminanalysis.html.

Chapter 8: Getting Away from It All

1. "Resignation of President Richard Nixon," www.archives.gov/exhibits/american_originals/nixon2.html. Accessed November 21, 2006.
2. "John Ashcroft resignation letter," www.msnbc.msn.com/id/6446686. Accessed November 21, 2006.
3. Sarah Breinig, "How to Resign with Style and Get an Awesome Reference," www.where2begin.com/articles/write-resignation-letter/how-to-resign-with-style--get-an-awesome-reference.html. Breinig is an independent recruiter and job search coach and the webmaster of www.best-online-job-search-tools.com, where you will find information, resources, tools, and strategies to empower your job search. Accessed November 21, 2006.
4. Kauser Kanji, "How to Resign with Style and Dignity," i-resign.com, www.i-resign.com/uk/resigning/how-to-resign.asp.
5. First page at www.business-letters.com/resignation-letter.htm. Accessed November 21, 2006.
6. Allison Hemming, *Work It!* (New York: Simon & Schuster, 2003), 192.
7. Cynthia Ingols and Mary Shapiro, *Take Charge of Your Career* (New York: Barnes and Noble, 2004), 173.

Chapter 9: Getting Your Travel Documents in Order

1. Richard C. Busse, *Fired, Laid-off or Forced Out* (Naperville, Ill.: Sphinx, 2005), 188.
2. Ibid.
3. "COBRA Questions and Answers," www.cobrainsurance.com/COBRA_FAQ.htm#What%20is%20COBRA? Accessed November 21, 2006.
4. Ibid.
5. Busse, *Fired*, 190.

6. Alan. L. Sklover, *Fired, Downsized, or Laid Off: What Your Employer Doesn't Want You to Know about How to Fight Back* (New York: Henry Holt, 2000), 180.

7. Ibid., 181.

8. Ibid., 200.

9. Ibid., 172.

Chapter 10: Asking Yourself the Tough Questions

1. Andre Bustanoby, "Why Pastors Drop Out," *Christianity Today* (January 7, 1977).

2. George Barna, *Today's Pastors* (Ventura, Calif.: Regal, 1993), 52.

3. Joseph L. Umidi, *Confirming the Pastoral Call: A Guide to Matching Candidates to Congregations* (Grand Rapids: Kregel, 2000), 13.

4. John C. LaRue Jr., "Forced Exits: Preparation and Survival," *Your Church* (July–August 1996): 64.

5. John C. LaRue Jr., "Forced Exits: Personal Effects," *Your Church* (November–December 1996): 64.

6. Ibid.

7. Ibid.

8. Gary L. McIntosh and Robert L. Edmondson, *It Only Hurts on Monday* (Carol Stream, Ill.: Church Smart, 1998), 171.

9. David L. Goetz, "Forced Out," *Leadership* (Winter 1996), 42.

10. Sharonrose Cannistraci, "Ministers Have No Protection against Wrongful Termination," *Protect the Church: A Legal Resource for Ministries Newsletter*, n.d.,1–4.

11. Cited in Karen Krakower, "Clergy in Crisis: Who Ministers to the Ministers?" *Mosaic*, June 1997, www.bengston.org/MTM/NewsArtl/news02.htm.

12. "American Baptist Delegates Celebrate Clergy/Congregational Relationship," report from the NACBA Convention, June 3, 2003, www.nacba.net/Article/AB_Clergy_Church.htm.

13. See George Henson, "Churches of Refuge Help Fired Ministers," www.baptiststandard.com/2001/1_15/pages/refuge.html. Accessed January 4, 2007.

14. Terri Lackey, "Forced Termination, Depression Top Calls to LeaderCare Helpline," Baptist Press, May 13, 2002, www.baptistpress.org/bpnews.asp?ID=13358.

15. Brooks R. Faulkner, *Forced Termination: Redemptive Options for Ministers and Churches* (Nashville: Broadman, 1986), 98–99.

16. Mary Anne Coate, *Clergy Stress: The Hidden Conflicts in Ministry* (Tiptree, Essex: Courier International, Ltd., 1989), 148–67.

Chapter 11: Dragging Your Family to the Magic Kingdom

1. Davis Duggins, "11 Questions You Should Ask at Home before Accepting a New Ministry," *Pastor's Family* (June–July 1998): 18.

2. Laura Winter, "On the Move," *Pastor's Family* (December 1998–January 1999): 6.

3. Paul A. Mickey and Ginny W. Ashmore, *Clergy Families: Is Normal Life Possible?* (Grand Rapids: Zondervan, 1991), 82.

4. Cited in Daniel L. Langford, *The Pastor's Family* (New York: Haworth Pastoral Press, 1998), 66.

5. Mickey and Ashmore, *Clergy Families*, 72.

6. Tom Elliff, *10 Questions a Pastor Should Ask His Wife Every Year*, LifeWay Christian Resources, www.lifeway.com. Elliff is the pastor of First Southern Baptist Church of Del City, Oklahoma, and chairman of the Southern Baptist Convention Council on Family Life.

Chapter 12: Updating Your Passport

1. According to the United States Department of State, over 12.1 million passports have been issued in 2006, http://travel.state.gov/passport/services/stats/stats_890.html. Accessed November 21, 2006.

2. Many thanks to Redeemer's Bible Fellowship, Roseburg, Oregon, and their search committee chairman, Mike McNett, for this and other helpful insights shared with the author on November 15, 1989.

3. Among the best resources in print, we suggest Karl Weber and Rob Kaplan, *The Insider's Guide to Writing the Perfect Resume* (Independence, Ky.: Thomson Learning, 2001), www.petersons.com. This volume contains numerous examples of cover letters and resumes related to the many circumstances the job seeker may face.

Chapter 13: Communicating Your Travel Plans

1. Katharine Hansen, *A Foot in the Door: Networking Your Way into the Hidden Job Market* (Berkeley, Calif.: Ten Speed Press, 2000), 10.

2. Micheal Jon Boersma, "The Relationship between Mentoring and Ministry Satisfaction among Early Career Protestant Clergy" (Ph.D. dissertation, Biola University, 1994), 107.

3. "Job Networking Basics for Beginners," Resumagic, www.resumagic.com/networking. Accessed November 21, 2006.

4. William S. Frank, "The Career Advisor: The 12 Biggest Job Hunting Mistakes," CareerLab, at www.careerlab.com/art_12mistakes.htm. Accessed November 21, 2006.

5. "Morning View: Networking Made Easy," *City Insider*, La Mirada, Calif. (January 20, 2006): 18.

6. Hansen, *Foot in the Door*, 17.

7. Mark Begly, "Networking for Dummies," FaithInTheWorkplace.com at www.christianitytoday.com. This article first appeared in the *Regent Business Review*, issue 2, Regent University, Virginia Beach, Va.

8. Paul D. Stanley and J. Robert Clinton, *Connecting: The Mentoring Relationships You Need to Succeed in Life* (Colorado Springs: NavPress, 1992), 33.

Chapter 14: Unexpected Detours

1. Erik H. Erikson, *Childhood and Society* (New York: W. W. Norton, 1950).

2. Daniel J. Levinson et al., *The Seasons of a Man's Life* (New York: Knopf, 1978).

3. Gail Sheehy, *Passages* (New York: E. P. Dutton, 1974).

4. Eddie Gibbs, "Leadership Matrix," *Your Church* (January–February 2006): 8.

5. Gayle Worland, "Clerics Get Their 'Call' Later: Divinity Students Are Older as They Move into the Pulpit," *Chicago Tribune*, April 8, 2004. Cited in *Pulpit & Pew: Research on Pastoral Leadership*, www.pulpitandpew.duke.edu/clerics%20get%20the%20call%20later%.html.

6. Ibid.

7. Lynne Meredith Schreiber, "Praying for a New Job," *AARP Newsletter* (May–June 2005): 1.

8. Barbara W. Davis, "Charting Your Course at Midlife," 6, http://pubs.cas.psu.edu/freepubs/pdfs/ui287.pdf. Accessed January 4, 2007.

9. Carolyn S. Self and William L. Self, *A Survival Kit for Marriage* (Nashville: Broadman, 1981), 129.

10. Gwen W. Halaas, *Clergy, Retirement, and Wholeness: Looking Forward to the Third Age* (Bethesda, Md.: Alban Institute, 2005), 1.

11. Ray W. Ragsdale, *The Mid-Life Crisis of a Minister* (Waco, Tex.: Word, 1978), 31.

12. Terry Hershey, *Soul Gardening: Cultivating the Good Life* (Minneapolis: Augsburg, 2000), 21.

13. Halaas, *Clergy, Retirement, and Wholeness*, 88.

14. Ragsdale, *Mid-Life Crisis of a Minister*, 57.

15. Janet Fishburn, "Male Clergy Adultery as Vocational Confusion," *Christian Century* (September 15–22, 1982): 922. Cited in www.religion-online.org/showarticle.asp?title=1338.

16. H. Feldman et al., "Impotence and Its Medical and Psychological Correlates: Results from the Massachusetts Male Aging Study," *Journal of Urology* 151 (1994): 54–61.

17. Halaas, *Clergy, Retirement, and Wholeness*, 32.

18. Barbara Bartlik and Marion Z. Goldstein, "Practical Geriatrics: Men's Sexual Health after Midlife," *Psychiatric Services Online* 52 (March 2001): 291–306, http://ps.psychiatryonline.org/cgi/content/full/52/3/291.

19. David J. Powell, "Understanding People in Life's Second Half," The Center on Aging, Older Adult Ministries newsletter (2006): 2, www.gbod.org/coa/articles.asp?=reader&item_id=14791.

20. H. Newton Malony and Richard A. Hunt, *The Psychology of Clergy* (Harrisburg, Pa.: Morehouse, 1991), 128–29.

21. Halaas, *Clergy, Retirement, and Wholeness*, 33.

22. David C. Morley, *Halfway up the Mountain* (Old Tappan, N.J.: Revell, 1979), 26.

23. Davis, "Charting Your Own Course at Midlife," 6.

Chapter 15: Using a Travel Agent

1. Robert Dingman, *In Search of a Leader: The Complete Search Committee Guidebook* (Westlake Village, Calif.: Lakeside Books,1989), 206–7.

2. Robert L. Pearson, "A Job Hunter's Guide to Executive Recruiters," Kennedy Information, Inc., 2005, www.executiveagent.com/career/archives/20050303_main.html.

3. Joe Borer, "How to Judge a Headhunter," *Ask the Headhunter: The Insider's Edge on Job Search and Hiring*, www.asktheheadhunter.com/gv980309.htm. Accessed November 21, 2006.

Chapter 16: The Long Wait till Dawn

1. The Reformed Church of America provides its churches with a comprehensive *Pastoral Search Handbook*. A downloadable version is available at their website, www.rca.org.

2. Robert Dingman, *In Search of a Leader: The Complete Search Committee Guidebook* (Westlake Village, Calif.: Lakeside Books, 1989), 44.

3. The Evangelical Mennonite Mission Conference provides its churches with *A Guide to Pastoral Search Committees in EMMC Congregations*, which outlines several helpful aspects of the candidating process. A downloadable version can be found at www.emmc.ca.

4. Em Griffin, *Confessions of a Pulpit Committee, Leadership Journal* 4, no. 4 (Fall 1983): 109.

5. Ibid., 110.

6. Anonymous, "An Open Letter to the Search Committee," *Leadership Journal* 24, no. 4 (Fall 2003): 49.

Chapter 17: Are We Almost There?

1. William Charlan, *The Complete Idiot's Guide to Changing Careers* (New York: Alpha Books, 1998), 197.

2. Ronni Eisenberg and Kate Kelly, *Organize Your Job Search* (New York: Hyperion, 2000), 198.

3. Wendy Enelow and Shelly Goldman, *The Insider's Guide to Finding a Job* (Indianapolis: JIST Publishing, 2005), 154–55.

Chapter 18: Scouting the Land of Milk and Honey

1. William Bud Phillips, *Pastoral Transitions: From Endings to New Beginnings* (Herndon, Va.: Alban Institute, 1988), 59–62.

2. Joel Garreau, *The Nine Nations of North America* (Boston: Houghton Mifflin, 1981). The book is out of print, but websites do carry the essential information and can be accessed by typing "Nine Nations of North America" into any search engine.

3. The National Center for Education Statistics (NCES) is a ministry of the U.S. Department of Education. Public and private schools and colleges can be located and certain statistics found. As of this writing, the Web address is http://nces.ed.gov/globallocator.

4. Rolane Boersma, a credentialed elementary school teacher, graciously provided this comprehensive list. She has been a pastor's wife, has taught in the public school system, and currently coteaches a course on family life in ministry with the author.

5. The Web address is www.census.gov/econ/census02.

6. The Web address is www.fec.gov.

7. The Web address is www.census.gov.

8. The Web address is www.ncdc.noaa.gov.

Chapter 19: Obeying the Tour Guide

1. Landa Riley, "When Your Wife Resents Your Call," *Leadership* 24, no. 4 (Fall 2003): 55.

2. Garry Friesen, *Decision Making and the Will of God* (Portland, Ore.: Multnomah Press, 1980), 213.

3. Edmund P. Clowney, *Called to the Ministry* (Phillipsburg, N.J.: Presbyterian and Reformed, 1964), 83.

4. John Jackson, "Pastorpreneur," *Leadership* 24, no. 4 (Fall 2003): 60.

5. Ibid.

Chapter 20: Can I Afford This Trip?

1. Marc Mencher, "Compensation Negotiation: Making It a Win/Win Situation," *Gamasutra* (August 12, 2005): 1, http://www.gamasutra.com/features/20050812/mencher_01.shtml.

2. Steven Case et al., "Myths in Your Own Mind," in *Compensation Workbook: Resources for Local Church Ministers* (Task Force of the Ministers' Council, American Baptist Churches, USA, n.d.), 8, www.mmbb.org/clergy_workbook_i.cfm.

3. Joe Hodowanes, "Career Cycles: Compensation Negotiation Is a Delicate Matter," *Tampa Bay Tribune,* April 4, 2005, 2, www.employment.tbo.com/careerseeker/MGBCXCV767E.html.

4. Sherrie G. Taguchi, "Seven Tips for Smarter Compensation Negotiation," *WetFeet* (n.d.): 1, www.wetfeet.com/Content/Articles/S/Seven%20Tips%20for%20Smarter%20Compensation

5. Case et al., "How to Pay the Pastor," in *Compensation Workbook*, 1.

6. "Q Tips: Critical Compensation Tips: Key Salary Negotiation Advice," *Quintessential Careers*, www.quintcareers.com/tips/salary_negotiation_tips.html. Accessed November 21, 2006.

7. Case et al., "Compensation Workbook: Resources for Local Church Ministers," in *Compensation Workbook,* 15.

8. Walter Williams et al., *Indiana-Kentucky Synod Minimum Compensation Guidelines Workbook,* 2007, 4, www.iksynod.org/filestodownload/2007%20Clergy%20Compensation%20Guidelines.pdf. Accessed November 22, 2006.

9. Case, et al., "Compensation Workbook," 35.

10. Donald W. Joiner and Norma Wimberly, *The Abingdon Guide to Funding Ministry* (Nashville: Abingdon Press, 1997). Cited in Glenn C. Daman "A Fair Salary: Ask and You Shall Receive," *Ministry Health* 46 (n.d.): 2, www.ministryhealth.net/mh_articles/046_gd_how_to_get_a_fair_salary.html. Accessed November 22, 2006.

11. Williams et al., *Indiana-Kentucky Synod*, 8.

12. Wendy S. Enelow and Shelly Goldman, *Insider's Guide to Finding a Job* (Indianapolis: JIST Publishing, 2005), 198.

13. The United Church of Christ, "Negotiating Pastoral Compensation," 6, http://www.wcucc.org/ClgyComp.htm. Accessed November 22, 2006.

Chapter 21: Arriving at Your Destination

1. U.S. Census Bureau, *Domestic Migration across Regions, Divisions, and States: 1995–2000*, August 2003, www.census.gov.
2. *What's the Origin of Bury the Hatchet?* Staff report by the Straight Dope Science Advisory Board, May 11, 2004, www.straightdope.com.
3. Roy M. Oswald, *New Beginnings: A Pastorate Start-up Workbook* (Bethesda, Md.: Alban Institute, 1990), 74.
4. This list was published on the Century 21 Real Estate website, www.century21.com. The site includes games you can play with your kids to help them with the transition to a new neighborhood.
5. Robert W. Dingman, *In Search of a Leader* (Westlake Village, Calif.: Lakeside Books, 1994), 200.
6. Robert H. Ramey Jr., *The Pastor's Start-up Manual: Beginning a New Pastorate* (Nashville: Abingdon, 1995), 85.
7. Kevin E. Lawson, *How to Thrive in Associate Staff Ministry* (Bethesda, Md.: Alban Institute, 2000), 28. This is an outstanding resource of helpful concepts and ideas for creating highly effective senior-associate working environments.
8. Ibid., 28–31.
9. Ibid., 176–87.

We want to hear from you. Please send your comments about this book to us in care of zreview@zondervan.com. Thank you.